Praise for *Beyond Intelligence:*
Secrets for Raising Happily Productive Kids

"Dona Matthews and Joanne Foster present parents with an evidence-based sweet spot between tiger mom and creative laissez-faire. Find advice on how to raise a child who is both disciplined and flexible, both wisely compliant and confident in one's own path." — Rena Subotnik, Ph.D., Director of the American Psychological Association Center for Gifted Education Policy, Washington, DC

"*Beyond Intelligence* is a refreshing and much-needed update on intelligence and its development." — Scott Barry Kaufman, Ph.D., author of *Ungifted: Intelligence Redefined*; Co-founder of The Creativity Post; Scientific Director of Imagination Institute, University of Pennsylvania

"If you only have time to read one book on parenting, make this the book... *Beyond Intelligence* is itself a highly intelligent guide to parenting." — Rosemary Evans, Principal, University of Toronto Schools

"*Beyond Intelligence* is a must-read book for parents, educators, and professionals. Matthews and Foster provide an erudite yet personal and compassionate perspective on how to promote children's intelligence and help them overcome obstacles in order to be more resilient and successful in life. If you want to help children be smart AND happy, read this book!" — Tracy Dennis, Ph.D., Associate Professor of Psychology, Hunter College, City University of New York; and parent

"*Beyond Intelligence* is laced with common-sense (and occasionally counter-intuitive) implications for parental practice, in which the need to deeply listen to, and understand, the child takes precedence over quick-fix commercial products or educational quackery. This book offers a refreshing alternative, and I recommend it unreservedly." — Barry Hymer, Ph.D., Professor of Psychology, University of Cumbria, United Kingdom

"By far the best book I have read on child development... It deserves to be a national best seller and it is a 'must read' for educators and parents." — Janet King, President and Founder of Kids Now

"*Beyond Intelligence* is the definitive almanac to help parents navigate and understand how to identify and nurture optimal learning for one's child. [It is] also a resource that can be referred back to time and time again as a parent interfaces with the joys and challenges encountered when raising a child to be successful." — Josh Silvertown, Ph.D.; Biomedical Researcher; President, Executive Director and Co-founder of Dream Catcher Mentoring

"Readers will benefit from the manner in which Matthews and Foster accurately address all of the current issues that modern parents face and do so in a logical and easy-to-read manner. The summaries at the end of each chapter make this book into much more than a one-time read, but a resource that can be returned to over throughout a persons "parenting" life." — Howie Grossinger, Director/Owner Camp Robin Hood/Camp Walden/Madawaska Camps

"*Beyond Intelligence* is a wise and balanced approach to optimizing children's intelligence based on the latest research on learning, development, and neuroscience, and complemented by the authors' extensive experience. It honours the complex ways in which children develop, giving practical recommendations for sensitive guidance at each stage of development. The book is a treasure trove for parents and teachers alike." — Marion Porath, Ph.D., Professor of Educational and Counseling Psychology and Special Education, University of British Columbia

"Thank goodness Dona and Joanne have written another book! By sharing personal stories, research, and practical strategies, Drs. Matthews and Foster have created a handbook that should sit on every parent's shelf. As an elementary school principal and a parent, I applaud the authors' nuanced approach to the discussion around intelligence and its implications for children, parents, and schools." — Nancy Steinhauer, award-winning school principal, and parent

"*Beyond Intelligence* carries a beautiful message — our kids all have unique abilities and challenges. Take the essence of each individual child and run with it to achieve the best possible result. With the expertise of these highly qualified writers, each personality trait deserves enriching, and each perceived problem has a thoughtful, hands-on, and concrete solution." — Shelley Peterson, bestselling Young Adult novelist and parent

Beyond Intelligence

Also by the Authors:

The Routledge International Companion to Gifted Education: Toward a Conceptualisation Fit for the 21st Century, T. Balchin, B. Hymer, and D. J. Matthews (Eds.)

Not Now, Maybe Later: Helping Children Overcome Procrastination, J. F. Foster

The Development of Giftedness and Talent Across the Life Span, F. D. Horowitz, R. F. Subotnik, and D. J. Matthews (Eds.)

Being Smart About Gifted Education: A Guidebook for Parents and Educators (2nd edition), D. J. Matthews and J. F. Foster

Beyond
Intelligence

Secrets for Raising
Happily Productive Kids

Dona Matthews, Ph.D.
Joanne Foster, Ed.D.

ANANSI

This edition published in 2014 by
House of Anansi Press Inc.
110 Spadina Avenue, Suite 801
Toronto, ON, M5V 2K4
Tel. 416-363-4343
Fax 416-363-1017
www.houseofanansi.com

Distributed in Canada by	Distributed in the United States by
HarperCollins Canada Ltd.	Publishers Group West
1995 Markham Road	1700 Fourth Street
Scarborough, ON, M1B 5M8	Berkeley, CA 94710
Toll free tel. 1-800-387-0117	Toll free tel. 1-800-788-3123

House of Anansi Press is committed to protecting our natural environment. As part of our efforts, the interior of this book is printed on paper that contains 100% post-consumer recycled fibres, is acid-free, and is processed chlorine-free.

18 17 16 15 14   1 2 3 4 5

Library and Archives Canada Cataloguing in Publication

Matthews, Dona J. (Dona Joyce), 1951–, author
Beyond intelligence : secrets for raising happily productive
kids / Dona Matthews and Joanne Foster.
Includes bibliographical references and index.
Issued in print and electronic formats.

ISBN 978-1-77089-477-8 (pbk.).—ISBN 978-1-77089-478-5 (epub)

1. Child rearing. 2. Success in children. 3. Parent and child.
4. Children—Intelligence levels. 5. Child development. 6. Brain—
Research—Popular works. I. Foster, Joanne, 1953–, author II. Title.
HQ769.M3758 2014   649'.1   C2013-906997-6
C2013-906998-4

Library of Congress Control Number: 2014935195

Cover design: Michel Vrana
Text design and typesetting: Gordon Robertson

 Canada Council   Conseil des Arts   ONTARIO ARTS COUNCIL
for the Arts   du Canada   CONSEIL DES ARTS DE L'ONTARIO
We acknowledge for their financial support of our publishing program
the Canada Council for the Arts, the Ontario Arts Council, and the
Government of Canada through the Canada Book Fund.

Printed and bound in Canada

 MIX
Paper from
responsible sources
FSC
www.fsc.org   FSC® C004071

 ANCIENT FOREST ™
FRIENDLY

We would like to dedicate this book to our mothers, who nurtured our creativity, curiosity, and love of learning—Joyce Eleanor Matthews (née Drake) and Clara Ruth Stein (née Shapiro)—and to our grandchildren—Theo, Sasha, Cara, Allie, and Jake. We hope these treasured little ones will experience the wonder of creativity, and the joys of developing their curiosity, love of learning, and more.

Contents

Introduction		1
1	Starting with Intelligence	5
2	Intelligence and Creativity	27
3	The Changing Demands of Parenting: Diapers to Diplomas	51
4	A Parents' Guide to Tests and Assessments	87
5	Education: Parents' Roles at School	107
6	Education: Teachers' Roles, Responsibilities, and Requirements	129
7	Decision-Making about Schooling	153
8	Possible Complications	175
9	The Social Context: Friends and Others	209
10	Raising Children to Thrive	233
	Endnotes	249
	Index	271
	Acknowledgements	287
	About the Authors	289

Introduction

*"The way you manage change is as important
as the change you manage."*

– ANONYMOUS

HOW CAN PARENTS best support the development of their children's intelligence, creativity, resilience, character, and well-being? And how can they encourage their children to succeed in a world of challenge and change, where no one can predict what tomorrow's opportunities might be?

Beyond Intelligence is designed to address these questions. We've written it to help you support your children's development, foster their talents and abilities, and enable them to thrive. You don't need a lot of money at your disposal to enhance your children's learning and intellectual growth. In fact, there's nothing quite as powerful as listening to a child, reading to her, communicating with her, and staying attuned to her individual needs.

The best nurturing happens in the natural flow of family life. Children's intelligence, resilience, motivation, and many other capacities develop when their parents allow them enough time and opportunities to discover who they are and what they're interested in. These capacities are further enhanced when parents help their kids acquire the enduring values and habits that will serve them in good stead as time goes by. Throughout this book, we show parents how to transform everyday circumstances into opportunities for their children to develop and activate their intelligence, and to apply their efforts successfully and productively.

In *Beyond Intelligence*, we unravel widely held misconceptions about ability, and about what it means for children to become smart, and stay smart. Most importantly, we address what they need to become happily productive in their lives. From infancy through adolescence and beyond, children develop in ways that are unique, fascinating, and diverse. As is the case with intelligence and talent, there are specific things parents can do to jump-start and enhance creativity. We offer suggestions that enable parents to respond more fully to their children's real learning needs, curiosities, and interests, thereby kindling their enthusiasm for learning.

Through questions, anecdotes, and examples, we reveal strategies that can transform the experience of parenting, making it more interesting and meaningful—as well as more fun for parents and children alike. Recognizing that most parents lead busy lives, we open each chapter with an overview, and end with a brief summary of practical suggestions, the take-home messages of the chapter.

Parents are rightly concerned about the profound and rapid changes that affect their children. They ask questions like "What is the effect on developing young brains of the technological explosion we're experiencing?"; "How do I handle the barrage of sex and violence in the computer games, music, film, television, and other media sources my kids are exposed to every day?"; "What kinds of careers will there be in the future?"; and "How can I prepare my daughter to earn a living when she grows up?"

The skill set that enables people to be successful in today's changing world is not what it was twenty or even ten years ago. As always, intelligence and a strong work ethic will give kids an important edge. But more than ever, those attributes need to be paired with creativity, adaptability, and other open-minded attitudes. It's also important to pay careful attention to your children's involvement with technology, and to be attuned to the different ways they may be affected by world events.

Perhaps surprisingly, however, it's just as important as it ever was—and maybe more so—to attend to children's needs for love, guidance, patience, reassurance, social interaction, emotional stability, physical play, and intellectual stimulation.

How you raise your children to cope with disruptions, troubles, and disappointments on a daily basis can make all the difference in how your kids will respond to these occurrences. Will they tune out or feel overwhelmed? Or will they be open to change, and confident in their ability to adapt and to solve problems? Challenge can be invigorating, and change can be positive. It's important for children to be supported in learning how to cope with difficult circumstances, and to learn how to adjust to new situations or surroundings.

In this book, we refer to real situations experienced by families with whom we've worked. (We use pseudonyms, with some exceptions as noted in the endnotes.) We also call upon up-to-the-minute research on how to raise well-balanced, intelligent, and happily productive children—kids who can adapt and succeed in fast-paced, complicated, and unpredictable times.

The future of the planet depends on children getting the learning opportunities they need, when they need them, so they can make mindful choices, and so their interests and strengths can become qualities and accomplishments they share with the world. In *Beyond Intelligence*, we help parents figure out how to make that happen, one child at a time, in straightforward, cost-effective, and life-affirming ways.

CHAPTER 1

Starting with Intelligence

"Intelligence is the ability to adapt to change."

– STEPHEN HAWKING[1]

WHAT DOES IT MEAN when people say a child is intelligent? That's the big question we address in this chapter, as we lay the foundation for considering the practical details of parents' roles in raising happily productive children. Here, we make the case against putting limits on kids' potential, and consider some of the problems associated with testing. After describing many different kinds of intelligence, and discussing the importance of attitudes and mindsets to children's academic and achievement outcomes, we answer the question "What is intelligence?"

Let's start with a quiz to get you thinking about children's intelligence, and parents' roles in how intelligence develops:

QUIZ: PARENTS AND INTELLIGENCE

Each of the following statements is either true (T) or false (F).

1. By the time a child is three years old, his intelligence level is set for life. (T/F)
2. The more you praise a child for his intelligence, the more confident he'll be. (T/F)

3. Some people are creative, and some aren't. (T/F)
4. Parents should protect their children from setbacks, obstacles, and experiences of failure. (T/F)
5. Highly intelligent children have more social and emotional problems than other kids. (T/F)
6. Children with advanced intellectual abilities are natural leaders. (T/F)
7. The faster a child completes tests and assignments, the smarter the child. (T/F)
8. You can spoil a baby by being too available and responsive. (T/F)
9. The best way to choose a school for your child is to look at the rankings that compare schools. (T/F)
10. Intelligent children don't have learning problems. (T/F)
11. In a family where the siblings have different interests and strengths, parents have to decide who is most deserving of family resources. (T/F)
12. A child who's experiencing bullying should be allowed to solve that problem on his own. (T/F)

If you answered "false" to each of these questions, you got a perfect score. If you thought some (or all) of these statements were true, you're not alone: each statement represents a common misconception about intelligence. Over the course of *Beyond Intelligence*, we'll explain the truth about each of these ideas, and lots more, too. To begin with, we'd like to address one of the most dangerous misconceptions about children and their intelligence: the idea that some kids are destined for success because of their high intelligent quotient (IQ), while others have limited potential.

Smashing the Crystal Ball

It's all too common for parents to hear comments like these from other parents, teachers, family members, friends: "Annabel is a lovely girl, but she'll never go to college. Her IQ just isn't high enough." "Manuel is a superstar! You can expect great things from him!" "Caleb has so much potential. He'd do well at school if only he'd apply himself."

It's a popular misconception that some children have a higher potential for learning and achievement than others. The more that's discovered about how the brain continues to change across the lifespan, however, the more support there is for the view that learning is a gradual, open-ended process, and that an individual's potential cannot be accurately measured, much less predicted.[2] If someone forecasts success or failure for a given child, the wise parent will pick up whatever crystal ball is being used—an intelligence test, comparisons with family members, or anything else—and smash it.

Parents often have questions about what intelligence really is. Finding answers can be surprisingly tricky. Several years ago, the American Psychological Association (APA) asked eleven renowned experts on intelligence to provide a definition.[3] The team of psychologists generated eleven different views, and weren't even close to a consensus. The task force members did agree on three important dimensions of intelligence, though: there are individual differences in how people interact with the environment; these differences are not stable; and assessment results vary depending on the judgement criteria selected.

The first point of agreement, regarding differences in people's interactions with the environment, may seem obvious at first glance. But it's worth noting by parents because educators and psychologists sometimes ignore it when deciding on school placements or when interpreting children's test scores. Examples taken from files of children we've worked with include Jackson, who at the age of four was energetic in his curiosity, and approached new people and situations with enthusiasm. He loved answering adults' questions. He participated with enthusiasm— and a high degree of success—in an intelligence testing session. Isabella, on the other hand, was quieter and more reticent at the same age, happiest in familiar environments. She was uncomfortable in the testing situation, and didn't answer as many questions or do as well as Jackson on the test. The task force psychologists emphasized that differences in temperament, personality, and behaviour, like we see with Jackson and Isabella—differences that resulted in markedly different IQs—shouldn't be mistaken for differences in intelligence.

The second area of agreement across the APA task force psychologists was that these individual differences in interactions with the environment are not stable, even within a given person across time or situations. When Isabella was seven, she became interested in mathematical problem-solving. Her parents found opportunities for her to develop this interest, and when she was ten, she went to a summer camp that specializes in math enrichment. The little girl who had been cautious in approaching unfamiliar situations at the age of four had become more confident by the age of ten. She had learned to welcome new experiences, especially in her areas of interest. Because of the intellectual challenges she experienced, and her increased confidence in problem-solving situations, Isabella's intelligence test score was considerably higher at age ten than it had been at age four. Her story illustrates the fact that test scores—even IQ—can change dramatically from one testing to another.

The task force also agreed that assessment results vary depending on the criteria used to assess intelligence. As Jackson got older, he became an avid reader. He was fascinated by history, and loved debating with friends and family. He didn't much enjoy doing math or solving spatial problems, such as jigsaw puzzles or building activities. He would have done better than Isabella on an intelligence test based on reasoning with language, whereas she would have done better than him on a test that emphasized spatial problem-solving or reasoning with numbers. Parents don't always realize that intelligence tests vary in these ways, and that the type of test can make a big difference in their children's scores. Descriptions of the specific items that have been included, and of the focus of the intelligence test used, are often omitted when results are communicated to parents.

The three points that the APA task force agreed on show how thinking about intelligence is changing. It used to be thought that some people were born smarter than others, and stayed smarter, but experts are moving toward seeing intelligence as a set of processes that an individual actively engages in over time. Instead of describing certain people as intelligent (and others not so much), most experts today would say something more specific and action-based. For example, "Isabella is the one to go to if you have a math question to solve." They're conceptualizing intelligence as a process that's fluid, active, and responsive, both to individual will and also to various kinds of experience and circumstance.[4]

Increasingly, then, intelligence is about "doing" intelligent things in certain situations, rather than "being" exceptionally smart. It's about learning, and about change over time. It looks as if theoretical physicist Stephen Hawking had it right when he said, "Intelligence is the ability to adapt to change."

Based on what's being learned now about brain development, psychologist and author Frances Degen Horowitz makes a strong argument that intelligence develops: it is not innate, and most people have a lot more capability than they ever develop.[5] All children have a tremendous capacity for intelligence, no matter what anyone might predict. In the rest of the book, we discuss practical strategies for parents who want to ensure their children have the chances they need to succeed, and to develop their own intelligence. For now, we ask, "Can intelligence be measured?"

What's Your Score? (And Does It Matter?)

Whether or not you've ever taken an intelligence test, you've almost certainly encountered or read about people who claim to know their IQ, and who set some store by that number.[6] Typically, IQ tests measure abstract reasoning, general knowledge, and short-term memory. They're used widely around the world, in a variety of different versions—including online—some much more reputable and better designed than others.[7] These tests were originally created to assess learning problems, and that continues to be their main (and best) use. They're also used sometimes when teachers or parents think a given child is exceptionally bright, and might require special learning opportunities.[8] Either way, it's worth spending a few minutes thinking about the strengths and limitations of these tests.

There are many reasons for individual children to get less-than-stellar IQ test scores, reasons that have nothing to do with their intelligence. We introduce you to three of the children we'll be discussing throughout the book, Paula, Caryn, and Roberto:

- Paula, a bubbly little girl with curly dark hair and a big smile, loves solving puzzles and went into the IQ test keen and curious. After taking the test, she told her mother she'd like to do that every day.
- Caryn, who makes friends everywhere she goes, enjoys creating drama productions with her friends, and hates wasting time on anything that doesn't result in a useful product she can share with others. "We didn't do anything worthwhile," she grumbled as she and her father headed home from the IQ test.
- Roberto is a quiet boy with a quirky sense of humour and a serious interest in math and physics. He woke up on test day with the flu, but he went to his appointment anyway, knowing it had been arranged months ago. His head hurt, and he could hardly stay awake, but he worked through to the end.

It's not hard to see why the final scores gave a truer reflection of Paula's abilities than Caryn's or Roberto's. Paula enjoys the test-taking process and is happy to participate in activities that have no other purpose than to challenge her ability to think.[9] Her score that day was a pretty good indicator of what she was capable of doing, at least in the areas assessed by the test. On the other hand, a preference for active creative production (like we see with Caryn), and illness at the time of testing (as Roberto experienced), meant that Caryn's and Roberto's scores were much lower than Paula's, and didn't reflect their ability very well at all.

Other reasons capable learners sometimes don't do well on IQ tests include apprehension about making mistakes, worries about family problems, difficulties understanding different communication patterns (on the part of the tester or the child), and physical needs such as hunger.

In addition to individual differences in test-taking abilities and interests, there are serious larger-scale criticisms of IQ tests. One of these is the narrow range of skills tested. Although social and emotional abilities are important aspects of people's successful real-world functioning, they're barely touched on. Creativity is an essential component of discovery in every field—science, mathematics, technology, the arts, and more—but isn't assessed. Other aspects of intelligent behaviour, such as motivation, drive, and persistence, aren't measured at all well by IQ tests.

Another problem with intelligence tests is the way the scores are interpreted. Many people—including professional educators—assume that IQ is permanent. They think that no matter when a person is tested—age 2, 12, 22, or later—her score is her score. Forever. Some parents question this assumption and ask, "If a child doesn't do well on an IQ test, that means she'll never do better, right?" The answer is—very simply—"No." Many children (like Isabella) who don't score very high the first time they're tested do better if they take the test again a few years later.

Another question we sometimes hear: "Does a high IQ in childhood mean a high IQ in adulthood?" Our answer is "Not necessarily." Those who score exceptionally high the first time they're tested are unlikely to do as well in subsequent testing sessions.[10] And the younger a child is when he's assessed, the more likely it is that his scores will change substantially over time.[11]

Alfred Binet was one of the first psychologists to design a test for intelligence, in the late nineteenth and early twentieth centuries.[12]

Even back then, before the findings on neural plasticity, he recognized that intelligence can change over time, and that the extent of a test's capacity is to provide an assessment of strengths and limitations at a given point in time. As cognitive psychologist Scott Barry Kaufman describes, Binet pointed out that "individuals' intellectual development progresses at variable rates, due to different rates of maturation, as well as differences in intellectual experiences. . . . With practice, training, and above all method, we manage to increase our attention, our memory, our judgment, and literally to become more intelligent than we were before."[13]

One of the most important criticisms of IQ testing concerns the persistent scoring differences across race, geography, and socio-economic status. For decades now, in spite of many attempts to reduce the gap, there continues to be a large difference favouring children from white and Asian suburban middle-class homes. Many observers are now suggesting that the best way to address the scoring gap is to provide stronger supports for parents, and better early childhood education across the population.[14]

In addition to all the limitations we've mentioned, IQ scores have little to do with how effectively children adapt to different environments, how well they learn from experience, whether they're likely to invest the hard work over time that's necessary for success, or how they deal with obstacles. Yes, an IQ score has something to do with how well a person understands complex ideas and is able to perform certain kinds of reasoning tasks. It also has a lot to do with how well he took a certain test on a particular day. But it doesn't tell very much at all about how he'll respond to failure, or deal with challenges and changes over time.

> *"I was dyslexic, I had no understanding of school work whatsoever. I certainly would have failed IQ tests."*
>
> – RICHARD BRANSON

Given that intelligence develops across the lifespan, and that intelligence test scores are a poor predictor of life achievement, it's best to avoid thinking about differences in children's potential on the basis of their IQ. A good rule of thumb for parents to keep in mind: a high IQ is a meaningful indicator of advanced reasoning ability (as well as excellent test-taking skills) at a certain point in time, but a lower score may or may not indicate less advanced intellectual ability.

So Many Ways of Being Smart

Pablo Picasso is known for his exceptional visual/spatial abilities, but he had a serious learning disability, and found academic studies next to impossible. Albert Einstein is highly respected for his discovery of the theory of relativity and for his philosophical writings, but he didn't speak until he was three years old, and his elementary teachers described him as a "foolish dreamer." Winston Churchill—an extraordinary political leader during the Second World War—is another example of an exceptionally high-achieving adult who had trouble with schooling in his early years.

Rather than speculating about the IQs of Picasso, Einstein, and Churchill, it makes more sense to think of each one as having a profile of abilities, doing exceptionally well at some activities, and not so well at others. That's as true for children today as it was for these eminent people who had problems with school-based learning.

Cognitive scientist Howard Gardner has written about these ideas, and suggests that there are at least nine major intelligences.[15] From his perspective, instead of having a single IQ, each of us has a profile of intelligences. Any given person might have one or more of her intelligences highly developed, others average, and still others below average. Extremely rare is the person whose profile shows consistently high or low ability across all nine intelligences.

The intelligences that Gardner proposes are the following:

- *linguistic*: reading, writing, speaking, and reasoning skills, in one's first language as well as other languages—especially evident in writers and lawyers;
- *logical-mathematical*: solving problems of logic, detecting patterns that involve numbers, and reasoning deductively—needed in the work of accountants and physicists;
- *spatial*: visualizing objects as they change form or move, and understanding spatial rotations and directions—used by architects and sculptors;
- *bodily-kinesthetic*: moving one's body through space, co-ordinating muscles, and exercising physical strength—honed by surgeons and athletes;
- *musical*:—making sense of sounds, rhythms, and tones—as evident in musicians and conductors;
- *intrapersonal (or emotional)*: understanding oneself and regulating one's emotions—as seen in members of the clergy and people we think of as wise;
- *interpersonal (or social)*: showing empathy, leadership, and the ability to get along well with others—important for businesspeople and teachers;
- *naturalistic*: being attuned to nature and the outdoors—as seen in gardeners and ecologists; and
- *existential*: being sensitive to spiritual matters and metaphysical ideas—required by religious professionals and philosophers.

IQ tests assess linguistic, logical-mathematical, and (to a lesser extent) spatial and interpersonal intelligences. None of the other five intelligences identified by Gardner is addressed. Because the multiple intelligences approach includes so many different kinds of ability, it's closer to the APA task force emphasis on individual developmental differences than is the IQ-based definition of intelligence (which is typically expressed as a single test score).

Parents and teachers know that some kids are great at reading, writing, and arithmetic, but have problems with social interactions. Other kids are terrific at getting along with others, but struggle with anything requiring physical co-ordination or spatial orientation. Still others might find music or sports easy to learn, but hate settling down to tasks requiring reading and writing. Understanding each child as having his own profile of experiences and intelligences leads to respect for the wonderful diversity in the ways of becoming smart, and enables parents to encourage each child's unique interests and abilities.

Another perspective that extends beyond typical understandings of intelligence theorizes a meaningful difference among analytical, practical, and creative intelligences. Consider this statement from Helen Gurley Brown: "My success was not based so much on any great intelligence but on great common sense." Gurley Brown was a publishing innovator who brought *Cosmopolitan* to life, and is often credited with starting the industry that resulted in *Sex and the City* and other American pop culture phenomena.

Now consider this statement from Ingmar Bergman: "I throw a spear into the darkness. That is intuition. Then I must send an army into the darkness to find the spear. That is intellect." Bergman was a Swedish film and stage director (*Scenes from a Marriage, Cries and Whispers,* and dozens more). His work focused on big questions of the human condition such as mortality, alienation, loneliness, and faith.

Brown's and Bergman's bodies of work illustrate the distinctions that interest psychologist Robert Sternberg.[16] He observes that conventional intelligence tests don't measure much other than academic skills, and argues that any comprehensive understanding of intelligence should also incorporate real-world expertise, and creative applications of that expertise. Stephen Hawking's definition of intelligence as the ability to adapt to change aligns well with this position: intelligence is best measured by how well an individual deals with the opportunities and challenges he encounters.

Sternberg proposes three different intelligences. They're not meant as supplements to Gardner's nine intelligences—linguistic, logical-mathematical, et cetera—thus adding up to twelve. Nor do they contradict or supplant Gardner's approach. Instead, they provide another window on what intelligence is.

Analytical intelligence is the capacity to analyze ideas and reason abstractly. It's measured quite well by IQ tests and is usually emphasized in academic studies. The second of Sternberg's intelligences is *practical* (or contextual), which is more closely allied to "street smarts" or "common sense" than to IQ, and includes the ability to succeed in personal and professional contexts, as illustrated by the career of Helen Gurley Brown. The third is *creative*, and that's the intelligence required for innovative work such as Ingmar Bergman's.

These different kinds of intelligence, incorporating people's life experiences, apply not only to adults but also to children. For example, Abby has a keen analytical mind and particularly enjoys the "compare and contrast" questions on exams. She's always done well at school, and her teachers tell her she'll enjoy university when she gets there. Kai's exceptionally good at figuring out how to make mechanical things work, and how to solve practical problems that arise. He often has difficulty with academic tasks, though, and doesn't like going to class. One of his teachers told him he'd probably never finish high school. Vera gets lost in books, and spends class time daydreaming, imagining new endings and challenges for the various characters she encounters in her reading. She thinks school is deadly dull, and barely gets by. Her teachers have told her she'd do much better if she paid attention, but there isn't much at school that captures her attention the way that books and writing do.

Although schools more frequently celebrate the accomplishments of children like Abby, and don't always recognize the abilities demonstrated by Kai and Vera, Sternberg would say that each of these children is intelligent, and that it's wrong to think of one as more intelligent than another. It would be great for society if schools (as well as parents) valued and fostered children's practical and creative abilities as highly as they value and work on further-ing analytical intelligence. More children would feel competent and successful, and more would go on to become fully engaged in all sorts of lifelong learning ventures.

"Nothing activates as many areas of the brain as music."

– DONALD HODGES[17]

Music education

The "Mozart Effect"—which claims that listening to certain kinds of music, such as Mozart's sonatas, makes children smarter—became wildly popular several years ago. It was later shown to have very short-term results (fifteen minutes) on only one form of intelligence (spatial reasoning). Studies indicated that listening to Mozart's sonatas without any other interventions doesn't improve children's overall intelligence in any useful or practical way.[18]

New advances in neuroimaging are enabling scientists to learn more about how the brain works. They're documenting improved efficiency in children's brains following sustained music education, as a result of better-developed and co-ordinated neural networks.[19] As might be expected, the effects increase with the intensity of training: professional musicians have significantly better-devel-oped neural networks than other people, in several brain regions.[20] Benefits don't come from a few minutes of listening to a particular form of music, but rather accrue over time, with systematic learn-ing, effort, and practice—as is true in all areas of endeavour.

There's growing evidence that challenging and well-designed music education enhances the math and language centres of chil-dren's brains. Improvements have been shown in cognitive dex-terity, auditory discrimination, working memory, and speech and language pathways.[21]

Canadian researchers who specialize in learning, memory, and language development in children are studying musical training as an experience that depends on neural plasticity—the changing nature of the brain's functioning and its ever-evolving re-organization in response to experience. They're investigating how interactive music-based learning can improve certain aspects of verbal intelligence among preschoolers.[22] What they're finding is that these musical learning experiences are beneficial for all children. And, by providing alternative pathways to brain development, music education that is systematic and child-friendly is particularly important for those who have trouble learning in more traditional academic ways.

Language study

In much the same way that learning music enhances the development of certain aspects of children's intelligence beyond music itself, learning other languages also fosters intellectual development beyond the obvious benefits of being able to read, write, and speak another language. A child who learns a second or third language will have a better understanding of her native language, and will be able to read it and write it with more fluency and proficiency. She'll also be able to think better in some important ways, experiencing gains in her working memory, attention, problem-solving, and planning abilities. As she gets older, if she retains her bilingualism, she'll also be less likely to experience cognitive decline than her peers who speak only one language.[23]

Scientists are still on the frontier of understanding how the brain develops, and what that means to parents and others interested in children's growth and well-being. What we know now is that, as with music education, when children participate in different kinds of language activities, including second language learning, it both enriches their lives and strengthens their intelligence. As time goes by and more is known about brain development, additional areas of study will almost certainly be identified

that are as good at stimulating overall brain development as 1
education and second language acquisition.

Mindsets and More

Carol Dweck has spent the last three decades studying people's
perspectives on their successes and failures, and she's made a
startling discovery: those who think of intelligence as developing incrementally, step by step, with effort and practice, do better
across measures of academic, career, and psychological success
than those who see intelligence as fixed at birth.

Dweck's findings are consistent with neuroscientific evidence
showing that the brain actively develops from before birth, and
across the lifespan.[24] The opportunities an infant has to interact
with her world make a difference to her developing intelligence.
The same can be said for a young child's engagement with the
environment, and it is also true through adolescence and adulthood. Even for children with profound developmental delays,
and adults in the early stages of dementia, a surprising amount of
learning is possible.

Dweck distinguishes between what she calls a *fixed mindset*
and a *growth mindset*. These different mindsets lead to surprisingly different outcomes.

Individuals with a fixed mindset think that some people are
inherently intelligent (that is, they're born smart) and others are
not. They also think that those who are lucky enough to be born
smart have a better likelihood of high-level achievement. You
might recognize this as a traditional understanding of intelligence, whereby a person's IQ can be measured once, even in early
childhood, and be considered a true measure of their intellectual
ability and potential from that point on.

Those with a growth mindset, by contrast, think of intelligence
as developing over time, given the right supports, motivation,
and opportunities to learn. They resist identifying some children

as having more intellectual potential than others. They perceive, instead, that human ability is far too complex and variable to use for predicting people's limits or future successes.

Mindsets make a big difference to people's subsequent achievement and fulfillment. Those with a growth mindset have greater confidence and are more willing to take intellectual risks, and they're more successful academically and professionally than those with a fixed mindset. Those with a fixed mindset are more self-critical, more prone to negative judgements of themselves and others.

It might sound like mindsets are one more way to categorize people, just a different version of the intelligent versus not-so-smart categorization, but that's not the case. In fact, mindsets are habits, and can be learned or unlearned. Parents and kids who start out with fixed mindsets can make choices and change their mindsets. As one might hope, educators and others are moving away from a fixed mindset and increasingly adopting a growth mindset when it comes to thinking about children's abilities.[25]

Two examples illustrate the difference between the two mindsets. Paula, the little girl mentioned earlier who loves solving puzzles, is constantly discovering new ways to grow and learn. When she encounters an obstacle or has trouble understanding something, it just makes her work harder. She invests more effort in the problem she's experiencing, and asks for help, or finds another way to master the situation. Next time she experiences that kind of challenge it's no longer an obstacle, or she finds it more manageable. At least partly because of that growth mindset, her competence and confidence are increasing as she gets older.

On the other hand, there's Alexander. He's a boy whose parents have praised him frequently for being very bright, telling him how proud they are of his superior intelligence. He's developed a habit of tackling only those tasks he knows he can do successfully. He becomes agitated when things don't come easily to him. Alexan-
\s a fixed mindset. He believes that people are either smart
smart, and that this doesn't change over the course of their

lives. This way of thinking—combined with his belief that his parents think highly of him only because he's smarter than other kids—have made him apprehensive about making mistakes. He's afraid that any kind of failure will show him up as belonging to the not-so-smart category, instead of the highly intelligent category that is the source of so much gratification for him. Unless his attitude becomes more growth-minded, these fears of failure will reduce the likelihood of his taking on big challenges. This, in turn, will almost certainly lead him to narrow his activities and pursuits.

Whereas Paula's enthusiastic approach to challenges is helping her master more and more knowledge and skills, Alexander's situation provides an unfortunate case of a self-reinforcing downward spiral. The more he continues to resist tackling challenging learning opportunities, the more his fears that he isn't really as smart as people think he is are likely to come true. His fixed mindset works against his developing his abilities to as high a level as possible.

> *"It's not always those who start out the smartest who end up the smartest."*
>
> – CAROL DWECK[26]

Is there any consistent pattern of behaviour for those who end up smarter than they started? Or those who might start out showing signs of high intelligence, but never quite live up to that? Dweck and her colleagues say yes, there are some clear patterns of differences, and these patterns can be taught and learned. Or unlearned.

Most parents are surprised to hear that praising children for being smart is actually detrimental to their learning. It harms their motivation and compromises their performance. Rather than telling children they're "bright" or "intelligent" or "talented" xander's parents did, believing they were encouraging his self-confidence), it's better to praise them for what they accomplish through practice, study, persistence, and good strategies. This adjustment in a parent's choice of words makes the difference between sending an implicit message of judgement about the child and his innate ability—which he can't change—and an explicit message about his behaviour—which is under his control. It's a relatively small change for a parent to make, but it can have an enormous impact on a child's life.

Instead of saying, "You're so smart," try to offer encouragement that also provides specific feedback so the child can build upon that. For example, you might tell your daughter you love her expressive flair when she plays the guitar, or you find her essay fascinating because of the examples she uses to support her views, or you're impressed with how she persists in tackling the finer points of a math problem.

You might ask your son about his school work in a way that appreciates his effort, and also encourages him to think about his options, learning strategies, or interests. "You raise some interesting questions in this paper. Which ones do you want to know more about, and where would you begin to look?" It's not the end of the world if occasionally you tell your child he's brilliant, but the more specific you can be with your praise, the better it is for his learning and development.

Another difference between the fixed and growth mindsets is the attitude toward hard work as it applies to intelligence-building. From the fixed mindset perspective, anyone who has to exert himself at a task, or learns something slowly, isn't very smart. From the growth mindset perspective, however, high ability develops over time—often by struggling and persisting. David McArthur, a well-loved teacher in Mississauga, Ontario, frequently told his struggling young students—many of them English Language Learners—"Practice makes better," often whispering afterward, "Perfect is boring!" When he died unexpectedly, parents, teachers, and students honoured his memory by sharing stories about his positive attitude, including how he encouraged people to go far beyond what they would otherwise have been able to achieve.

Parents can help children understand that thoughtful attention to detail (which is usually slow and effortful) enables learning to occur, and ability to increase. Malcolm Gladwell made an insightful observation when he wrote, "Practice isn't the thing you do once you're good. It's the thing you do that makes you good."[27]

It's a common misconception that intelligent people master new ideas quickly and easily. This is true only when the "new" ideas are close to concepts they've already mastered, in which case the ideas aren't really very new. Rather than saying that working hard means someone isn't smart, it's more accurate to say that working hard—which means confronting challenges and moving ahead methodically—is what makes a person smart. It's also true that if a child doesn't have to work hard at school, she needs more challenging learning opportunities.

Take the case of a young dancer learning to do a pirouette. No matter how talented she is, the learning and strengthening process is slow and arduous. The position of each muscle in the body must be learned with precision, one step at a time. The dancer has to practise the movements again and again if she's going to execute a graceful twirl, rather than complete a clumsy twist or incur a serious injury. Those who go on to become prima ballerinas are renowned not for the speed with which they master new steps, but rather the apparently effortless beauty of their performance. This apparent effortlessness is built on tedious attention to every detail in the learning process, including harder work and longer hours of preparation and practice—not shorter hours—than their less accomplished peers.

Another important difference between those holding the fixed and growth mindsets concerns their approaches to failure. It's not often a child says, "Hooray! I made a mistake! What does that tell me?" Or a parent says to his child, "It's actually *good* you failed that algebra test. Now we can go through the questions and see what you need to work on." But these are exactly the kinds of responses you'll hear when someone with a growth mindset encounters an obstacle.

Those with a growth mindset welcome setbacks and criticism as opportunities for productive self-discovery and intelligence-building. We're not recommending that parents aim for their kids to fail, but rather that when failures and disappointments arrive—which they inevitably do when people are learning, growing, and taking on challenges—they should be seen as learning opportunities.

People with a fixed mindset tend to feel judged and evaluated, both by themselves and others, and they're more likely to shy away from potentially difficult situations. They're apt to get embarrassed, angry, frustrated, or look for someone to blame if, for example, they don't do well on a test or an assignment. Parents can help their children realize that although failure is disappointing, it can also be informative. This growth-minded outlook leads to kids learning from their mistakes and stretching themselves beyond their comfort zones—seeking challenge and then building on it. Not surprising, then, that the growth mindset is associated with higher academic and career achievement levels over time.

According to people who have worked with Barack Obama, this attitude toward obstacles has characterized him at least since his university days: when something doesn't go well, he habitually asks what there is to learn from it. No matter what you might think of his politics, his growth-minded approach to challenge helped take him all the way to the White House. Twice.

So, What Is Intelligence?

Based on everything we've discussed in this chapter—the APA task force deliberations, research findings across several fields, and our own understandings and experience—this is our view of what comprises intelligence: *Intelligence is the ability to under-*

stand complex ideas, adapt effectively to the environment, overcome
obstacles, engage meaningfully in various forms of reasoning, and
learn from experience. It develops incrementally, and varies across
time, situations, and domains.

When intelligence is unpacked in this way, it isn't as mysterious
as it appears when it's all wrapped up in conjectures, predictions,
and test scores. Current research is showing that intelligence is far
more dynamic and vibrant than people once thought. The important thing when it comes to parenting is to celebrate intelligence
in all its forms, as it develops in every child.

Parents can help children build their intelligence by remembering—and reminding them—that it develops over time with
opportunities to learn, and that there are many different ways of
being intelligent.

Our Secrets: Starting with Intelligence

1. Be wary of discussions of your child's "potential." All
   children have a tremendous capacity for intelligence, no
   matter what anyone might predict, or how well they do
   on an intelligence test.
2. Think about intelligence as a process rather than an
   innate essence that some people have more of than others. Intelligence is more about doing than being.
3. Remember that intelligence develops incrementally,
   and varies across time, situations, and domains.
4. Support your child's particular kinds of intelligence.
   Each child has his own profile of different intelligences.
5. Think carefully about the implications of any test results
   your child achieves, especially IQ. Scores don't always
   mean what they seem to mean.
6. Look for and encourage children's involvement in music
   and second language learning experiences. These are
   valuable for all kids, but especially for those who don't
   learn in traditional academic ways.

7. Support your child in acquiring a growth mindset—the attitude that ability develops one step at a time, with hard work, persistence, and patience.

8. Don't praise your child for being intelligent. It's better to be specific with your praise, by focusing on what she's doing and how she's doing it.

9. Do praise your child for working hard. Thoughtful attention to detail (which can be painfully slow, challenging, and effortful) is how intelligence grows.

10. Learn to have and display an open mind about obstacles, criticisms, and mistakes. Avoid blame. Think constructively about failures, seeing them as opportunities for learning about what needs more work.

Einstein observed that "the true sign of intelligence is not knowledge but imagination." For parents, going beyond intelligence means nurturing a child's imagination as well as his intellect, and helping him cultivate his creativity. That's what the next chapter is all about.

CHAPTER 2

Intelligence and Creativity

"Wisdom begins in wonder."

– SOCRATES

A S WITH INTELLIGENCE, most people think they know what creativity is. But when they start thinking deeper, they usually have some questions. What is creativity? How does it connect with intelligence? What can parents do to foster their child's creativity? In this chapter, we address all of these questions, and provide plenty of practical suggestions for parents.

Insect Force and the Venus Fly Traps

Thinking about creativity brings to mind the story of a nine-year-old boy whose parents were worried because he'd become impassioned with developing a video game, so much so that he'd lost interest in school.

> Nicholas started kindergarten as a keen learner. By grade four, however, his marks were slipping. He told his parents, "School's not fun anymore. I just want to stay home."
>
> Meanwhile, Nicholas was spending countless hours creating a video game called *Insect Force and the Venus Fly Traps*. In his game, insects and plants battled it out in a

world filled with fantastic arenas, combination vehicles, and hundreds of exotic characters and hybrid animals. Once he'd designed it, he decided he wanted to market it. He generated ideas about how to do this, all neatly recorded in a special marketing notebook.

Although Nicholas's parents were proud of his imagination, his knowledge of science and technology, and his tenacity, they were worried that his preoccupation with the video game was damaging his intellectual development. "He'd work through the night if we let him, and even miss meals. He loses all track of time. What should we do? We don't want him to compromise his schooling!"

After discussing their worries with us, Nicholas's parents took their concerns to his teacher. They talked about how they could work together to capitalize on his interests, so he could continue to develop his strengths in science and technology. They also wanted to reinforce Nicholas's hard work and perseverance, important habits of mind they thought would diminish if he continued to lose interest in school.

With his parents' support and his teacher's help, Nicholas took his video game to several city-wide science fairs. He also participated in a weekly computer lab at the local high school. Nicholas told his teacher he'd like to form a game-making club at school. The teacher helped him set that up, so he was able to spend time working with other kids who were interested in making their own video games.

Nicholas began to appreciate school again. The teacher suggested that Nicholas might benefit from working with a mentor the following year. She said she could try to find someone in science or the high-tech industry who could connect with him on a regular basis to talk about his projects, ideas, and plans.[1]

In our discussions with Nicholas's parents, we'd emphasized the need to be flexible when thinking about his learning and education. We'd told them that the best way to get him engaged in school again was probably to capitalize on his interests. Given his keen motivation, his video game activities had seemed an obvious place to start.

It turned out Nicholas's parents were lucky. He had a teacher who was willing to think creatively and invest some extra effort to help Nicholas succeed.

This story raises several questions about the value of extracurricular activities in children's lives, the importance of academic achievement, the responsibilities of teachers, the role of parents in children's education, and many others.[2] But for now, our focus is on whether or not Nicholas is creative.

Although most people would say, "Yes, Nicholas is obviously creative," some experts would disagree.[3] They'd argue that real creativity doesn't apply to children at all, but should be reserved for innovators like Einstein and Picasso, people who move whole fields of endeavour forward in some important way. Others prefer to distinguish between *Creativity*—Einstein's and Picasso's—and *creativity*[4]—such as a young child's attempts at finger painting, or an adult's gardening or woodworking activities, or Nicholas's video game design. Before weighing in on one side or the other of that debate, it might help to think about the underlying question: What *is* creativity?

What Makes Someone or Something Creative?

One widely used approach to understanding creativity incorporates originality, flexibility, fluency, and elaboration.[5] An overlapping view defines creativity as a mix of originality, flexible thinking, purpose, aesthetics, and motivation.[6] A third perspective focuses on the product, rather than the process—the capacity to make original, high-quality products, as judged by a group of experts in that domain.[7]

While each of these understandings of creativity (as with others that have been proposed) is well-considered and defensible, we suggest an approach that's more practical for parents and teachers. Daniel Keating sees creativity as the bringing together of domain-specific knowledge, divergent thinking, critical thinking, and effective communication.[8] At first reading, this may sound quite theoretical, but with a little further thought, it provides a parent-friendly framework for supporting kids' creativity.

> *"I saw the angel in the marble and carved until I set him free."*
>
> – MICHELANGELO

To begin with, how might this four-point understanding of creativity apply to Nicholas and his video game? He started out with some competence both in biology and in game making (domain-specific knowledge). He generated novel and inventive ideas about how to make his game more fun, challenging, and interesting (divergent thinking). He systematically figured out which of his ideas might work best, choosing the ones he wanted to spend time fine-tuning (critical analysis). Finally, he thought about how to market his game design in order to sell it to others (communication).

Looked at this way, Nicholas's work on his video game project did indeed demonstrate creativity. Not the Creativity of a Picasso or Einstein, perhaps, but the creativity that parents and teachers can encourage, and that may, in time, lead to larger-scale Creativity.

It's not unusual to hear someone say, "I'm just not creative," as if this is an easy yes/no categorical judgement, like saying that some people are tall and some are not so tall. While there aren't many people who transform whole fields of endeavour, creativity is a reachable goal for everyone. Those four learnable foundations are a good place to start. Let's consider each one separately.

Domain-specific knowledge

Domain-specific knowledge is as essential to creativity as it is to intelligence. Simply put, you can't be creative (or intelligent) until

> *"Genius without education is like silver in the mine."*
>
> – BENJAMIN FRANKLIN

you have some knowledge and skills to work with. If you don't have a strong vocabulary and well-honed understanding of language use, you'll have a hard time being a creative writer, no matter how brilliant your perceptions or ideas might be. A common theme across biographies of creatively accomplished people— whether writers, inventors, mathematicians, or others—is a solid mastery of their chosen area of interest.[9]

Judy Anne Breneman, a quilt-maker, said it very well:

The general public tends to think of creativity as an unpredictable occurrence that strikes a few gifted people. Creativity is thought to flow from such people with little or no effort. . . . As researchers study the nature of creativity they discover a very different picture. . . . Creativity may seem to appear by magic but in truth it comes from a deep well of information.

An occasional creative inspiration won't get us far. Instead we need a deepening understanding of our craft as well as increasingly refined skills in order to expand our creativity. Without knowledge we cannot draw from our memory to find unique and interesting ideas or objects to pull together. A weaver needs to know the possible materials and patterns she might use. . . . Without skills we can envision a unique quilt, painting or poem but will not be able to bring the dream to life.[10]

Too often, parents think that focusing on knowledge and skills will rob their children of creativity. Quite the reverse. It's that very knowledge that enables creative possibility.

> *"The best way to have a good idea is to have lots of ideas."*
>
> – LINUS PAULING

Divergent thinking

Divergent thinking is often what comes to mind when people think about creativity—the imaginative "out-there" ideas that surprise us with their originality. Divergent thinking is the zany, quirky, idiosyncratic dimension of creativity, the spontaneity that distinguishes it from everything else we do. It's what Nobel-winning scientist Linus Pauling was referring to when he said, "The best way to have a good idea is to have lots of ideas." Imagination is the effervescence that bubbles beneath the surface of creative thinking.

When Caryn was four, she invented similes to help her make sense of the world as she experienced it. Observing the way some flowers close when the sun goes down, she said, "Night is bedtime for flowers. The flowers curl up and go to sleep, like I do."

Caryn's mother told us her daughter had endless ideas that led in many directions, from experiments with cooking ("What if we added peanut butter to the chicken soup?"), to inventing costumes and stage sets for her plays, and, in time, to deeper explorations of diverse intellectual areas.

Senka Naimji, a teacher, wrote this about the role of divergent thinking in the creative process:

Have you ever noticed how a cucumber plant sends forth tendrils as it grows? They're designed to wrap around something in the environment to give the plant some support as it gets bigger.

Tendrils are like the plant's divergent ideas. They shoot out in many directions, and if one of these tendrils affixes itself to a nail in the fence, then it wraps tightly around that nail and grows upward more strongly from there.

Many tendrils go nowhere. There's nothing for them to attach themselves to. They eventually dry up. Still, one respects the plant for sending a tendril out to nowhere, for taking that risk. Sometimes, a tendril going nowhere on one day will happen to latch on to something that wasn't there the day before. One could say that some tendrils are ahead of their time.

It's good to honour and encourage the many tendrils of a child's imagination, because those tendrils are the ideas that inspire all creative productivity.

> *"Creativity arises out of the tension between spontaneity and limitations, the latter (like the river banks) forcing the spontaneity into the various forms which are essential to the work of art or poem."*
>
> – ROLLO MAY

Critical thinking

Critical thinking is the activity that helps people decide which innovative ideas to pursue, and how to pursue those ideas productively. Rollo May, a psychologist who investigated creativity, emphasized the role of disciplined thought—or critical thinking—in all creative achievement. His simile of the riverbank is apt: without the limits imposed by critical thinking, great ideas are spilled aimlessly in every direction, and end up going nowhere.

In his book *Creating Minds*, Howard Gardner explored the life and work of Sigmund Freud, Albert Einstein, Pablo Picasso, Igor Stravinsky, T. S. Eliot, Martha Graham, and Mahatma Gandhi as examples of transformational creators in seven different fields.

Among the few similarities across these individuals was that each had an extraordinary capacity for critical thinking in his or her field.[11] The capacity to select the best of many ideas for a huge investment of time and energy is a necessary component of productive creativity.

"Self-expression must pass into communication for its fulfillment."

− PEARL S. BUCK

Communication

Communication is the fourth cornerstone of creativity. Once Nicholas had developed his *Insect Force and the Venus Fly Traps* video game, he wanted to share it with others. Marketing—or some other way of sharing one's ideas broadly—is an example of the communication dimension of creativity. Nicholas had to spruce up and assemble his storyboards for the various characters and plotlines, and create a compelling and coherent package that he could show to others, in order to market his game design.

Sophisticated communication skills are required for productive creativity. A musician can have all the musical knowledge in the world, and be able to generate great melodies, but if she can't communicate her ideas effectively, whether through performance or composition, her brilliance will never be heard. An architect who envisions innovative buildings but can't get his ideas translated into effective working drawings might as well be doodling in the sand. As Pearl Buck's quote suggests, for creativity to come to fruition, ideas have to move past the idea stage, out of people's heads, and into the real world.

It's also important to establish balance among these four aspects of creativity. Too heavy an emphasis on knowledge can crowd out original thought. Too much divergent thinking can result in an unfocused scattering of time and energy. Too much critical analysis can scrap every new idea that's generated. And too much focus on communication at the expense of content, ideas, or critical thinking processes can lead to superficiality. Parents can help their child find a productive balance by discussing each of these four dimensions of creativity, and thinking together about how it applies to their areas of interest.

Creativity is what happens when content mastery, divergent thinking, critical thinking, and communication skills all come together in balance, in the service of a goal. Because each of these components is teachable (and learnable), this four-pronged approach provides something tangible for parents to work with. It leads to specific directions for nurturing children's creativity, and applies not only to areas conventionally associated with creativity—such as music, painting, and dance—but also to mathematics, science, technology, and every other domain. By supporting their children in strengthening each of these four dimensions of creativity, parents increase the likelihood that their children will be happily productive in their adult lives.

Ten Creative Thinking Habits

Like intelligence, creativity develops step by step over time, in a process that involves mastering challenges and difficulties. In the same way that intelligence demands effort, so too does creativity. People can choose to advance their intelligence—or not; and they can choose to cultivate their creativity—or not.

According to Robert Sternberg, "Children as well as adults are creative, not by virtue of an innate ability, but by virtue of a set of decisions. In essence, they decide for creativity."[12] If children are going to adapt successfully to the rapidly changing world, they must learn to "decide for creativity,"[13] and Sternberg suggests a ten-point plan for helping them do just that. We've thought about how his ideas contribute to children's developing abilities, and we discuss here how parents can use these ten points to support their children in making creativity-minded decisions for themselves.

Redefine problems

The first point in the deciding-for-creativity plan is to redefine problems. This means looking at things open-mindedly and not accepting the status quo approach to situations. For example, in the second half of the nineteenth century in France, Edouard Manet and his colleagues redefined how artists looked at painting, and paved the way to what became known as Impressionism. They painted scenes of everyday life, and emphasized moods and effects rather than lines and details. They took painting out of the studio and into the real world, redefining the artist's problem as the capturing of an impression of a scene or person, creating an image that was true to a feeling state, rather than a physically objective reality.

Young children can be very good at the spontaneous redefinition of problems. Sometimes they choose to see a mud puddle as an opportunity for going barefoot and experiencing the delightfully squishy ooziness of it, rather than a mucky hazard to be carefully sidestepped. Sometimes they decide that a puddle bears examination; who knows what lurks therein? And, sometimes, they decide on puddles as face paint. Parents can help their children learn creative habits of mind—and build their intelligence—by staying open to problem redefinition, and by pointing out instances when they encounter this kind of thinking in their own daily lives.

Analyze your ideas

A second way to decide for creativity is to analyze your ideas. Although it's great to encourage divergent thinking like the mud puddle redefinitions, no one's ideas are always good. Not Einstein's, not Picasso's, not anyone's. Skepticism is an important component of creativity—the critical thinking component. Children need to learn to critique their own ideas. This includes deciding which ones are worth pursuing, and which should be abandoned or saved for later. (Mud puddle face paint, for example, is sometimes best saved for later.)

Nicholas had a seemingly endless supply of ideas for his video game. At first he devised dozens of characters he found funny or odd. However, when he realized that his design might be marketable, he revisited his choices and became more selective. Each of the characters had to be carefully crafted if the game was going to be popular with his friends and others.

Parents can support their children's creativity by critiquing their own ideas in the company of their children, and by asking their children questions that help them learn how to do that for themselves.

Sell your ideas

Somewhat paradoxically perhaps, the more important, innovative, or groundbreaking an idea, the harder its creator has to work to gain acceptance for it, at least in the beginning. Selling your ideas is the third skill needed in deciding for creativity. Many of the best-known novelists started their writing careers with years of near-starvation and failure. J. K. Rowling, George Orwell, John Grisham, Kathryn Stockett, and Ernest Hemingway are a few of the writers whose work might not have seen the light of day but for their persistence, not just at writing their books, but also at selling them. Both Freud and Einstein struggled for years trying to get attention for their groundbreaking theories before they could get them published, much less read or understood by influential people in their fields who would consider taking the ideas further and putting them into practice.

Sometimes parents become irritated when their children's suggestions are not immediately accepted by teachers or others. Having to fight for their ideas actually helps children become creative. Learning to make a case sufficiently compelling so others want to buy into it is an essential part of creativity. By showing their children how to strengthen their skills of persuasion, parents can help them develop their social intelligence and communication skills, as well as their creativity.

Remember that knowledge is a double-edged sword

Although one needs knowledge in order to move beyond what's known, that very knowledge can interfere with the ability to see possibilities, and that's the point of the fourth dimension of deciding for creativity: knowledge is a double-edged sword. A person who believes he knows all he needs to know about something can be resistant to new perspectives and understandings. Parents who listen to their children, as well as teaching and guiding them, can keep their own creativity vital, while at the same time appreciating how fresh eyes can sometimes see things more experienced eyes might miss.

Caryn's statement about flowers going to sleep like people is one of those observations that can refresh an adult's understanding, if he's listening. Parents who realize that learning is a lifelong endeavour listen to their children's ideas for many reasons, including because they realize that people with less knowledge— like children—can have surprising ways of perceiving problems or arriving at solutions that they, with all their knowledge and experience, might never have imagined.

Surmount obstacles

The fifth point—allied to the decision to sell one's ideas—has to do with surmounting the obstacles that are an inevitable accompaniment to creativity. Any time people challenge how things are done, they're setting themselves up to encounter opposition. The more groundbreaking the work, the truer this is. Einstein said, "If at first the idea is not absurd, there is no hope for it." He also said, "Great spirits have always found violent opposition from mediocrities." Famous examples of oppositional treatment of groundbreaking ideas include the widespread criticism experienced by Stravinsky when the *Rite of Spring* was first performed, and Galileo's condemnation from the church for his seemingly outrageous claim that the world goes around the sun instead of vice versa. Here's a less famous example:

> When Michele was in grade five, she wrote a book report. It contained all the elements required: plot, character, setting, theme, et cetera. She worked hard, and thought she'd done a good job. She was devastated to receive a zero on the assignment. Zero! The reason? She'd written the entire report in rhyme. The teacher had expected an introduction, main body paragraphs, and a conclusion, all in prose.
>
> Michele went home and fumed, but a couple of days later she brought in a book report in the conventional format, using the ideas she'd included in the poem. The teacher reconsidered, graded the two assignments together, and gave Michele a high mark for her work. Instead of being overcome or infuriated by the injustice of the zero, Michele surmounted the obstacle, and learned something important about the art of negotiation.[14]

The question is not whether people with creative ideas will confront roadblocks, but rather how they'll perceive and respond to the hurdles and rejections they experience. Some of our own best writing has been done in response to an editor, reviewer, or publisher criticizing our work. We have to let our indignation settle first, of course, and then we begin to ask ourselves what we need to do to make the work stronger, clearer, or more persuasive. Parents can support their children in deciding for creativity by showing them how to respond productively to opposition, making use of problems as opportunities to strengthen and fine-tune their ideas.

Take sensible risks

Learning to take sensible risks is the sixth aspect of deciding for creativity. One of the hazards experienced by children who take risks (Nicholas, Caryn, and Michele come immediately to mind) is that schools usually cater to conventional thinking, and in fact are designed to foster it. On tests, for example, students will usually do better with safe answers. Children risk experiencing punishing consequences such as lower grades or conflict with teachers when they exercise their ingenuity or share novel ideas in the classroom.

Joanne took a creative writing class in high school, and one day she wrote a paper entitled "Thoughts of a Store Mannequin Facing out the Window on a Busy Street." That was the whole paper. Just the title at the top of a blank page. It was a risk, but was it sensible? Was it an A paper or a D paper? (You decide . . .)[15]

Sadly, even in art, music, and creative writing classes (where one might assume creativity would be encouraged), teachers too often penalize children who take risks in their work. We've all heard stories of people who've gone on to become renowned artists, musicians, and writers after failing art, music, or creative writing classes as children.

You want your child to take creative risks, but you don't want her to experience disproportionate consequences. One solution to this conundrum is to teach your child to keep an eye on the long term. While encouraging her creative risk-taking, also help her learn about compromise. This means analyzing the risks associated with creativity, and deciding which ones are worth taking. Reassure her that once she's proven herself capable in her field, she'll get to take all the risks she wants, but she has to get there first.

Keep growing

Even for those who start off deciding for creativity, there's a temptation to settle into more comfortable habits and behaviours as time goes by, and the seventh decision for creativity is to keep growing. Picasso said, "All children are artists. The problem is how to remain an artist once you grow up." Freud expressed something similar when he said, "What a distressing contrast there is between the radiant intelligence of the child, and the feeble mentality of the average adult."

Some people achieve initial success and then stall, perhaps becoming experts on their initial good idea, but never moving forward from there. It's particularly sad when they resist others' new ideas with the same intensity they encountered when they were starting out.

The only way to stay creative is to keep looking for challenges, and devising innovative ways to meet them. Children learn this best by seeing their parents demonstrate it. Bravo for parents who continue to meet challenges head on in their own lives, stretching their creative tendencies in new directions, or squishing their bare toes through mud puddles just to celebrate the creative possibilities in everyday life.

Believe in yourself

Those who go out on a limb for their creative ideas can find themselves stranded there alone, and sometimes for a long time. Believing in oneself is the eighth way to decide for creativity. A reasonable response to rejection from those who want to protect the status quo is to vow to play it safe in the future. Prudent, perhaps, but not very creative. Proposing innovative ideas means being wrong from time to time, and this can feel embarrassing, maddening, or demotivating. Part of the thrill of creativity is the risk-taking, but a potential cost is losing confidence in oneself.

The story of Michele's rhyming book report could have turned out quite differently if she and her teacher had not been able to come to a reasonable compromise. Michele's desire to take creative risks with her writing might well have been eroded—which would have been a shame, because she's become an avid writer who's learned (among other things) when it's okay to use rhyme, and when it's best to stick to prose.

In order to keep deciding for creativity—as with intelligence—children need to learn to have faith in their abilities, so they can withstand criticism and recover from errors. When Paula—the girl from chapter 1 who loved solving puzzles—had trouble understanding something, it just made her work harder. She trusted that with effort and help, eventually she'd figure things out. Children need reassurance and encouragement in acquiring that faith. They should know that even if they're not generating good ideas at any one moment, the time will come again when they do.

Tolerate ambiguity

F. Scott Fitzgerald wrote, "The test of a first-rate intelligence is the ability to hold two opposed ideas in mind at the same time and still retain the ability to function." The ninth way to decide for creativity is to tolerate ambiguity. Almost always with creative work, there are prolonged, uncomfortable stages where each of two (or more) mutually exclusive ideas has a hold, and things just won't fall into place. In order to be creative, you have to be able to live with that kind of ambiguity long enough to get it right.

In the early years, children need certainty in order to feel secure. They live in a world of heroes and villains, friends and enemies, right and wrong—although who or what might fit into each category varies from one moment to the next. For example, Alicia might have been six-year-old Brenna's best friend yesterday, but they can't stand one another today. Perhaps neither one understands that it's okay to have a best friend who's annoying sometimes. Before the age of ten or eleven, most children can't handle the nuances of meaning, the ambiguities and complexities that are recognized by a more mature intelligence. It's wise, then, to wait until kids are old enough to understand ambiguity before teaching them to tolerate it, and even then, be patient: it's intellectually tough to master, and can take a long time to fully grasp.

A good way for young people to learn about the ambiguity inherent in most complex ideas is to participate in staged debates on controversial topics. Animal rights, say, or homeschooling. Kids are assigned randomly to one side or another, and debate in teams on their assigned position. After a set time, the sides switch. The team that was attacking the idea has to defend it, and vice versa. At the conclusion, each person is asked to formulate his personal position, including the strengths as well as the weaknesses of each side. The final stage of this process is for each person to reflect on the experience. Did the debate experience change your mind on the topic? Would you have reached as thoughtful an understanding of the issues if you'd defended just one side, and not the other?

Misha Abarbanel is a teacher who has coached Ontario high school debaters to success at provincial, national, and international debate competitions. Here's how he describes the benefits of debating: "Organized debating cultivates research skills, communication and language abilities, organizational skills, self-confidence, creativity, cooperation, respect, reasoning, empathy, and more. It also helps kids develop an appreciation of nuance and complexity."[16]

Although ambiguity is much less comfortable than certainty, it's essential to creative work, and invaluable in refining ideas. Parents can help their children appreciate the joys of creativity, showing them that the rewards of a creative life are rich. They should also help them realize that one of the prices is the discomfort that can come from ambiguity, sometimes for long stretches at a time.

Find what you love to do, and do it

Biographies and interviews with people renowned for their exceptional creativity emphasize the need to love your work in order to stay with it, and that's the tenth way to decide for creativity. Mozart wrote, "Neither a lofty degree of intelligence nor imagination, nor both together, go to the making of genius. Love, love, love, that is the soul of genius."

People are at their most creative when doing what they deeply enjoy. Parents can support their children's creativity by helping them explore what they take pleasure in doing, and then providing the necessary opportunities and supports to try it out. Perhaps it's a violin and music lessons, or a block of granite and a set of stone chisels, or a membership in a science museum. Then again, it might be each of these over a period of time, as the child experiments and decides what she wants to take further. Ultimately, it's the love of what one is doing that enables the sustained effort, discipline, and perseverance required for creative achievement.

Creativity can be developed. It isn't a fixed ability or personality trait that some people are born with while others are not.[17] Parents can encourage their children to decide for creativity, and in the process arm them with essential skills for success in a rapidly changing world. Perhaps better still—because the best way to teach anything is to live it—parents can decide for creativity for themselves.

Timelessness: Experiencing the State of Flow

Creatively productive people in every field (across the sciences, arts, sports, and humanities) experience a state that Mihaly Csikszentmihalyi—a psychologist and creativity expert—calls *flow*.[18] Flow is total immersion in an activity, characterized by a feeling of energized focus, concentrated involvement, and loss of a sense of time. When people experience it, they almost always want more. It's like a euphoric drug that motivates further and deeper engagement in the activity that prompted the flow experience in the first place.

> *"In the creative state a man is taken out of himself. He lets down a bucket into his subconscious, and draws up something which is normally beyond his reach. He mixes this thing with his normal experiences and out of the mixture he makes a work of art."*
>
> – E.M. FORSTER

How does flow happen? First, it's associated with *clearly defined goals*—concrete short-term plans, as well as reasonable long-term aspirations. Nicholas's intense engagement in designing his video game suggests that he experienced creative flow when he was working on *Insect Force and the Venus Fly Traps*. He was moti-vated by his desire to create a video game that combined his love of insects and nature. He enjoyed the process, and spent hundreds of hours on the project. He devised specific short-, interim, and long-term goals as he worked on developing characters, settings, computer coding, and all the rest that went into it.

The second requirement for flow is *a balance between ability level and degree of challenge*—that is, the activity is neither too easy, nor too difficult. Nicholas wouldn't have been so motivated by an assigned school science project on a plant (even the Venus Fly Trap). That would've been too simple (and boring) for him. Nor would he have invested hundreds of hours in mastering botanical textbooks. That would've been aimed at a higher level of scientific knowledge and reading comprehension than he could've happily grasped at age nine. The game he devised required him to work very hard at mastering scientific and computer software ideas at a level that was tough enough to challenge him, and easy enough for him to manage.

The third requirement for flow is *direct, immediate feedback*. That includes commendation where earned, as well as constructive criticism. Direct immediate feedback is built into certain pursuits. For example, when designing video game software, you know very quickly if you're doing it right, because it works, whereas if you make a mistake, it won't work. That immediacy worked in favour of Nicholas staying with his project.

Parents can encourage flow experiences by helping their children define realistic goals for themselves, both short-term and long-term; by making sure the goals are tough enough to be chal-lenging, and also easy enough to be doable; and by providing feedback, as needed.

Curiouser and Curiouser

In response to the question "What are the three attributes you most want to see in your child?" very few people include curiosity in their list. Instead, they usually say happiness, intelligence, integrity, creativity, respect, confidence, perseverance, and more—all of which are enormously important.

Wise parents realize the value of curiosity in spurring the development of other highly valued attributes like intelligence, creativity, and perseverance. For example, Eleanor Roosevelt said, "I think, at a child's birth, if a mother could ask a fairy godmother to endow it with the most useful gift, that gift should be curiosity."

Curiosity is important not only for stimulating inquiry, but also for igniting a child's imagination and motivating her learning. By giving rise to important questions—the who, what, when, where, why, and how of the world she encounters—curiosity directs a child to meaningful answers, and furthers her intelligence. Curiosity is what makes her want to know more about life, keeps her engaged, and has the potential to fire up the sort of passion that drives highly creative accomplishments. What a great name to give the Mars rover: *Curiosity*.

In *Teach Your Children Well*, Madeline Levine writes, "Stay curious with your child. . . . Sit with her while she watches the clear liquid you poured into the bathtub turn into a burst of coloured bubbles that dance and disappear with her slightest breath. . . . Your child is both awakening to the world and becoming a trained observer. Curiosity and observation are at the heart of learning."[19]

Things go best for children who stay "chronically curious,"[20] kids who learn to think critically and creatively, question relentlessly, and delight in discovery. As Alistair Cooke said, "Curiosity is free-wheeling intelligence."

If you ask your child, "What is it that makes you learn new things?" or "What are the three best things a fairy godmother could bestow on a baby?" you just might discover that he already knows that curiosity is the secret answer.

QUIZ: PARENTING FOR CREATIVITY

We've designed a yes/no quiz to guide parents in thinking about what they're doing to nurture and support their children's creativity. Although some questions apply to children who are school-aged and older, it's never too soon to start thinking about these ideas, attitudes, and perspectives.

1. Do I expose my child to a wide range of experiences, in many domains—cultural, intellectual, scientific, athletic, and technological? (Y/N)
2. Once my child has identified one or more areas of interest, do I support her in learning more about those areas? (Y/N)
3. Do I welcome digressions from the usual rules and ways of doing things? (Y/N)
4. Is it okay for my child to hold ideas that differ from my own? (Y/N)
5. Do I celebrate my child's playfulness, spontaneity, and curiosity? (Y/N)
6. Do I experience my errors as opportunities for learning? (Y/N)
7. Do I welcome my child's errors as opportunities for learning? (Y/N)
8. Do I welcome collaboration? Do I recognize my child's contributions to joint efforts? (Y/N)
9. Do I encourage my child to think openly, patiently, and generously about the ideas of others? (Y/N)
10. Do I encourage my child to communicate as freely, honestly, and effectively as possible? (Y/N)
11. Do I listen carefully to what my child has to say? (Y/N)
12. Do I provide direct and immediate feedback to my child's efforts? (Y/N)

The items are in no particular order, and the quiz is open-ended, waiting for your creative additions. And, because of its yes/no format, there's room to go back and think about *how* and *what* you do, or don't do, readily.

Creativity is too spontaneous to be reliably measured, so there isn't a score attached to this quiz. However, people who have lots of "Yes" answers are probably already encouraging their children to be creative, as well as intelligent. On the other hand, every "No" provides fresh ideas for nurturing these strengths.

Both creativity and intelligence are fluid and dynamic processes. They're not fixed at birth as attributes some people have more of, and others less. Creativity and intelligence build upon each other as they develop, enabling a child's brain to make more and more neural connections, leading to further cognitive development, which in turn leads to increasing competence.

Our Secrets: Intelligence and Creativity

1. Support your child's creativity and his intelligence by encouraging him to find and develop his passions.
2. Foster your child's creativity by emphasizing each of these four essential aspects: (i) knowledge, (ii) divergent thinking, (iii) critical thinking, and (iv) communication skills.
3. Help your child balance these four aspects so there's not too much focus on any one of them.
4. Model in your own life the ten decisions for creativity: (i) redefine problems; (ii) analyze your ideas; (iii) sell your ideas; (iv) remember that knowledge is a double-edged sword; (v) surmount obstacles; (vi) take sensible risks; (vii) keep growing; (viii) believe in yourself; (ix) tolerate ambiguity; and (x) find what you love to do, and do it.
5. Help your child apply these ten decisions in his life.

6. Nurture and support your child's curiosity. Welcome her questions, and find the answers together. Celebrate her explorations and discoveries.

7. Take the Parenting for Creativity quiz, and see if it gives you any further ideas.

All of this raises questions about how ability actually develops, which is the focus of the next chapter.

CHAPTER 3

The Changing Demands of Parenting: Diapers to Diplomas

"I'm not a genius. I'm just a tremendous bundle of experience."

– BUCKMINSTER FULLER

WE'VE DISCUSSED how intelligence and creativity develop over time, with opportunities to learn. This perspective opens doors to exciting possibilities, but also raises difficult questions. What kinds of opportunities are appropriate, and when? What should parents do—and not do—to support their child's optimal development over the years? What's a good balance between work and play? These are the questions we address in this chapter.

Because each developmental stage has its own particular experiences and challenges, and requires different supports, resources, and parenting skills, we've divided this discussion into four age groups: the early years (birth to five), childhood (five to eleven), early through mid-adolescence (eleven to fourteen, and fifteen to seventeen), and late adolescence into young adulthood (eighteen-plus). Strategies that work well in the early years of children's lives (for example, organizing their social activities, or choosing their reading material) can cause problems later on.

Writer and broadcaster Paul Tough describes the challenge parents face to grow along with their children. In an interview on National Public Radio in the U.S., he said:

> When kids are really young—when they're in their first year or two of life—my sense from the research is you can't be too loving. What kids need at that point is just support, attention, parents who are really attuned to the child's needs. But at some point somewhere around one, or two or three, that really starts to change and what kids need is independence and challenge. And certainly as kids get into middle childhood and into adolescence, that's exactly what they need. They need less parenting. They need parents to really stand back, let them fall and get back up, let them fight their own battles.[1]

Feel free to sample your way through this chapter. In the interest of efficiency, you may want to read only the section that applies to your child at his current stage. Alternatively, you may want to read through the chapter in its entirety, so you can review what's already occurred in his development, think about what's happening now, and get ready for what's coming.

One of the themes you'll see running through this chapter is the interaction between work and play. From the early years into adulthood, and in different areas, intelligence develops in a moving arc from play to work, and back again—with a lot of work—to play. Recent studies done by Rena Subotnik and her colleagues show that patterns that lead to high achievement in all domains trace a general line from playful exploration, through skill acquisition, through increasing mastery, to creative performance or productivity.[2]

People often take positions on one side or the other on the relative importance of work versus play in intelligence-building and achievement. Thomas Edison stated, "Opportunity is missed by most people because it is dressed in overalls and looks like work." He believed that achievement is the result of hard work. The author Joseph Chilton Pearce, on the other hand, said, "Play is the only way the highest intelligence of humankind can unfold." He argued that the highest achievements come from play. Current findings in the neurosciences and psychology are showing they were both right.

The Early Years: Building a Better Brain

Simply by taking pleasure in spending time with a baby, a parent is actively encouraging her child's developing intelligence. An adult who responds to a baby's sounds and actions with smiles, affectionate body language, and echoing gurgles is engaged in the earliest and most important form of brain-building. From birth until age five or so, warmth, safety, and responsiveness—as well as variety and complexity of stimulation—are the factors most likely to lead to subsequent achievement.[3]

Andrea Nair has filmed a delightful short video in which she discusses five simple ways to bond with an infant. She includes holding the baby close to your heart in skin-to-skin contact, looking into the baby's eyes, singing to the baby, giving the baby a lotion massage, and responding to the baby's facial expressions. By mirroring back a baby's expressions, you're telling the baby you're listening.[4]

In contrast with some interpretations of the "Tiger Mother"[5] approach, the early years should not be a circus of non-stop multisensory cognitive stimulation. On the contrary. The research is clear that as long as basic requirements for physical safety and nutrition are satisfied, it's the child who feels loved, valued, and respected, and who lives in a home that provides lots of emotional warmth, who has the sturdiest foundation for developing her abilities.

The nine months of pregnancy and the first few years of life are times of intensive brain-building. By a baby's birth, she has about 100 billion brain cells, or neurons. As neurons make connections with one another (synapses), they create pathways throughout the brain. Neural networks are formed as the pathways intersect.[6]

Synapses that are used often are strengthened, and those that aren't used are pruned out. During the active building and pruning process of the first few years, the young child's brain develops by means of her sensory and emotional experiences.[7] Although this process of neural sculpting begins during pregnancy and continues across the lifespan, it's most active in the early years.

A young child's environment weaves itself into her brain, changing both the structure of the brain and its functional pathways. When she's awake, each of her five senses—sight, smell, touch, hearing, and taste—sends information to her brain. That information is filed away via synapses, neural pathways, and networks, allowing her to more easily understand subsequent similar or related experiences. What happens in the early years influences the person she'll become, shaping what she'll find interesting, and what she'll be able to do easily and well. And as her brain changes, the nature of her experiences of the environment change, in a never-ending loop of interaction between her brain and her experience.

Given that a young person's brain is so dynamic and absorbent, the young person herself benefits from living in a language-rich home environment,[8] and from as many different kinds of experience as possible. It's best when these circumstances occur amidst a spirit of playful exploration, in the company of kind, patient, and enthusiastic adults. As the baby gets a little older, the adults should do their best to respond to her utterances as much as possible, at a level that makes sense to the child. Parents should ask questions, too. The young child learns most when she's engaged in thoughtful, relaxed conversations about her activities, and is stimulated to think about the connections she's making to the people, places, and things she knows or wants to know.

"*All the wisdom in the world about child-rearing cannot,
by itself, replace intimate human ties, family ties, as the
center for human development, the point of departure
for all sound psychological thinking.*"

– SELMA FRAIBERG[9]

A parent once asked us about an expensive toy she'd bought
that claimed to teach young children about texture differentiation and sound discrimination, while developing both fine and
gross motor skills. We said yes, it was a good toy, but we weren't
sure it was any better than a pot and a wooden spoon. There are
countless inexpensive options for providing babies, toddlers, and
preschoolers with healthy brain-building experiences. Here's a
start:

CHECKLIST:
BRAIN-BUILDING EXPERIENCES

- *books*: read aloud with expression, pleasure, and interest
  ("Did you notice the look on the rabbit's face?" "Can you
  make that look?" "What's going to happen next?")
- *inventive activities:* finger puppets, sandcastles, songs
- *interactive science and natural history museums*
- *traditional museums*: stamps, hockey, butterflies—where
  an adult engages children in conversations about what
  they're seeing
- *musical performances*: impromptu family sing-alongs, side-
  walk buskers, karaoke, opera, symphony orchestras, open-
  air concerts
- *art experiences*: sculpting with playdough or wet sand, making collages from bits and pieces of things found around the
  house, creating chalk drawings, going to galleries

- *drama experiences*: puppet shows, improvisation, children's theatre
- *shops*: food, clothing, hardware, pharmacy—chatting about where things come from, how they're made, who might use them, what they're used for
- *mystery boxes*: filled with items to investigate and feel (bamboo, seaweed, pebbles, wood chips)
- *walks in different neighbourhoods*: talking about buildings, design, human activity
- *walks in nature*: a backyard, local parks, and conservation areas—examining and discussing age-appropriate details of plant and animal life
- *television or videos, watched together*: about people, nature, history, faraway places
- *zoos*: especially petting zoos, where children can have a multisensory (touch, sight, smell, sound) interaction with animals
- *farms, ponds, orchards, beaches*
- *the kitchen*: cooking and then eating together (and cleaning up, too)
- *closets, bookshelves, and kitchen cupboards*: potential treasure troves of discovery, with endless opportunities for learning about categorizing and sorting
- *photo albums*: taking pictures, then arranging, sorting, displaying
- *sports activities*: both watching and participating
- *unstructured playtime*
- *travel*: around the block, through a nearby neighbourhood, or into an online adventure abroad

As important as intellectual stimulation is to a young child's developing brain, however, it's not enough. A child also needs opportunities for reflection if he's going to connect new information to what he already knows, consolidate what he's learning, and work out what he wants to do next.[10] Recent research shows that too heavy a focus on the instruction component of learning—

without ample rest between learning sessions—actually reduces the amount a person learns.[11] As we discuss later in this chapter in connection with the importance of unstructured playtime, the wise parent ensures a good balance between a child's activities and his quiet times.

You may remember Roberto from chapter 1, a child who persevered with an IQ test in spite of having the flu. He was exceptionally strong in mathematical areas. His parents told us he'd always enjoyed counting things, even as a baby.

"We had a mobile over his crib," Roberto's father told us, "with a string of brightly coloured blocks on it. He'd move the blocks one at a time until he had the whole set on one side. Then he'd do the same thing, back to the other side. After we saw him do that a few times, we started counting with him. He'd laugh and do it again, and soon counting together became our nightly ritual, our family lullaby."

"That's right," said his mother. "Later we added twists, adding or subtracting the blocks, or connecting the numbers to something Roberto could relate to, like fingers or toes, or stuffed animals."

Her husband continued. "As he got older, he started counting whatever he could find around the house. We'd make up number games with piles of things—crayons, Legos, and uncooked pasta—and before long, Roberto was multiplying and dividing."

"Then we created arithmetic booklets for him," his mother said. "He was so intent on learning. His kindergarten teacher told us he was able to answer third-grade questions."

Intellectual development usually begins with the kind of shared playful experience that Roberto's parents provided. They took pleasure in their son's increasing understanding of math concepts—without pushing him too hard or too fast—which in turn increased his enjoyment and interest in mathematical activities. Given their own mathematical inclinations, they naturally saw his activities connecting to numbers, and so fostered those interests, rather than something else.

Roberto's parents gradually stepped back from his education. By the time he was eight or so, they were no longer inventing or actively participating in his learning, except on his request. But they continued to give him emotional support, and he knew he could go to them with questions or concerns. They were smart enough to know when and how to back off, and to let the learning become Roberto's.

Parents with different interests might see and encourage other abilities. Given the same experience of a baby moving coloured blocks back and forth on a mobile, a mother interested in physical movement might move her body to the right as her child shifts the blocks that way, repeating her actions with the left side, perhaps creating a dance to accompany the baby's movements. A parent attuned to visual aspects of the environment might focus on the colours of the blocks, saying, "Red like a strawberry, yellow like a sunflower, green like a frog, and blue like your rain hat" as the child moves the blocks from side to side. Someone interested in music might invent rhythms or melodies to accompany the blocks as the baby moves them across the string.

In each case, the parent's response encourages the baby to feel a sense of mastery and engagement as neural pathways are being created and strengthened in a particular domain, whether mathematical, bodily-kinesthetic, visual, musical, or something else entirely. When fun, encouragement, and shared pleasure are part of the mix—as was the case in Roberto's family—a child becomes motivated to learn more. The child's interests and development might well take different directions than the parents', but in general, what gets reinforced is most likely to develop further.

Children who have happy and successful early learning experiences in one area or another are more likely to be motivated to keep learning in that area, at a rate that exceeds that of other children. Sometimes called "The Matthew Effect,"[12] this is one explanation for how giftedness develops: an initial small advantage gets larger and larger over time.

An example of the way a child's early pleasurable experiences can be converted into high-level learning can be seen in a child's musical development. When a young girl or boy is just beginning to play the piano, things go best when the teacher makes the learning enjoyable. With time the child's pleasure will come more from a sense of accomplishment and achievement—which will require dedication, discipline, and more demanding instruction—but in the early years, the most motivating experiences are playful.[13]

Motivation can be fostered, and of course it can also be dampened. Particularly in the early years, a parent's responses can make a difference to whether or not a child will choose to develop certain skills. Kelly Masci, a parent, told us this story:

A few years ago, when my son was two, he was tossing a ball at the garage wall. I saw him eyeing a small spider web. Before I knew it, he threw the ball and, astoundingly, he actually hit it! As we watched the spider scurry away, I realized I had a choice—I could admonish him for his actions ("You ruined the spider's web! Poor spider!"), or not.

I looked at my son's worried face, and said, "What a great throw! How about aiming for another spot?" He picked up the ball, pointed at a paint splotch, aimed, and hit it. I asked him to do it again. Sure enough, he was right on target.

His happy relief that I hadn't scolded him, coupled with his excitement about doing something well, made me think that sometimes the way we respond to a child's actions, even if they appear trivial or inconsequential, can change how they feel about themselves—and perhaps even how their lives will unfold. (And, incidentally, later that day, I found an opportunity to talk about what a determined and industrious spider might do next.)

Kelly's response to her son's ball-throwing supported his motivation to do his best in a skill-developing activity he'd devised for himself. If he continues to experience the "steady drip of daily life"[14] as encouraging his athletic abilities, he's going to be more motivated to keep working at his physical skills.

Some children appear intensely motivated to learn from a very early age, and that's what Ellen Winner observed in a study of exceptionally talented young people.[15] In a group of children identified as prodigies, but otherwise very different from each other, she identified a "rage to master," an urgent desire to take learning as far as possible.

A rage to master, or passion for learning in a given area, is also seen in children who aren't identified as prodigies. While it's wonderful if children are internally motivated to learn, managing their intensity can be challenging for parents, as this account illustrates:

Robin's big extended family had gone home from the party, and the two-year-old birthday girl was sitting on the living room floor surrounded by a mess of toys, puzzles, books, crumpled paper, and strands of ribbon. She was focused on three sets of brightly coloured letters that had come with magnetic boards and illustrated cards with words stencilled on them.

She selected an alphabet card and set it in place on one of the magnetic boards. She knew the letter names by heart, and now she was determined to learn the sounds that the letters made in words.

Robin asked her mother to go through the alphabet with her, saying aloud the reading sound of each letter as she put it into its spot: "Ahh, Buh, Kuh, Duh, Eh, Fuh, Guh . . . " They repeated the process, again and again, until Robin could sound them out by herself.

They were both exhausted, but Robin insisted on one more thing: she needed to make a word, and read it, on her own. She carefully selected the "DOG" card, and put the letters into place, while sounding out "Duh, Awe, Guh. DOG!"

Although it was hours past bedtime when she finally went to sleep, she woke up early the next morning, determined to learn more words. Before long, Robin was reading independently.[16]

This story illustrates how parents can help their children's interests become abilities, by paying attention to what those interests are, responding to them as they emerge, and providing structure and encouragement for their development. It also illustrates how a rage to master combines the hard work Edison was talking about when he said that people miss opportunities because they're dressed in overalls and look like work, and the attitude of play that Pearce argued is fundamental to intelligence. Although what Robin was doing might have looked like hard work to someone else, for her it was a form of play. It was what she most wanted to do, far more interesting than anything else at the time.

We should add that a passionate engagement in learning can go too far. It's useful to distinguish between harmonious and obsessive passion.[17] People who are harmoniously passionate experience their area of passion as enhancing their pleasure in life; they feel in control of their activities and their lives. Those who are obsessively passionate are emotionally dependent on pursuing their activity; they experience a rigid persistence that interferes with their pleasure in the activity, and in other dimensions of their lives. Obsessive passions can lead to early burnout, so it's important that parents watch for this, and work to encourage the balance and pleasure inherent in harmonious passion.

Whether or not a child demonstrates an intense desire to learn, talent development starts out feeling like fun, just as Robin thought it was more fun to puzzle out letters and words than play with her other toys. Over time, deep engagement in an activity progresses to being actual work. That entails many, many hours of practice, motivated by the engagement in the learning process that began earlier in the more playful exploration phase. Parents can stay alert to the natural rhythm of talent development. It starts with play, and increasingly incorporates the effortful work involved in serious practice and perseverance, leading to higher levels of challenge—eventually finding its way back to play again at the highest levels of competence.[18]

One final topic to touch on before considering the next developmental stage: child care in the early years. It can be stressful to fight your way through the thicket of conflicting opinions and recommendations. Should one parent stay home if at all possible, until the child goes to kindergarten? Should all children go to preschool? What's the child-care option most likely to lead to intelligence-building and to well-being across the lifespan?

The most comprehensive study on this topic is longitudinal research done in the U.S. by the National Institute for Child Health and Human Development (NICHD).[19] The study began in 1991 with over one thousand infants from a variety of family situations and locations throughout the United States. It was designed to explore how quality, quantity, and type of child-care settings affect children's long-term development, including health, behaviour, and cognitive outcomes.

Overall, the NICHD findings showed that children who were cared for by stay-at-home mothers didn't develop differently than those who were primarily cared for by others, whether nannies, fathers, extended family, or daycare workers. What really matters to the well-being of young children is the parental and familial characteristics they experience, including warmth, responsiveness, and the right kinds of stimulation, as we discuss throughout the book.

The researchers did find some differences across the different circumstances, though. Children who participated in better care settings showed higher levels of language, cognitive, and social development than those who experienced lower-quality care. This is consistent with research conducted by Megan Gunnar and her colleagues, who found that children's stress levels rise when they're in settings where they don't receive ample attention, support, and guidance from the care provider.[20]

The amount of time spent in care also matters. Children in the NICHD study who spent more time in non-maternal care in their first four and a half years of life had more behaviour problems (aggression and lack of co-operation), as well as more minor illnesses (upper respiratory and stomach), than those with fewer hours in care. This conclusion is consistent with Gunnar's findings that children in daycare situations have higher levels of cortisol (a stress hormone) than children being cared for at home by their parents, and that this increases with the number of hours in care.[21]

The third major finding is that the impact of the type of childcare setting varies by age. Children attending child-care centres do better socially and cognitively in the early years, but also have more minor illnesses up to age three, and more behavioural problems when they enter kindergarten. Gunnar's findings led her to conclude that centre-based care is inherently more stressful than home-based care for children younger than three, and that parents should keep to a minimum the number of hours their infant or toddler spends in centre-based daycare.[22]

Although the NICHD findings show that children can do fine even in less-than-ideal care circumstances, the child's intelligence and well-being—including his cognitive, emotional, and social development—are enhanced by a care environment that incorporates all the components we discuss here. That includes safety, responsivity, quiet times, kindness, humour, playfulness, language stimulation, multi-sensory stimulation, and opportunities for unstructured play, both alone and with others. This is as true for home environments as it is for non-parental care situations.

Although young children experience stressors in care situations, that doesn't mean it's always best for a child to have a stay-at-home parent. It doesn't do a child a whole lot of good to spend all day every day with a parent who's irritable or impatient much of the time because she resents her baby for keeping her away from a career she loves, stimulating interaction with other adults, or an income she'd rather have. The quality of a child's experience—

including the likelihood of his engaging in intelligence-building activities—is enormously affected by the attitude and patience of his caregiver.

The bottom line is that there is no good or bad child-care option, in and of itself. What works for each family is unique to that family, and changes as the family's situation changes. No matter what child-care provisions are made, what's most important in the early years is warmth, love, and affection, in an environment that's safe, stable, and predictable, where a small child feels listened to and valued. When a child is also receiving a variety of stimulation, and lots of opportunities for playful engagement and exploration, she's getting a head start on the important next stage of life—childhood.

Childhood: Developing Interests, Habits, and Skills

During the years from age five through eleven, as in other stages, many of the most important intelligence-building skills are not academic or intellectual.[23] The habits of mind acquired during childhood—persistence, patience, respect, integrity, imagination, responsibility, and more—underlie an adult's willingness to do the hard work over time that can result in high-level intelligence and achievement. Where do these habits of mind come from? How can parents encourage and nurture them?

Eric always loved books. When he was a baby his parents took turns sitting in the rocking chair with him, reading his favourite stories aloud over and over. *Pat the Bunny* (tap, tap, tap, scratch, scratch, scratch) was the first of the many books he wore out.

Once Eric was able to read on his own, he discovered the Hardy Boys adventure series. He read each one from cover to cover, often more than once. He enjoyed many genres, and soon found that he preferred history, politics, sports, and intrigue. He'd go to the library and take out stacks of books.

He'd reserve new titles before they arrived. Several times a month, librarians would call the house and leave messages, saying, "I have another book on hold for Eric." He often read late into the night—sometimes with a flashlight strapped to his forehead. Although he read quickly, he also paid close attention to detail, and his vocabulary grew rapidly.

Today he's a lawyer, and his ability to read quickly but carefully has served him well, both in the arduous years of law school, and now that he's a practising professional. And he still likes to read for hours at night—sometimes with an elasticized headlamp.[24]

This story provides a simple illustration of a complex process that's one of the most important secrets of raising happily productive kids. It starts with a child having an interest the parents take pleasure in nurturing. By enabling access to the necessary learning opportunities, and letting the child own as much as possible of the learning experience, his interest can develop into an ability, and eventually strengthen as time goes by. If he stays motivated, invests the necessary effort, and continues to obtain the learning challenges and opportunities he needs, it can eventually lead to greater achievement and fulfillment.

> *"We are what we repeatedly do.*
> *Excellence, then, is not an act, but a habit."*
>
> – ARISTOTLE

The years from five to eleven are a time of rapid brain development. Neural pathways are being established, pruned, and strengthened for different areas of skill, depending on the child's experience. Broad exposure to many different kinds of activities—such as the intelligence-building options we listed for young children—continues to be valuable, but at increasingly sophisticated levels that

match the child's developing ability. Many children begin to identify areas of special interest during this period, gravitating toward
language-based activities, as Eric did, or science, math, music,
athletics, or something else entirely.

When a child invests considerable time and energy in a particular interest, his parents can help him investigate further learning
opportunities. That might mean looking for lessons at a higher
level of difficulty, or for ways to acquire the necessary sports or lab
equipment or art supplies.

It's important to encourage children's developing interests,
but it's also possible for parents to be too enthusiastic in providing support. A child's motivation can be eroded if he feels that his
parents have taken over his learning.

When Sunil was seven, he told his mother he wanted to play
the guitar. He hadn't shown much interest in music prior to
this, and she was delighted. He selected a beautiful guitar,
and she bought that for him, along with a series of lessons
with a highly recommended teacher. Every Wednesday, she
picked him up from school and took him across town to his
lesson. Each day after school, she reminded him he had to
practise. After about four weeks, he wasn't practising at all,
so she imposed a rule that there would be no screens—no
TV, computer, phones, pads, or video games—until he'd finished his thirty minutes of daily music practice. Before long,
Sunil and his mother were at loggerheads. She resented the
investment she'd made, and he had come to hate the guitar.
His teacher suggested they take a break from the lessons. He
never did go back to the guitar, and after a few years, Sunil's
mother gave it away to a friend.

This story might have gone differently if Sunil's mother had
been patient, supporting his interest but waiting to see how it
developed before investing too much time and money. She might

have responded to his first expression of interest by renting a guitar and arranging for one or two introductory lessons with a local teacher. Perhaps after a few weeks of trying out the instrument, he would've asked for his own guitar or more lessons. That would've been a good time for his mother to discuss with him how committed he was, including whether or not he wanted to do the daily practice needed for progress.

As a child's interest becomes more serious, he should be as active in making decisions about what experiences to pursue as his age and maturity allow. For example, when Roberto was eight, he wanted to compete in math contests, so his parents helped him locate a club at the local community centre where kids worked together with a volunteer teacher to prepare for math competitions. Roberto loved his weekly meetings with the math group, and worked hard between sessions on the sample contests the teacher found for them. Had his parents insisted he pursue something else instead—higher-level math workbooks, for example, or more challenging academic courses—his motivation might have diminished, both in math and in other areas of learning.

Like adults, most children have preferences not only about *what* they learn, but also about *how* they learn. Some prefer to work alone rather than with others, or to tackle challenges provided at school rather than exploring extracurricular options. It's good to take these preferences into account, both to enhance the likelihood of a child enjoying her learning experiences so she continues to be motivated, and also to enable her to experience some autonomy. When kids feel ownership over their own learning, they're far more likely to stay engaged and motivated.[25]

As children move through childhood, they experience a number of challenges, not the least of which is establishing a healthy life balance. This should include a mix of enough intellectual stimulation, physical exercise, and sleep, as well as play, reflection, social activities, and time with family. Helping children manage this kind of balancing act can demand everything of a parent's creativity, planning, and negotiation skills. For example, if Roberto's parents are worried that his life is too sedentary, they might give him per- mission to attend the math competition workshops on the con- dition that he walk, jog, or bicycle the six blocks there and back every week. Or they might have him suggest physically active out- ings in which the whole family can participate.

Reaching a balance of priorities is wonderfully satisfying, but it's only ever a momentary achievement. Children's needs, desires, concerns, and interests are always changing, as are family situa- tions. The balance point is a rapidly shifting and multi-dimen- sional target, so parents can expect some disequilibrium along the way. Their challenge is to continue to aim for balance, enlisting help from their child, and moving forward together.

If a child's interest develops into a real strength, it becomes harder for his school to provide the learning challenges he needs. Putting a student like Roberto in the usual second-grade math class when he was already functioning at a grade-seven level might well have squelched his enthusiasm for learning. He needed much more advanced work than his grade two classmates.

Elsewhere in this book (chapters 5 and 6), we discuss practi- cal details of how parents can work with teachers to help them match school curriculum to a child's levels of ability, like Roberto needed if he was going to keep growing mathematically. Here, however, we emphasize the importance to his all-around devel- opment of his moving to higher levels of competence according to his ability. Devising a good learning match is more likely to maintain his interest, and his increasing mastery of skills will also free his attention for the demands of creative and critical thinking.[26] The student who's already acquired the basic phys- ics and math concepts can move more rapidly into specialty areas. Perhaps it will be particle physics or theoretical physics. Who knows, he might even devise new approaches to quantum mechanics one day.[27]

"The cure for boredom is curiosity. There is no cure for curiosity."

– DOROTHY PARKER

Unstructured playtime is an important—and frequently underestimated—secret of raising happily productive kids. Over the past few decades, children's play has become more about toys, educational puzzles, electronic games, et cetera, than about activities that children invent for themselves. Kids' time is too often overscheduled by adults. What's left over is increasingly gobbled up by electronic devices. There's little time left for spontaneity, curiosity, improvisation, and discovery.

Many parents think their children's time should be tightly scheduled in order to maximize their acquisition of certain skills. They think this will give their kids an edge at school, in life, or in the competitions to get into the "best" schools and universities. But even Amy Chua—the original Tiger Mom—is backing off from this position.[28]

There's growing evidence of the value of time being left free for imagination, exploration, collaboration, invention, and even boredom. Depriving kids of these experiences robs them of essential opportunities for developing important skills such as managing their feelings, moods, time, behaviour, and intellectual focus. These skills are prerequisites to real achievement and fulfillment in the long run. Kids who spend good chunks of their time building forts, playing house, constructing narratives of pirates, paupers, cowboys, and circus clowns, and thinking about what to do next, are more likely to take ownership of their own learning.[29]

Jerome Singer has been studying daydreaming since 1955.[30] He distinguishes among three different kinds of mind-wandering activities: positive constructive daydreaming, which is playful, imaginative, and creative; guilty-dysphoric daydreaming, which tends to involve obsessive fantasies; and poor attentional control, which impedes the ability to concentrate. It's impossible to tell just by looking at someone which kind of daydreaming is going on, but it's important not to assume that a child who's staring off into space is wasting time.

Rebecca McMillan, Scott Barry Kaufman, and Jerome Singer wrote an article called "Ode to Positive Constructive Daydreaming,"[31] in which they review the findings of the past six decades of research in this area, and sum up the benefits associated with positive constructive daydreaming. Examples include self-awareness, creative incubation, memory consolidation, future planning, moral reasoning, and more.

So, although it may seem that children are wasting their time when they're spending a Saturday afternoon doing nothing much at all, kids involved in imaginative play may actually be investing their time as productively as possible. When making up rules and games, they're exploring and discovering what they enjoy doing, what they want to learn more about, and how to interact successfully with others. Even boredom is important—it can be the best possible catalyst for self-discovery, determination, and creativity. It's best if parents refrain from giving kids scripts and props for play, and instead allow them to invent their own ways of playing and learning, at least for part of every day.

Children do need planned stimulation and enrichment opportunities—classes, clubs, books, puzzles, building toys, educational activities, museums, performances, outings, et cetera—but their lives shouldn't be so jammed up with these good things that there's no time left for unstructured play, or reflection on what they're experiencing. Somewhat counterintuitively, an exclusive focus on enrichment and achievement can actually impede cognitive and emotional development. Do-nothing times can be the most productive times of all.[32]

Marilyn Price-Mitchell has written about the importance of silence in a noisy world, the silence that allows kids to *think*—about what they enjoy doing, and what their hopes and dreams and values are. This is the silence needed for deep problem-finding and problem-solving.[33] Dr. Price-Mitchell describes five ways that parents can foster self-reflection in their children: (1) invite conversations that ask kids to go deeper—into their feelings, fears, excitements, and worries; (2) explore attitudes and assumptions; (3) honour the validity of thoughts and feelings, without judging; (4) act in ways consistent with thoughts and feelings; and (5) engage in conversations that matter to their kids, thereby encouraging young people's curiosity and desire for growth.

While it's important to make enough time in a child's life for unstructured play, silence, and daydreaming, it's equally important to ensure that he experiences the pleasures that can be found in working hard and achieving small daily goals. Household chores can be an important component of finding a healthy balance in everyday life.

Although tasks related to meal preparation, tidying, cleaning, or laundry might be seen by kids (or their parents) as drudgery to be avoided, some parents actually welcome household chores. There are few tasks better suited for teaching about the pleasures that come from taking responsibility for something that matters, making a real contribution to the family, and achieving tangible outcomes, all of which contribute to kids' self-esteem. In addition, chores provide an opportunity for parents to improve family harmony while giving their children practical tools for managing their lives.

The long-term consequences of parents' doing too much for kids—starting in childhood with household chores—can be feelings of entitlement. An entitled adult can be crippled by his inability to manage the small tasks of daily life, to say nothing of the larger challenges of careers and relationships. An adult who's taken responsibility for household chores from childhood on has an advantage in achieving productive, confidence-boosting, and fulfilling independence in adulthood.[34]

One of the reasons parents give for relieving their kids of chores around the house is that it's easier for them to do the chores themselves. Even when they assign kids household tasks, many parents say, the kids don't do them, or don't do them well.

It's true that the parent who orders, "Clean up your room!" risks overwhelming the child, and will probably meet with resistance or sloppy task completion. Although chores can seem simple to an adult who does them repeatedly, tasks may appear complex to a child, or take time for kids to learn and for parents to teach. It takes even longer before children can perform these tasks independently, so they eventually become habits.[35]

Some kids actually enjoy doing household chores. The keys to making that happen are to show patience, offer step-by-step instruction, and give them time.

How long a chore takes to learn depends on its complexity. A big undertaking, like cleaning a bedroom, can be broken into smaller tasks—making the bed; getting rid of garbage; putting away clothes, toys, and games; and sweeping or vacuuming. The smaller tasks can then be taught, one at a time.

This methodical approach, implemented in a spirit of encouragement and collaboration, applies to musical, mathematical, athletic, and other endeavours. When a systematic approach to learning is embedded in normal daily life, as in the case of household chores, it becomes second nature, and enables kids to see large or difficult tasks as doable. Later, they can draw upon these lessons and be stronger and more successful for having acquired them early on.

Early Adolescence through Mid-Adolescence: Peril and Possibility

Through the early and mid-adolescent years—from eleven to eighteen—changes are happening all at once, in every area of a person's life. Teens are dealing with confusing and often conflicting worries about peer pressure, integrity, family demands, popularity, their unique identity, sexuality, academic decision-making, career ambitions, and more.

It's challenging being a teenager, but in many ways, it's almost as challenging being a teenager's parent.[36] With the onset of a child's adolescence, parents' jobs get a lot more complicated. Their teenager continues to need support for developing her psychosocial skills, such as perseverance, relationship-building, and responsibility. However, she also needs help in strengthening her intellectual abilities, mastering more complex emotional and social skills, becoming accountable for her decisions, and moving toward independence.[37] She won't always ask nicely for this help, and she may not show much gratitude for several years yet. No wonder so many parents get frazzled as their children go through their early to mid-teen years.

> *"Adolescence is a period of rapid unexpected changes. Between the ages of eleven and sixteen, for example, a parent ages as much as twenty years."*
>
> − ANONYMOUS

Most adults understand that times of change in their own lives are inherently stressful. They know about the vulnerability they experience when they're leaving a job or starting a new one; getting married or divorced; buying, renting, or selling a home; or dealing with serious illness or bereavement. As challenging as transitions are for adults, though, they can be far more so for young people. Teenagers haven't yet defined their identities or had much experience navigating major life changes. Most teens haven't acquired the coping skills and resilience they need in order to manage change with equanimity.

Early adolescence in particular (age eleven to fourteen) is a sensitive period, much like early childhood in its impact on subsequent outcomes.[38] The brain is changing dramatically, particularly in the prefrontal cortex (associated with behaviour monitoring and self-control), and in the communication between this area of the brain and other regions. It's also a time when neural pathways that aren't much used are being pruned, when it's even possible to reverse brain patterns that were established during infancy and childhood.[39]

Examples of transitions that early adolescents can experience include moving into a new neighbourhood, responding to changes in family structure, and leaving a local elementary or middle school to go into a big high school. Even transitions as apparently "normal" as these can be jolting for those who haven't acquired much resilience, and don't receive the necessary guidance and support through the transition.

Here's a tale of some teenagers experiencing a difficult change:

The advancement class from grades five through eight was like a wonderful greenhouse where all the conditions were perfect for learning and friendship. Moving to high school was like being planted out into the middle of the summer's heat and drought. All of a sudden, each of the students was alone, and had to fend for him or herself.

They'd originally been pulled from neighbourhood schools across the city for the segregated advancement class, and many of them found it hard to fit back into a broader cross-section of students when they each went to their own community high schools. They'd all skipped one or more grades before getting into that special grade five class. So, in addition to being strangers in the established social groups they were entering, they were younger than the rest of the kids. Other members of the teenage world didn't seem to learn, think, or express themselves the way they did. They were twelve and thirteen, advanced academically, perhaps, but going into a formidable crowd of much more socially savvy fourteen- and fifteen-year-olds.[40]

If only someone who understood the nature of early adolescence had prepared these students for their new environments, their experiences might have been different. A transition supervisor—perhaps a parent working together with a teacher, or a guidance counsellor or psychologist—might have organized visits from graduates of the previous year's advancement class to talk about their transition experiences. What surprised them? What tripped them up? What did they wish they'd done differently? These veterans could have advised those in the current class how to prepare to attend a large high school with older kids who'd known each other for years.

The transition supervisor might have arranged exchange visits with students from other programs or schools. Maybe a series of debates, community volunteering opportunities, or science fairs, with time for snacks and informal conversation. There, the advancement class students could meet their grade-level peers on relatively even ground where (although younger than the others) they could contribute.

Had this transitional support been provided, it's unlikely that going off to high school would have been quite so devastating. The students from the advancement class wouldn't have felt so much like hothouse plants being plunked directly into an arid field.

Early adolescence is a time of stress and vulnerability not only for kids, but also for most parents. As parental demands change, some parents are saddened by the loss of easy closeness. Psychologist Madeline Levine recommends, "Once you've grieved a bit for what is lost, think about all that is gained: A child who is learning to be independent, to make good choices, to carve out an identity, to cultivate multiple relationships, and ultimately to make his or her particular contribution to the world."[41]

Early to mid-adolescence is an ideal time to acquire "grit."[42] Like infancy and early adolescence, late adolescence (eighteen-plus) is another transitional time when those who haven't had much experience with failure can experience profound distress that may upset the course of their development. So the years from eleven to eighteen are an opportunity for parents to provide the buffering support that can help their child learn to manage the challenges that will come along a few years later.

A young adult who's used to succeeding at everything he attempts can be thrown off course when he encounters others who are just as good as he is, or even better than him in some way. Tony's story illustrates this concern:

> Tony was an exceptional young trumpet player. He lived for his practice sessions, sang scales as he walked to and from school, and couldn't get enough of Miles Davis, Chet Baker, and Arturo Sandoval. Tony rose quickly to the top of players at his age level in his hometown. By the time he was fourteen, he was playing first trumpet in the city-wide high school orchestra. No one was surprised when he was accepted to Juilliard on a scholarship.
>
> That's where his story changed course. He was a terrific player, with a beautiful lyrical sound—Juilliard couldn't take that away from him—but he met others with more stamina, better rhythm, cleaner intonation, and a stronger mastery of sight-reading. Before this, all through his years at school, he'd never worked with anyone close to his ability level. But being a great trumpet player was who he was. Ever since childhood, Tony had built his identity on his musical virtuosity. He was devastated, humiliated, and close to a breakdown when he quit Juilliard and returned home in his second year.[43]

No matter how exceptional a person is in a given domain, there's always someone who's mastered some aspect of it better. And the more exceptional the person is compared to others his age, the more likely he is to go along for some years before encountering a serious challenge to his supremacy. The older a person is when he experiences real challenges and setbacks, the harder these setbacks are to manage. It's important for a child to experience obstacles early enough in the learning process so they don't cripple his confidence or shatter his developing identity. Tony did not have the benefit of that lesson during his teenage years.[44]

It so happens that Tony's story ends well. He spent two years at home with his family, helping his parents by earning some much-needed additional income. They insisted he go back to school and continue his music studies. They believed in his talent, and were confident in his success if only he persevered. He was accepted into another strong conservatory, where he excelled. He went from there to a satisfying career playing the trumpet in a top orchestra.

Tony's experiences illustrate the important roles that parents play in helping young people develop the resilience they need for managing setbacks. Kids who experience jolts like Tony did should be reassured that they have everything they need to keep on learning, growing, and succeeding.

The likelihood of problems can be reduced by giving kids early experiences with learning how to manage big challenges. For example, sixteen-year-old Michele had been taking singing lessons for years. She had studio experience and had won Canadian vocal music awards for her demos.[45] She'd been involved in recitals, competitions, and community theatre productions. Next, she wanted to sing the national anthem at Toronto's largest sports stadium prior to a Major League Baseball game. Here's what happened:

> Together, Michele's parents helped her get ready to work up to the stadium event and fulfill her goal. They encouraged her to perform songs in front of small and then larger audiences, always preparing thoroughly, so she wouldn't have to worry about the notes and lyrics at performance time.
>
> Her parents helped her learn to appreciate the co-operative aspects of auditioning, rehearsals, and staging. She began to extend her comfort zone, so she'd be ready to face the massive crowd when she appeared on the giant stadium screen, and on national television.
>
> Although Michele took a huge risk that might have

resulted in an embarrassing flop, the singing of the anthem was a success. She thoroughly enjoyed the experience, and the family has fabulous memories, and audio and visual keepsakes from that day.[46]

Michele's experience of singing "O Canada" in front of a Blue Jays crowd of over 30,000 people left her with feelings of pride, accomplishment, and excitement. She knows the power that comes from setting very high goals, and working hard and persistently toward meeting them.

Drawing on the work of Carol Dweck and others, Maureen Neihart recommends something she calls the "inner game of achievement." It's characterized by goal-setting that is "SMART": Specific, Measurable, Attainable, Realistic, and Timely. Because of her national anthem experience, Michele recognizes she has the support she needs to take on almost anything that comes along, and that—when the challenge is SMART—it's worth doing. No matter what happens next in her life, she's learned how to translate her dreams into reality.[47]

It's this kind of thinking that keeps dancers working on their twirls, inventors labouring on their creations, authors toiling on their writing, and parents improving their parenting skills. SMART goal-setting involves taking the necessary steps to activate aspirations, embrace a growth mindset, and surge forward— an ambitious formula that has spurred many journeys from small beginnings all the way to positions of power and influence. Parents can also make a huge difference by how they model responses to the failures and roadblocks in their own lives, and how they respond to the obstacles their kids encounter.

By the time their children become teenagers, parents have to learn to back off considerably. Adolescents should be making many of their own decisions, and (the hard part for many parents!) accepting the consequences of those decisions when they prove less than wise. As much as most parents hate to contemplate this, a failed high school course because of a series of questionable decisions about completing assignments is far better than a failed career opportunity later in life. If you want your children to be making good decisions when they're adults, it's wise to start their learning about decision-making and consequences in childhood, so it can be ramped up through the teen years.

A combination of cognitive, social, and emotional changes occurs at adolescence, including a movement toward independence. By eleven or twelve, kids are better able to define and pursue their own interests, but they also need to figure out who they are (identity), and how to chart their own paths (autonomy). And this learning curve continues throughout adolescence. Teenagers benefit from a reduction in rules, and appropriate—but not controlling—guidance from parents and others. In short, if adolescents are to take ownership of their lives and become able to make good decisions, they need to make their own mistakes, and learn from them. Another story illustrates this point:

Erin was an independent thinker, which got her into trouble when she was in high school. She failed several courses. There were years when she skipped more classes than she attended, and she ended up at five different high schools within a span of six years.

Her mother—who was an educational expert, providing counselling to parents whose kids were having problems with school—worked diligently, encouraging Erin to become interested in school, helping her find one program after another, each time hoping this one would be better than the last. Homeschooling, alternative schools, strict-discipline schools, academically rigorous schools—you name it. Nothing worked, or not for long. Erin continued to experience school as a terrible bore, and to devise creative ways to escape it.

It wasn't until Erin was sixteen that things turned around. It was then, in the midst of one more of her mother's attempts to get her daughter to see the importance of getting a good education, that Erin looked levelly at her mom and said, "Maybe if you stopped caring so much about school, I would care more."

Tough as they were, those were the words Erin's mother needed to hear. She was hurt, but realized she was too invested in her daughter's success. It wasn't easy, but she learned to let go of her ambitions for Erin's future, trusting that she would make a good life for herself, whether or not she finished high school.[48]

Independent young people who have the intellectual and social/emotional skills to excel don't always do so. There are many reasons why kids might legitimately question the value of school—for example, classes can appear irrelevant, the work might be too easy, the rules may be too strict. A wise parent learns to move aside before she becomes one of those reasons.

Each case is unique, but it might be of interest to know that Erin eventually completed a challenging university degree, while winning scholarships and awards. She became the author of her own success only when her mother learned to respect her autonomy, and began to trust her to work things out for herself.

Late Adolescence and Early Adulthood: Higher Learning

Even as your child reaches the end of his high school years—and then reaches beyond them—he still needs your support and guidance. This is true whether he's at home or living independently. The years from eighteen to twenty-three—late adolescence or early adulthood—are years of higher learning, whether he's attending a college or university, seeking employment, starting up his own business, or beginning a career.

Many parents and guidance counsellors believe that college or university is the best pathway to a successful career. That's not always true. It's important for parents to recognize there are as many pathways to success and fulfillment as there are individuals. By keeping an open mind about what's next, parents are able to provide their child with the guidance and support she'll need through these challenging years.

> *"Learning is a treasure that will follow its owner everywhere."*
>
> – CHINESE PROVERB

Some highly intelligent young adults are impatient to get on with their lives even before high school graduation, and can't bear the thought of spending more years immersed in a course of study that's designed, monitored, and evaluated by others. Some of today's most successful entrepreneurs didn't complete a college degree—Bill Gates, Steve Jobs, and Richard Branson come immediately to mind. For young people who don't want to attend post-secondary school, there are many avenues for continued learning, including apprenticeships, independent study, trade school, business enterprises, travel, community service, and other non-academic experiences.

Others who do plan to attend college or university may want to think about some time out. Increasingly, high school seniors are deciding to take one or more years off before continuing their formal education. Parents can be leery of this educational break, picturing their kids sleeping until noon every day, wandering about aimlessly or worse, and losing all ambition to succeed. However, gap years can provide kids with opportunities to work and raise money for college expenses, investigate alternative career options, and acquire self-knowledge, leading to wiser choices of study later on.

As with other kinds of sabbatical, many people return to their formal education after a gap year refreshed and keener to learn than they've felt in a long time. They usually bring more maturity to their university experience, and are better able to handle the social pressures of first-year college than those who go there directly from high school. Prestigious institutions like Oxford, McGill, and the Massachusetts Institute of Technology regularly grant deferred admission status to students who take gap years. Harvard's dean of admissions, William Fitzsimmons, said about the gap year experience, "It's a time to step back and reflect, gain perspective on personal values and goals, or to gain needed life experience in a setting separate from and independent of one's accustomed pressures and expectations."[49]

Parents can help make gap years productive—whether before or between years of college—by encouraging kids to think ahead about how they intend to spend their time. Who should they contact to set things up? What schedule will they put in place? What's the fallback if things don't proceed well? Being prepared can make the difference between a less-than-satisfactory experience and a meaningful one.

Mentorship arrangements can also provide students with deeper understandings of areas of interest, informing decisions about future courses of study, and sometimes even providing openings into careers. A mentor can help a young person explore his options, participate more actively in a subject area, or reach a goal. He can offer suggestions about useful courses, possible connections, and resources. Whether it's culinary arts, scriptwriting, kinesiology, or any of a thousand other pursuits, a mentor can be well positioned to help a young person make informed decisions—both during and after high school.

Sometimes a young adult has more than one area of strength, and isn't sure which to pursue wholeheartedly, and which to abandon or relegate to a secondary position. Although it sounds like a blessing that any parent would want for a child, this dilemma— sometimes called "multipotentiality"—can be confusing and frustrating for someone who's anxious to get on with her life. A gap year experience or mentorship can be invaluable in situations like this.

Parents can support their kids in navigating through such an impasse by suggesting they consider their short-term and long-term goals. They can also encourage them to ask questions of professionals in the fields of interest. They can assure their kids that with time, effort, and flexibility, they'll ultimately carve out their own unique pathways to success. That might mean a creative integration of their areas of interest, or professional pursuit of one interest while following another as a serious hobby. Or it might involve following a particular interest for some time, with the intention of taking up another later on.

As Tony experienced when he went to Juilliard, exceptionally capable kids can sometimes experience serious and potentially damaging blows to their confidence when they make the transition to college. They can find they're up against stiff competition for the first time in their lives, and aren't the most competent students in class. Depending on their experiences prior to college, and the nature of the challenges they encounter when they get there, some are shocked to discover they can't coast through courses like they did in high school.

College or university is different than high school. As seen in the story of the advanced class kids, making the transition to a post-secondary institution can be daunting, or even damaging. Sometimes, college-bound students are leaving home for the first time. Even if they're happy to be heading off on their own, moving into an unfamiliar situation can be scary. Perhaps there's less privacy, study space, or peace and quiet than they're used to. Certainly there's less support from family and other well-established social networks. Going to university—whether in their hometown or far away—can be lonely.

Participation in well-planned on-campus orientation activities can help smooth the way for first-year students, and provide opportunities for relationship-building. Involvement in campus and community life—groups, clubs, teams, organizations—is great for meeting people, while also enriching the college experience. Parents can share stories about their own college days, or those of others they know. There are endless possibilities for learning and personal growth, but there are also widely publicized hazards of the first-year experience, including too much late-night partying; easy access to drugs, alcohol, and sex; pressures to conform to an all-fun-no-work student culture; and an increased risk of mental health problems. It's wise to think about the potential pitfalls ahead of time.

Encouraging kids to fine-tune their study, time-management, and organizational skills before heading off to college can't hurt (if they listen), but students should also know about on-campus resources in case they need them. If they haven't already acquired basic independent-living survival skills, kids should be given a primer, preferably ahead of time. This includes how to shop for food, cook a meal, do the laundry, change a bed, and clean a bathroom. They should also be encouraged to familiarize themselves with local security services.

It's smart for kids to start thinking about and planning for college early, and parents can help them do that, while making sure they don't usurp ownership of the choice. Take a walk through a university campus together, or attend events that are taking place there. Drive past colleges when travelling, and keep track of what looks promising. Teens can be encouraged to request brochures and course catalogues, to find out what programs or specialty areas might be of interest, and what the prerequisites are. It's also helpful if they keep up-to-date portfolios of their accomplishments and awards at school and work, as well as in their hobby areas, including any references, all of which will come in handy when it's time to submit applications. It's never too early for kids to check out scholarship sources, start a savings plan, or take part in volunteer or leadership activities where they can contribute to the community and build networks, while sharing information and chatting about their plans with others.[50]

The biggest challenge parents face when kids leave home can come as a surprise: it can be very hard to loosen the safety net that much further. It's important that parents stay available for support and encouragement while learning to hold on less tightly (don't let go of that net altogether!) as they watch their children become young adults and move on into the world.

Although we've divided this chapter into stages, emphasizing different activities and skills—for example, the importance of play in the early years, solid work habits in childhood, and resilience throughout adolescence—all of these activities and skills cut across developmental stages. Time for play continues to be important throughout our lives, perseverance is a key to every type of achievement, and successful coping skills are important across the lifespan. The important dimensions of development are not confined to any one age or stage.

Our Secrets: Diapers to Diplomas

1. Respond to your baby's sounds and actions with smiles, affectionate body language, and echoing gurgles. Provide warmth, safety, and responsiveness.
2. Create a language-rich home environment. Talk with your baby and growing child. Listen and respond to her. Read to her. Engage her in conversations about her activities and your own.
3. Provide a variety of stimulating experiences from infancy through to the end of childhood (see Checklist: Brain-Building Experiences).
4. Be enthusiastic and positive. Encourage playfulness in your child.
5. Ensure your child has ample time for unstructured playtime, both independently and with others.
6. Be responsive to your child's and adolescent's interests as they emerge by offering guidance as needed, and enabling access to increasingly challenging learning opportunities (and materials) as required.
7. Let your child/teenager be as active in decision-making

as his age and maturity allow.

8. Remember that daily life offers ideal opportunities to embed a systematic approach to learning, whether through household chores or other responsibilities.

9. Create a healthy balanced lifestyle within your family, with time for reflection, intellectual stimulation, exercise, rest, play, and social activities, as well as time for one another.

10. Continue to model a growth mindset.

11. Ensure that supports and guidance are in place for transitions and times of adversity. Offer reassurance, and talk through issues that arise.

12. Respond thoughtfully to your adolescent's questions about academic and career decision-making. Consider together options such as mentorships, apprenticeships, gap years, and talks with professionals in the fields of interest.

Having given some thought over the past three chapters to supporting your child's development, are there any ways to find out how well your child might be doing at any given point in time? There are many kinds of tests and assessments that claim to measure children's development and, in particular, their intellectual growth. There are just as many questions and concerns surrounding all these measurements. How can parents make sense of the non-sense around the methods, controversies, and numbers? We take a look at this next.

CHAPTER 4

A Parent's Guide to Tests and Assessments

"Not everything that counts can be counted,
and not everything that can be counted counts."

— ALBERT EINSTEIN

Today, people think of Einstein as a genius, but his teachers saw him as something of a problem. If there'd been gifted programs in Munich in the late nineteenth century, it's unlikely he would have been nominated for testing, much less have made the cut. The situation was similar with Winston Churchill and Pablo Picasso, both of whom went on to demonstrate extraordinary abilities in one area or another, but whose early academic achievements were less than stellar.

As part of Dona's private practice as a psychoeducational consultant, she has conducted assessments of hundreds of children whose teachers or parents have concerns about their learning. In the process, she's learned a lot about what tests are able to test well, and what they don't begin to measure, as well as the questions that parents, teachers, and kids have about tests and assessments. As a classroom teacher, and later as an educational consultant and teacher educator, Joanne sees testing processes from the other side of the table, addressing the questions that arise when teachers try to apply assessment findings and recommendations to classroom practice.

We raise these issues in this chapter as we think about what parents need to know about tests and assessment processes, in the interest of raising intelligent, happy, and productive kids. After a brief review of basic principles, we make recommendations for good assessment practices. We respond to many of the questions parents ask us, such as "When should children be tested?" "What should we request by way of results and their interpretation?" and "What should parents tell their kids about their scores?" Although assessment policies are out of the hands—and beyond the expertise—of most parents, understanding the basics can go a long way toward becoming an informed and effective advocate for their child. Test-wise parents can help to secure a better match between their child's learning needs and educational opportunities.

Four Basic Principles

Before thinking about basic principles, we should briefly describe the difference between tests and assessments. A test—an IQ test, a math test, a hearing test—is one component of an assessment. An assessment is a comprehensive study of a person's strengths and weaknesses, using a variety of approaches, possibly including tests, inventories, questionnaires, interviews, observations, and reports from others. Tests yield scores, whereas assessments yield findings and recommendations.

The first basic principle for parents to keep in mind is that *tests of intelligence and ability are far more limited than human potential.* Because the brain continues to develop as long as it continues to be stimulated and challenged, the upper limits of a person's learning potential can't be defined or accurately measured. In fact, exercising the brain is a lot like exercising a muscle. There's increasing evidence that the "use it or lose it" principle applies to cognitive functioning over the lifespan as much as it does to physical fitness. Moreover, neuroscientists are demonstrating that the brain can do a lot to repair itself if needed, and can often find alternative pathways when more typical neural pathways are blocked for one reason or another.[1]

A test score should be seen as a temporary indication of a child's ability, as measured by a certain test at a certain point in time. Scores can change across time and circumstance, a principle that is demonstrated not only in the lives of Einstein, Churchill, and Picasso, but also in the lives of us all. Exceptional strengths can develop in children who don't initially qualify for advanced learning opportunities.

If your child makes the eligibility cut for a gifted program, it usually means she has some excellent thinking and test-taking skills. But if she doesn't make the cut, nobody should conclude she isn't really a gifted learner, or (if she came close) that she's "almost gifted." Instead, you might say she didn't satisfy the school's criteria for giftedness—that is, high enough scores on one or more specific tests at a specific time. She may have advanced learning needs in one or more areas, either now or in the future, and these didn't show up in the tests that were administered. As Einstein put it, too often what counts in a child's development isn't being counted, and what *is* being counted doesn't count in any important way.

The second basic principle concerns areas of ability. When at all possible, *test scores should be reported for different academic subject areas.*[2] People who have high-level abilities generally have strengths in particular domains—mathematical, linguistic, or spatial, for example—rather than across the board. For example, it makes more sense to say that certain people show evidence of advanced ability to solve mathematical problems than to categorize individuals as generically "gifted" (or "not gifted"), which implies they're amazing (or somewhat less than amazing) at everything.

An intelligent assessment of a child's learning needs provides information about the areas of study in which he is exceptionally advanced or experiencing problems, and how advanced or delayed he is compared to others of the same age. It identifies for teachers which academic subject areas need to be adapted to ensure the child continues to be intellectually challenged.

The third basic principle is that *intelligence occurs on a continuum*, not as a yes/no category. In many jurisdictions, children are identified as either falling into the gifted category, or outside of it. This can cause all kinds of problems. The difficulties for those in the "not gifted" category are usually more obvious. For example, being implicitly labelled as "not gifted" can lead to insufficient academic challenge and a sense of inadequacy. It can undermine a child's self-confidence, and result in academic disengagement.[3]

There are problems on the "gifted" side of cut-offs, too. One of these is that only rarely is the identification process used to determine with any degree of exactness how far advanced a given child is in specific subject areas. You may recall Roberto, a boy whose mathematical abilities were way beyond those of his classmates. Going into a gifted program did little to address his extraordinary mathematical advancement.

A good assessment of advanced learning needs includes information about how far ahead of age or grade peers an individual child is in different areas, as well as which areas might require special attention. People's abilities—like their height, weight, and everything else—happen on continuous, not categorical, scales.

The fourth basic principle is that *as people's interests change, and their experiences evolve, so do the nature and direction of their intelligence*. Assessment practices often assume that intelligence is stable. However, as researchers discover more about how abilities develop—with motivation, effort, and appropriate learning opportunities and challenges over time—it becomes increasingly evident that individuals' intelligence also changes over time.

The eight-year-old child who is an accomplished musician compared to others her age may lose her passionate engagement in music by age twelve, and become musically average by the time she's sixteen. Similarly, the child who has no interest in science in elementary school may have a great biology teacher in middle school, and discover a love for the subject that leads to high-level development and achievement in high school and adulthood. There's no time when interests and abilities are more fluid than they are in childhood.[4]

Here are the four basic principles as a checklist for you to consult when you've got assessment concerns:

1. Tests of intelligence and ability are far more limited than human potential.
2. Test scores should be reported separately for different academic subject areas.
3. Intelligence occurs on a continuum.
4. As people's interests change, and their experiences evolve, so do the nature and direction of their intelligence.

What Are They Really Testing?

Educational measurement and evaluation are riddled with controversies, misconceptions, and prickly politics. Concerns include the best age for testing, the criteria that should be used for assessing different kinds of abilities and problems, whether and how often to re-test, differences across jurisdictions in policies and practices, racial and socio-economic discrepancies in scoring patterns—and more.

> *"It makes sense to begin by asking these two guiding questions: 'If this child is not tested, what's likely to happen?' and 'If we do test, how will the information be used?'"*
>
> – DONA MATTHEWS AND JOANNE FOSTER[5]

One concept that helps simplify this puzzling area—for teachers as well as parents—is to remember that assessments are (or should be!) designed to contribute to children's learning processes. At their most useful, assessments inform a teacher's planning and instruction. The child's response to instruction—also known as "learning"—informs the next round of assessment.[6] The best assessment practices take into account the underlying principles we discuss in this chapter and elsewhere in this book: neural plasticity, domain-specificity, degree of advancement, developmental influences, and social milieu.

Many concerns about tests and assessment can be averted if parents and educators focus on matching children's learning needs and interests as these change and develop. In general, it's best to avoid putting labels—"gifted," "learning disabled," et cetera—on children, and to concentrate instead on providing intellectual challenges for all kids. With that in mind, parents with concerns about their kids—including issues having to do with possible giftedness, or problems compared to others of the same age—can ask teachers practical questions such as "How does our child learn?" "What are her areas of strength and weakness?" "What does she need right now in order to feel both challenged and supported in her learning?" and "How can we help?"

The starting point for answering these questions is usually an assessment (whether formal or informal) of what the child already knows in each subject area. Sometimes, a test of intelligence makes sense as a component of that assessment.

There are many tests on the market that contain the word *intelligence* in their names, and provide a score in the form of an intelligence quotient or IQ. Some of these are solidly respectable, but some are iffy and should not be taken as valid assessments of a person's cognitive ability. For example, a local newspaper recently ran a full-page advertisement entitled "Boost Your Brainpower!" which promoted *The Book of IQ Tests: 25 Self-Scoring Quizzes to Sharpen Your Mind.* This book uses "stumpers," and for $6.95 claims to "prove" the extent of people's intellectual prowess.[7] Although it might provide some good intellectual challenge (we don't know that it doesn't), any score that it generates would be questionable, and unlikely to show up in a professional assessment.

Of course, not all assessment tools are suspect. The most valid and reliable intelligence tests—the ones that give the IQ its reputation as a meaningful ability index—are individually administered by a psychologist with special training. When a child takes a psychometrically respectable IQ test, he spends one-on-one time (at least an hour, usually closer to two hours) with someone who's been trained to pay attention to what the child can do well, and what he finds troublesome. Taking such tests can be fun for an intellectually curious child, as they include a series of somewhat novel puzzles and quizzes that assess things like vocabulary, different kinds of reasoning, and short-term memory.

Too often, IQ scores are used as if they defined a person's once-and-forever global intelligence. When seen that way, they interfere with parents' and teachers' understandings of a child's real learning needs. An IQ score that's very high can confirm a student's need for gifted education, but because it's a composite score that combines several abilities, it doesn't help teachers know *how* or *where* or *how much* to differentiate the child's education. And, in the context of schools, those are the most relevant considerations.

Generally speaking, IQ tests make sense only when there are complications, such as learning problems that interfere with a child's ability to do well on the other kinds of measures we describe below—measures that provide a more targeted understanding of what a child needs in order to keep learning optimally. That is, intelligence tests make sense when they're used for their original purpose: understanding an individual child's learning problems.

Measuring Up

If you consider the differences across the lives, learning experiences, abilities, and interests of Roberto, Robin, Michele, and others we introduce in this book, it becomes obvious that there are countless ways children's development can be measured and nurtured. The best assessment practices are rooted in opportunities to learn, whether at home, school, or elsewhere. What really matters is whether a child is learning—that is, whether he's being challenged intellectually.

> *"Abilities and performance that are valued in school are not just discovered through identification strategies— they can be developed through access to rich, challenging learning experiences."*
>
> – BARRY HYMER, JACK WHITEHEAD, AND MARIE HUXTABLE[8]

A solid approach to assessment includes four information sources—academic achievement, reasoning, interest, and persistence—as they apply to specific subject areas.[9] This combination of information sources leads most simply and directly to teaching designed to match children's learning needs. There are many different tests and assessment approaches available that provide this kind of information. In *Being Smart about Gifted Education*,[10] we discuss the who, what, where, when, why, and how of assessing children's advanced learning needs.[11]

Testing intelligence is problematic, but testing creativity is worse. Here's a first-hand account that illustrates some of the issues associated with attempts to measure creativity:

I'm a professional artist and a musician, and I consider myself a creative person. My elementary and high school teachers may have had a completely different idea, however, since I rarely pushed the limits of creativity at school. I guard my privacy, and my art is extremely personal. I didn't *want* others to see it, unless they'd earned my trust. . . . I think it's much easier for extroverted students to demonstrate creativity than quieter students. And, it's possible they'll never demonstrate the extent of their creativity on *any* kind of formal assessment. Just because someone decides *not* to communicate her creativity for whatever reason doesn't mean that she's not very creative. Some of the most creative students are unable or unwilling to demonstrate their creativity in the form that teachers ask for. — Alexis[12]

Alexis's story illustrates some of the problems with assessment when it's disconnected from an authentic context of teaching and learning, or doesn't reflect a student's interests. We discuss how parents can support their children's creative development in chapter 2, but want to underline here that creativity is not something that can be reflected with any degree of meaning or accuracy in test scores.

The learning gap by race and social class is another big issue when it comes to tests and assessment, very much including at the high end of the achievement spectrum. In the United States, for example, African American students are about half as likely as white students to be in gifted programs.[13] Similarly, in Canada, it appears that First Nations, Metis, and Inuit students are half as likely as others to be identified as gifted learners.[14] The problem of under-representation of many different groups in gifted programming has been investigated exhaustively, resulting in important findings and recommendations.[15]

One of the solutions put forward in the past was to increase the numbers of minority, rural, and low socio-economic students in gifted education programs by changing entry requirements to these programs. More recently, however, we and many of our colleagues[16] have been recommending that the learning gap be addressed by investing greater efforts to support learning in *all* children, beginning at preschool or even earlier. Looked at in this way, minority under-representation in gifted education practices is not so much a reflection of racism, but rather a troubling symptom of much larger economic and cultural disparities.

New York City has recently initiated a pilot program that reflects the importance of early childhood education for disadvantaged babies and young children, starting at six months of age. As Sandra Aamodt and Sam Wang wrote in the *New York Post*:

> Early childhood is the most effective time to help disadvantaged kids, since early experience is critical for cognitive and emotional maturation. Brain development occurs in stages—if a child falls too far behind his or her peers, it becomes hard to catch up. For many disadvantaged children, by the time they start school, the academic skills gap is too wide to bridge. Instead, they can enter a vicious cycle of failure that reduces their interest in school, interfering further with their chances of academic progress.[17]

In addition to reducing the learning gap through early childhood programs, there are assessment approaches that can help mitigate socio-economic and racial disparities. Using multiple information sources is one of those inclusive approaches. This can be particularly important for children from minority and disadvantaged backgrounds, as they tend to perform less well on IQ and other standardized tests, but may nevertheless need more access to challenging programming and learning opportunities.[18]

If multiple measures are used to identify giftedness in underrepresented populations, however, three main conditions need to be considered—coherence, inclusivity, and collaboration.[19]

Assessment measures should be *coherent* with available educational practices. For example, when children's mathematical reasoning ability is tested, those children who do exceptionally well should be given appropriately advanced mathematical learning opportunities. Conversely, when more challenging mathematical programming is on offer, the best assessment tools are tests of mathematical ability, not tests of general knowledge or intelligence.

One of the big problems with using IQ as a measure of children's ability is the lack of coherence with schooling practices—that is, with what's actually happening in classrooms on a day-to-day basis. This may sound self-evident, but it's worth noting because this principle is frequently ignored in educational settings.

The second important condition of using multiple measures intelligently is that each measure should be used *inclusively* rather than exclusively. For example, in one jurisdiction where we worked, children have to achieve above a cut-off score on an academic reasoning test in order to be eligible for an enrichment program, but they also have to achieve above a certain score on a teacher checklist, as well as excellent grades. This leads to a situation where some of the most advanced students—those who opt out of their school work because they're bored—aren't accepted into the program either because their teachers don't see them as sufficiently diligent or motivated, or because they don't get high enough grades. Although they might achieve in the top one percent of the population in their academic reasoning scores, they miss out on the programming they need. Each of the measures in a multiple measures approach should provide another possible avenue for inclusion in the pool of children who require differentiated programming, not another way to be excluded from it.

Collaboration between parents and teachers from diverse backgrounds is the third dimension of the intelligent use of multiple measures approaches, especially when the objective is to increase minority achievement. When people from different walks of life come together to discuss priorities, concerns, and perspectives from their varying points of view, learning possibilities open up for everyone. A broader range of educational resources can then be provided for all children who need them.

Solving the Mystery: It's All about Mastery

There are so many pressing concerns about intelligence. Sometimes parents want to know what it takes to guide a remarkably clever child. Teachers wonder if they can possibly teach a group of students who have IQ scores higher than their own. Kids ask us what it means to be extremely bright. Parents worry about the praise, suspicion, or expectations that come when a child seems noticeably ahead of "normal." They ask if they should try to prevent their child's abilities from zooming ahead of others their age.

In order to consider concerns like this, it's helpful to understand what advanced intellectual ability is, and what it isn't.[20]

> *"I was considered by all my masters and by my father as a very ordinary boy, rather below the common standard in intellect."*
>
> – CHARLES DARWIN

The more that's learned about cognitive development, the more evidence there is that intelligence is an ongoing process that depends to a great extent on the temperament and will of the individual. Intelligence-building involves genetic predispositions, as well as all those moment-by-moment environmental influences that make up a child's experiences of life and the world. All learners are actively engaged in creating their own intelligence, and in developmental processes that are more complex than—but not as mysterious as—often imagined.

> *"I wasn't naturally gifted in terms of size and speed; everything I did in hockey I worked for."*
>
> – WAYNE GRETZKY[21]

Giftedness is a term that may be even more loaded than *intelligence*, in its cultural undertones and problematic implications. People as widely recognized for their accomplishments as Darwin, Gretzky, and Einstein shied away from describing themselves as gifted, so it's not surprising that many people think there are only a select few who are truly gifted, and declare that they personally are in the "not gifted" category. Even if they have children formally identified as gifted, or have achieved remarkable success in their own work, or teach students with the gifted label, many adults see giftedness as something intangible, and so superior as to be out of their own reach. They perceive it as mysteriously "other," often a bit scary or weird, and sometimes almost sacred.

One way to address misconceptions like this is to talk about the paradigm shift that's currently underway—what we've called a move from a "mystery model" to a "mastery model" of giftedness.[22] The mystery model is a belief in the innate, permanent, and mysteriously superior intellectual qualities of some select children—a belief that's not consistent with current knowledge about the brain and its development. The mastery model, on the other hand, focuses on practical educational implications for learners who are exceptionally advanced in one or more areas relative to their age peers. It's based on observations about the way abilities develop over time, with appropriate learning opportunities.

> *"I am neither especially clever nor especially gifted.*
> *I am only very, very curious."*
>
> – ALBERT EINSTEIN

Darwin's, Gretzky's, and Einstein's observations align with mastery model thinking. Each of these high achievers sees his achievements as resulting not from a mystical superiority, but rather from a great deal of hard work over time, motivated by passionate commitment, in a context of solid support and ample learning opportunities.

There's increasing momentum away from understanding intelligence as fixed, passive, and innate, and toward seeing it as a developmental process in which a person actively engages with ideas, environments, people, things, and circumstances. As more is learned about the brain and its development, it's becoming apparent that intelligence is less about *being*, and more about *doing*.

Parents often wonder, "Is my child gifted?" A more action-oriented—and better—question is, "Does my child have abilities that are advanced, compared to other kids his age?" This initial question can be coupled with "Does he have areas needing special attention?" and followed by "What can we do to help?"

The focus of these questions is on developing competence. Indeed, from our standpoint, the term *gifted* makes sense only when it's required to designate special learning needs at a given point in time.[23] The strength of this approach lies in its practical applications, including that identification of advanced learning needs and suitable programming are tied together, with no implications of mysterious origins. When seen in this way, for parents and teachers alike, the questions of giftedness and what to do about it are open to a world of possibilities—endless opportunities that can extend children's learning, both within and beyond the classroom.

Hidden Costs of Labelling Children

Although some children sail along remarkably well through a labelling process, others find their real needs get lost behind categorical designations.

> *"Neither I nor the student should use the label as an explanation or excuse for anything; we learn together how best to work with one another."*
>
> – GERRY[24]

Every child has many different needs, including social, emotional, physical, and intellectual, some of which can fade from attention once a categorical label (e.g., "gifted," "learning disabled," "attention-deficit/hyperactivity disordered") has been applied. The only advantage to being labelled—and this is not trivial—is that it sometimes leads to beneficial changes and accommodations.

Labels can mislead people into over-focusing on the similarities—and being blind to the differences—among people within a given category. As Scott Barry Kaufman writes:

When we split people up into such dichotomous categories [such as gifted/not-gifted, or fat/thin], the large variation *within* each category is minimized whereas differences *between* these categories are exaggerated. Truth is, every single person on this planet has their own unique combination of traits and life experiences.[25]

Because labels can mask strengths and weaknesses in children's learning profiles, adults may not realize that children who are labelled with learning disabilities or attention-deficit/hyperactivity disorder (ADHD) can have their academic strengths ignored, leading to boredom or disengagement from school. Similarly, students labelled as gifted may have learning or emotional problems that need attention, but that are hidden behind the gifted label.

> *"Telling children they're smart, in the end, made them feel dumber and act dumber, but claim they were smarter. I don't think this is what we're aiming for when we put positive labels—'gifted,' 'talented,' 'brilliant'—on people."*
>
> – CAROL DWECK

CHECKLIST:
DRAWBACKS OF THE GIFTED LABEL

Here are a dozen label-related drawbacks we've seen among children who've been designated "intellectually advanced" or "gifted":

1. *Imposter syndrome.* Some children (like Alexander, introduced in chapter 1) are afraid they aren't really as smart as others think they are, and that they will be "found out." This can result in kids choosing safe options, and avoiding taking intellectual risks.
2. *Self-doubts.* Some children worry when they experience a new gifted peer group and are no longer at the top of the class. They can lose the self-confidence they felt prior to being grouped with highly capable kids.
3. *Inaccuracy.* Labelling processes are far from perfect. When labels are used for purposes of educational decision-making, kids can be overlooked for programming they need, wrongly designated, or placed in programs that don't meet their learning needs at all well.
4. *Expectations.* Children labelled as intellectually superior or gifted sometimes experience unrealistic expectations from themselves, their parents, other relatives, or teachers.
5. *Complacency.* When a child perceives the gifted label as permanent, like a tattoo, it can lead to complacency, and a belief that he doesn't have to work hard because he's unusually smart.
6. *Narrow-mindedness.* Many children who are labelled have problems with the prejudices and misconceptions of others. Conversely, kids designated as gifted can be intolerant of children who aren't so designated.
7. *Elitism.* Some families don't like participating in what they experience as the elitism and exclusivity of the gifted

label or program. Others—and this may be worse for the children—seek the label for reasons of elitism.

8. *Leaving friends and neighbourhoods behind.* Children can have problems with changing schools and friends to get the educational programming that they're eligible for.

9. *Envy and rejection.* Some children find themselves the targets of negative responses from former friends and others who haven't acquired a similar label.

10. *Ability-masking.* A label masks children's individual profiles of strengths and weaknesses, and can lead to educational mismatches. For example, mathematically gifted learners like Roberto can be placed in generic "gifted programs" where their exceptional mathematical strengths may be ignored and underdeveloped. And, if a child has gaps in some subject areas, these also may not be addressed, especially if he's learned to compensate or hide such problems.

11. *Arrogance.* Arrogance can be used to cover up insecurity and self-doubt, and should be seen as a warning signal for these problems. It may also signify a fixed mindset.

12. *Uncertainty.* A label of any sort can cause confusion because of variations in people's perceptions of what it means. (Does "stylish," "large," or "comfortable" mean the same to everyone?)

Although labels can cause problems for kids, they can also bring benefits. Children who experience themselves as different from others can feel validated when their differentness is acknowledged, and they're helped to understand it. Nancy Steinhauer, an elementary school principal, said it well: "I think at times a label, *when explained properly*, can really help the child identify strengths and needs, and why the child is feeling different from peers."[26]

For Robin, who learned to read at age two, and who continued to be intensely engaged with mastering complex ideas, the gifted label worked as a ticket to educational programming that better matched her interests and abilities. Because the label was carefully explained to her as something indicating she was a good learner, it also helped her understand her lack of enthusiasm for the academic activities most of her classmates found engaging.

A wise parent uses a label, or allows its use, carefully and selectively. For some children, the most appropriate learning options require a specific designation, and in those circumstances, the benefits may outweigh the costs of the label. The important thing for parents to help children understand is that over the years they'll develop a wide range of intelligences, strengths of character, and insights that no IQ test could possibly measure, and that no label could ever define.

The closer assessment practices are to teaching and learning processes, the more likely they are to provide useful information about children's learning needs. Building on that, teachers require resources that allow them to become thoughtful ability diagnosticians, closely monitoring what individual children can and cannot do. This depends on easy access to many different kinds of assessment tools. Information can be gleaned from a child's history of academic achievement in different subject areas, as indicated by (1) school grades and other reports; (2) scores on high-ceiling tests of domain-specific reasoning and aptitude; and (3) information about interests, persistence, and motivation. Learning happens best when parents work with teachers, paying attention to these three information sources on an ongoing basis.

> "*Labels are for filing. Labels are for clothing.*
> *Labels are not for people.*"
>
> — MARTINA NAVRATILOVA

The goal of assessment should not be to label children, but rather to make carefully reasoned decisions that meet their ever-changing learning needs. When assessment is understood this way, parents become informed partners in the multi-faceted and collaborative process of discovering and rediscovering what their children need in order to thrive.

Our Secrets: Tests and Assessments

1. Four basic principles of assessments are (i) tests of intelligence and ability are far more limited than human potential; (ii) most children's development is uneven across subject areas; (iii) intelligence occurs on a continuum; and (iv) interests change over time, thereby changing the nature and direction of intelligence-building.

2. The best assessment questions for parents to ask are "How does our child learn? What are her areas of strength and weakness?" "What does she need right now in order to feel both challenged and supported in her learning?" "How can we help?"

3. The starting point for answering these questions is an assessment of what the child already knows, needs to know, and wants to know in each subject area.

4. Intelligence tests make sense when they're used for understanding learning problems, and when the results are explained well to parents.

5. The best assessment practices are rooted in classroom practice, when teachers take a diagnostic approach and use children's understandings to inform daily instruction.

6. Creativity is difficult to measure; creativity test scores aren't very useful or accurate.

7. A multiple measures approach should be used to identify children's advanced abilities. This is especially important

for under-represented populations. Measures should be aligned with available educational practices, be as inclusive as possible, and be collaborative in nature.

8. Giftedness is an exceptionally advanced subject-specific ability at a particular point in time, and in a particular context.

9. Parents should think carefully before allowing their children to be labelled as a result of an assessment. Although a label may be affirming, and serve as the ticket for admission into special programs, labelling can also have drawbacks.

10. The goal of assessment should not be to label children, but rather to provide information for making carefully reasoned decisions and meeting ever-changing individual learning needs.

Having thought about ways of assessing and understanding a child's learning needs, it's time now to think about how parents can support their children's developing abilities at school. This is the topic of chapter 5.

CHAPTER 5

Education:
Parents' Roles
at School

"Education is not preparation for life; education is life itself."

– JOHN DEWEY

W HAT RESPONSIBILITIES do parents have when it comes to children's schooling? What can they reasonably ask of their children's teachers—and how should they ask for it? How assertive should they be in fighting for their children's education? What rights do parents have? In this chapter, we address all of these questions concerning parents' roles in their children's schooling. We also describe classroom life from the teacher's point of view, and recommend strategies for parents who want to be effective advocates for their children at school.

Although parents sometimes feel hesitant about engaging with their children's schools, it's worth the effort. Parents can make a significant difference to their children's learning outcomes over the years. This is true for all parents, very much including those who come from culturally and socially diverse backgrounds.[1]

Many of the students at the Elizabeth Garrett Anderson School (EGAS) in London, England, are dealing with serious challenges in their home lives. In spite of this, EGAS has demonstrated its ability to sustain a school culture that supports high-level development in diverse learners—partly by including parents as important partners in their children's learning. The students come from many racial, linguistic, and religious backgrounds. So it's particularly meaningful that this is where U.S. First Lady Michelle Obama chose to talk to students and teachers about the importance of hard work, education, and high achievement, in a message broadcast around the world.[2]

Shortly after Michelle Obama's visit, we asked Jo Dibb, head teacher at EGAS, about her school's experience of this event. She replied: "Our students face huge disadvantages and yet still go on to achieve so much. Her [Michelle Obama's] words were powerful, and carefully chosen. They really reflected what we stand for as a school. The impact was tremendous on both students and staff . . . they all feel part of something special."[3]

We've since spoken in depth with many other head teachers and principals in the U.K., Canada, and the United States about intelligence-building and high academic achievement. Three themes have emerged from our conversations.[4] Firstly, school leaders identified *hard work* as instrumental for accomplishment. Secondly, they observed that clear, strong messages of *encouragement* from respected adults—including parents—can be powerful motivators for children to strive harder and achieve more. Finally, they said that educators and parents have to exercise *patience,* because change happens slowly, over time. A strong current that ran throughout the school leaders' observations was that school-wide support for hard work, encouragement, and patience requires good communication, and that all of this can propel everyone toward higher standards.

Parents who share these attitudes and create this kind of learning climate at home contribute enormously both to their own child's success and to the school's success. This is what Michelle Obama is referring to when she emphasizes the importance of attitude, supportive environments, and intentional effort in her own achievement and life experiences.

The Teacher's Point of View

Classroom teachers have to make tough choices. They labour under constraints that are invisible to many parents. These include paperwork, paperwork, and more paperwork (often with legal, financial, or professional consequences if not completed accurately and promptly); resource shortages; administrative requirements; and their own past experience (or lack thereof). Add to that an ever-changing curriculum; infinite discrepancies between students' current academic levels and the mandated grade-level curriculum; increasing demands for standardized testing, and the pressure to keep students' scores high; and educational politics. And let's not forget disruptive day-to-day scheduling changes and interruptions, and parents'—and students'—ongoing suggestions and demands. Is it any wonder that teachers don't always open their arms in welcome when parents have special requests regarding their child?

The fact that conscientious teachers have so many constraints and demands, and are involved in a constant juggling of priorities, doesn't excuse them from their most important and basic responsibility—providing the best possible education to each child. Nor does it mean that parents should just shrug their shoulders and avoid asking questions or making requests. Philosopher Bertrand Russell observed that "education has become one of the chief obstacles to intelligence and freedom of thought," and although that is too often true, it certainly doesn't have to be that way. We've seen plenty of examples of parents who've worked with schools to make an important difference for their children's education, and other children's as well.

Sometimes all it takes is a small change in attitude and understanding. For example, Paula, the little girl who thrived on solving problems, was sent to an advanced class when she was in elementary school. She began to think she wasn't very smart because she was slower than her classmates in learning to read.

> *"Teachers are expected to reach unattainable goals with inadequate tools. The miracle is that at times they accomplish this impossible task."*
>
> – HAIM G. GINOTT[5]

Paula's parents were worried about what was happening. She wasn't participating in class activities, and she was unhappy about going to school. Perhaps she wasn't as advanced as the other children in the class? Maybe she'd been misidentified? Maybe this was the wrong class for her?

They remembered she'd been an enthusiastic learner until a few months previously. They knew she was still exceptionally capable when it came to spatial reasoning tasks, and she continued to apply her excellent problem-solving skills to lots of things not having to do with school. They wondered if she'd be better out of the advanced class, but they also wondered if she'd be bored in a general education program.

Paula and her parents were suffering from the fixed mindset belief that being smart means learning everything quickly. They needed help moving toward a growth mindset and a broader understanding of intelligence.

Paula's teacher, who was a kind and intelligent professional (like most teachers we've met), worked hard to make sure her students were thriving. She was open to new perspectives, including learning about mindsets and multiple intelligences. She was keen to try out these approaches with her second-graders, including letting her students know what she was doing and why. We gave her some resources, and offered the same materials to Paula's parents for use at home.

Within a few weeks, things began to turn around, and Paula came to some important realizations. She recognized that she had several strengths, and that reading (so far) wasn't one of them. She understood she could learn to read better if she really wanted to, and if she was willing to work harder at it. Before long, Paula's enthusiasm for school returned. Instead of coming home dejected at the end of the day, she started bouncing through the door, excited to tell her parents what she'd been working on.

There are a number of factors that make Paula's story a happy one, starting with astute parents observing a problem that needed to be solved. Another positive factor was their persistence in trying to understand what was going on with their daughter, along with sufficient open-mindedness to question their own attitudes and beliefs.

Paula's problem was solved relatively easily because of a number of other serendipitous circumstances, including that the teacher was amenable to suggestions for professional development. The teacher also had administrative support that allowed her to make changes to the curriculum. For example, she incorporated multiple intelligences ideas into the students' reading activities, deviating somewhat from the normally prescribed lessons. The principal invited her to select a few new resources for the school. She displayed these in the school's library, and encouraged everyone—including parents—to share the information.

Once Paula's problem had been identified, the various circumstances for addressing it meshed well. Not all problematic situations work out so quickly or so easily, but if parents are patient and persistent—and if they can maintain their sense of humour and a respectful attitude—almost any school-related situation can be improved. Usually parents can facilitate this by working directly with teachers, without the expense of hiring outside consultants. As Paula's story illustrates, open dialogue and good resource materials can be helpful, as they encourage people to think matters through carefully, and to ask the right questions, at the right times, in a productive way.

A good starting point for parents is to ask for a meeting with the teacher to see her perspective on the situation they want to discuss. Sometimes the teacher is relieved the parents have noticed the problem, and is glad to have someone with whom to do some problem-solving. Other times the teacher doesn't perceive something is wrong until a child is functioning far below expectations in one subject or another, or there are behavioural issues.[6] In some cases, teachers don't respond well to parents' concerns that a child isn't learning as much, as quickly, or as enthusiastically, as they'd like. Very often where heightened abilities are involved, parents are the first to recognize that something needs changing.

Although it's not always easy to go slowly when a child's well-being is at stake, carefully planned small steps are more likely to make real progress than pushing ahead too aggressively. This holds true for many aspects of life, including schooling issues.

At the early stages of educational problem-solving, it's usually best to start with the classroom teacher. Things tend to go better if outside consultants are nowhere to be seen. School personnel are no different than other professionals in preferring to be given a chance to solve their own problems before an outside "expert" is called in. For the same reason, it's better, too, if the principal, superintendent, and other higher-ups are called in only as needed, later in the process. In Paula's case we'd been working with the school, so there were already consultants on board, but in most circumstances it's helpful for parents and teachers to talk through things together on their own. When it works (and it doesn't always), this informal approach yields the simplest and quickest outcomes.

If parents' initial request to meet with the teacher is warm, friendly, and positive, it communicates a desire for easy collaboration. The request can be made via e-mail or phone call, by saying something like "Hello, Mr. Ghomeshi. I'm Josie Alvarez's mother, and I've got some concerns about how she's doing. I know you're busy, but could we please arrange to meet one day soon?"

Some parents stride into their children's schools in a huff, loudly demanding immediate attention to changes they think should be made.

> Gizelle was deeply concerned. In her opinion, problems at Daniel's school had been festering far too long. Homework ignored by the teacher, quizzes left ungraded. Lack of communication. Poor test scores. She'd waited some time, hoping things would get better. A month ago, she'd had a chat over the phone with the teacher, who'd said she'd address the problems, but nothing changed. Or so it seemed to Gizelle. No one ever got back in touch with her. She'd boiled up a head of steam and decided it was time for action. She'd go to the principal with her complaints. Then the teacher would have to pay attention.

Most parents are more emotional (and less rational) when it comes to their children than in other areas in their lives. While they probably wouldn't go to a medical doctor or an employer in a huff about unquestioned assumptions, sometimes parents confront a teacher angrily out of a sense of frustration and helplessness. Some parents see teachers as their employees, and think it's within their rights to give instructions about how best to teach their children. Parents who feel like this will have to be extra polite if they want the teacher to make any changes at all for their child. Well, changes they'll be happy with, anyway . . .

While anxiety, anger, impatience, frustration, and other negative emotions are sometimes justified, parents who indulge in expressing them to a teacher are less likely to receive the kind of response they want. It's smart to open the conversation politely, respectfully, and co-operatively. As with any negotiation, making everyone feel appreciated, reining in any impatience, and setting a positive and collaborative tone greatly increase the likelihood of a successful outcome.

Parents who approach the teacher as the professional she is, framing their concerns and comments as questions, tend to get ahead—both farther and faster—than parents who arrive with suggestions, instructions, or (even worse!) accusations. For example, asking, "Have you noticed Brett seeming sad or disinterested lately?" is more productive than declaring, "Brett is very intelligent and totally bored by what you're giving him. You need to give him harder work," or "I don't know what you're doing at school, but our son used to be a lot happier."

We asked educators how parents can help them do a better job of building children's intelligence and meeting their individual learning needs. You might find it interesting, and perhaps a bit unsettling, to read some of the answers: "Children should be assessed on their merits—not the pushiness or naiveté or abilities or financial means (or anything else) of their parents"; "Parents have to know when to step forward, back, or aside. So often, they have no idea what's going on at school"; "What parents do at home should be in sync with what their child is doing at school."

When a parent is worried, there's almost always good reason, and there's something worth paying attention to. At the same time, however, some parents are clumsy or rude in their attempts to advocate for their children. By framing their concerns as thoughtful questions, parents increase the chances that a teacher will respond positively, and engage in useful problem-solving. They also reduce the likelihood that their requests will be met with skepticism, resistance, or outright denial of the problem, none of which ends up being very constructive.

Parents who approach a meeting with their child's educator as an opportunity for collaborative problem-solving are much likelier to receive a response like "Thanks for letting me know. That makes sense. Let's see what we can do for your son so we can tap into his strengths, and make sure he has the best possible learning experience."

"You need chaos in your soul to give birth to a dancing star."

– FRIEDRICH NIETZSCHE

Making Changes Together

Chaos and excitement surely have their place in motivating change and increasing intelligence. But working with your child's teacher requires the exact opposite—a carefully considered approach. It's rare that classroom change happens for a given child without thoughtful collaboration among parents and educators. Parents have an enormous influence on a child's physical, behavioural, social, and emotional functioning, all of which have a big impact on what kind of education will work best. Most children's attitudes emerge from their experiences at home, and—as happened with Paula—a child's attitudes can make all the difference in her experience of any situation, including classroom learning.

Parents can help teachers by providing information about their child—what she's like at home, what she enjoys doing, what makes her happy, enthusiastic, engaged, angry, or upset. They can find efficient ways to share their child's interests, enthusiasms, and extracurricular activities. It's important to emphasize "efficient" here, recognizing that teachers are typically under burdensome time constraints, and can't have long daily chats with parents about everything each of the children in their classes is doing, thinking, and saying when they're not at school.

Parents can offer a teacher useful information about a child by writing it out, starting by making a list of activities and interests, and then prioritizing it, maybe annotating any particularly interesting achievements or passions. A short (one-page) list is more useful than a two-hour video of a child's dramatic production, accompanied by script, diary notes, other parents' reviews, and costume drawings. (Yes, well-meaning parents do sometimes present portfolios like this to their children's teachers!)

The best educational outcomes occur when all participants—parents, teachers, and children—are actively engaged in the process together.

> *"It pays to plan ahead. It wasn't raining*
> *when Noah built the ark."*
>
> – ANONYMOUS

One of the problems that teachers can't solve on their own is a child's lack of self-discipline. Another is a child's belief that someone else is responsible for making every minute fun. Parents who want things to go well at school can start by setting high standards at home, and encouraging critical, creative, and cooperative habits of mind. They can ensure their children understand the importance of discipline and persistence, attributes they'll need for success in any environment, from preschool right through adulthood. Parents can also facilitate their kids' engagement in learning by being growth-minded themselves, taking pleasure in and gaining knowledge from their own day-to-day experiences.

Some children are exuberantly curious, perhaps by temperament. They find things to learn everywhere they go, looking for interesting connections between what they're being taught and other things they've already learned, reading independently, or detecting spatial or numerical patterns in the world around them. Others need support before they'll take responsibility for their own intelligence-building.

Somewhat counterintuitively, an expression of boredom can be a gift to a wise parent. A child who says, "I'm bored, Mommy!" is inviting a conversation about things to do, and ways she can begin to take ownership for her own learning. When children are very young, parents might get out some toys or books, or suggest some favourite activities. Unless the child is sick or genuinely exhausted, turning on the television or some other electronic babysitter will waste that golden moment. Although there's a time and place for technology in children's lives, and there are some excellent learning programs available, too much of it can encourage lazy habits of mind where the child comes to rely on entertainment created by others instead of inventing his own fun or discovering intellectual interests.

As children get older, the wise parent's response to an expression of boredom becomes something like "Wonderful! This is a good time for you to come up with some ideas about what you want to do. And while you're thinking about it, you can help me do the dishes." (Or fold the laundry, or straighten out the kitchen cupboards, or complete another chore the child usually finds tedious.) This strategy is best if it involves doing something together, because then it's a win-win choice. Either the child figures out what else he wants to do and is no longer bored, or the chore gets done and there's also time for conversation. The child who chooses the dishes, laundry, or straightening option often has something he wants to talk about with his parent.

People are bored when they haven't learned how to take responsibility for their own intellectual stimulation. Parents who think it's their job to keep their children entertained risk having kids who are bored at school, kids who grow up to be bored on the job, and perhaps in other areas of their lives as well. However, children who know that their education is, in part, their own to create have learned an important lesson for life and derive a lot more from their schooling.

By working co-operatively with teachers, parents play a pivotal role in their children's development at school and beyond.

Consider the case of Caryn, who we introduced in chapter 1. She enjoyed drama activities but didn't find academics very interesting. Her parents found some community-based extracurricular options for her to explore during out-of-school hours, and told her teacher about her interests. The teacher gave Caryn a chance to apply her passions and skills to some of her school work. For example, the teacher offered everyone in the class a choice between writing an account of the lives of early pioneers and collaboratively composing, directing, and participating in a play about one of the challenges the pioneers experienced. Caryn loved creating a script, and then acting it out with a friend. In fact, she later developed a second dialogue for science class, depicting what happened during a recent space launch.

Caryn's parents took an active and responsible role in her education, working in partnership with the teacher to inform her of areas of interest. By doing that, they greatly increased the likelihood that their daughter—who'd been showing signs of disengaging from school—would have a positive and meaningful school experience.

Schools vary considerably in the extent to which they individualize learning opportunities for students. Some schools routinely adjust instruction and assessment in response to kids' individual learning needs. This can take the form of alternative approaches to teaching and testing, providing a range of learning activities and challenges, and other strategies that help teachers adjust what they're doing in response to children's areas of strength and weakness. Other schools are not as accommodating. In some classrooms, everyone is given the same thing at the same time because they're the same chronological age. For parents who have concerns about their child's education, "being reasonable" means something different from one school environment to the next.

Remember Alexander? He was the student who was easily frustrated and afraid to tackle difficult work. There were many ways his teachers might have encouraged him to move toward taking bigger—but reasonable—risks. And his parents might have helped the teachers by providing information about difficulties he was experiencing, strengths they observed, and possible leadership indicators. But sadly, the teachers weren't particularly interested in adapting their program for children's individual learning needs, and his parents didn't want to risk his tenuous place in the program by asking for special consideration.

At some schools, Alexander's problem might have been relatively easily solved, but what works in one situation (such as the teacher incorporating specific changes into the curriculum to help an individual student) may not be considered so reasonable at another school. In this circumstance, Alexander's parents would do well to begin slowly, taking the lead with him at home, connecting with his teacher, and moving forward collaboratively, one step at a time toward necessary changes.

> *"Education's purpose is to replace an empty mind with an open one."*
>
> – MALCOLM S. FORBES

What Matters?

One of the most important things parents can do to support their children's education is to model and encourage a love of learning.

It's fine to trust in the school system (as merited), and to believe that teachers are capable professionals who will do everything possible to provide children with a solid education. However, it's also good for parents to be vigilant and proactive when it comes to their children's intellectual development, and not just let matters run their course, whatever that course might be.

CHECKLIST:
AN "A-LIST" OF WHAT MATTERS MOST IN
A CHILD'S EDUCATIONAL EXPERIENCE

These are the factors to pay close attention to, factors where parents can make an important difference:

- *authenticity:* Help your child find his own interests, values, and ways of being.
- *activities:* Provide a wide range of activities for your child. Do some of them together.
- *augmentation:* Encourage your child to build on his strengths.
- *autonomy:* Respect and foster your child's independence.
- *achievement:* Celebrate your child's achievements, and help him learn from his failures.
- *affirmation:* Affirm your child's essential humanity, as well as his unique abilities.
- *accountability:* As your child grows older, let him be increasingly responsible for his decisions.
- *attitude:* Model a growth mindset, and reinforce one in your child.
- *assumptions:* Identify and challenge your inferences and assumptions about intelligence and learning.
- *advocacy:* Work with other parents, teachers, administrators, and legislators toward getting important educational concerns addressed.

About Assumptions

Each factor on our A-list weaves its way through this book in many different forms. However, for now, we'd like to focus briefly on the last two points—assumptions and advocacy.

Albert Einstein said, "If you judge a fish by its ability to climb a tree, it will spend its whole life believing that it is stupid." Astute parents think critically about what they're reading, hearing, and seeing, and they work hard to avoid buying into the assumptions of others. Take Paula, for example. She was quick to solve puzzles, but she was slower learning to read. Her parents believed—without questioning their underlying assumptions—that advanced students are good at everything academic, especially reading, and are always quick to master new skills.

Once these assumptions were effectively challenged, however, Paula's parents recognized that ability isn't general across all areas of accomplishment. Different people have different strengths, so there's no reason to expect a child who's advanced in one area to be similarly advanced in other areas. Paula, her parents, and teacher were then able to see and appreciate Paula's areas of strength, and began to rectify her emerging problems with self-esteem and school.

Checking one's own assumptions is never easy, but it helps to try. Thinking critically about one's attitudes, perceptions, and conclusions goes a long way toward reducing the problems caused by faulty assumptions.

For example, sometimes parents worry because they can't afford expensive private schools, foreign travel, or exclusive clubs and lessons for their children. They make the assumption that by spending more money, they will be giving their child better learning experiences. That's an assumption very much worth challenging: the necessity borne of financial constraints can inspire creative ideas that work to children's long-term benefit.

Annemarie's story illustrates this. Like many parents, she's on a limited budget. She explained how she's been able to provide challenging learning opportunities for her ten-year-old daughter.

> Lena has such enthusiasm for learning! It's spilled over into all kinds of different interests so I'm always on the lookout for enrichment opportunities.
>
> I used to worry that Lena's education would be compromised because I don't have a lot of money, but I've discovered

some excellent activities well within my financial reach. For instance, Lena and I joined a community gardening group that restores untended lots in our neighbourhood, and gives residents allotments for growing food or flowers. Her interest in organic gardening has expanded to include cooking and environmentalism. We're also building a bird "hotel and spa" and planning other do-it-yourself projects to help the environment. She's also designed a mosquito-safe rain barrel for watering the garden, made out of recycled olive containers.[7]

There are many inexpensive and inventive resources that parents, teachers, and children can tap into for personal enrichment, extended learning, and fun. As Annemarie's story illustrates, parents' resourcefulness in finding and co-creating engaging learning opportunities can be an inspiration to their children, and nurture a spirit of innovation. Never make assumptions that a child's best learning opportunities depend on abundant finances. That's hardly ever true.

Opportunities for intelligence-building activities outside of school know no bounds. You can encourage your child to take up hobbies such as chess, second-language study, and music (including reading, writing, and singing, or playing by ear). Have fun learning together. Have open-ended discussions, with lots of questions. Generate analogies, metaphors, and puzzles, and ask your child to do the same. Role-play. When you don't know something, guess—and admit that you're guessing. Ask your child to look at current events from different points of view. Be resourceful, responsive to his questions, and attentive to his ideas.

Advocacy in Action

Wise parents are involved in teamwork. Working together, they become knowledgeable about local policies and practices, and can speak up effectively on behalf of their children's learning needs.

"If you have no will to change it, you have no right to criticize it."

– ABRAHAM LINCOLN

Schools in most North American jurisdictions are now required by law to offer a continuum of placements for children's learning needs across the spectrum.[8] Schools are also required to provide parents with information about special education services, and rights of appeal. However, what exactly is considered a special learning need, as covered by legislation? That depends on where you live. Regardless of the policies and regulations in place, parents usually have to take it upon themselves to become informed, often doing some research first, in order to know what to look for, and what questions to ask.

Most parents don't have the time or expertise to get involved in fact-finding investigations of their own. Luckily, there are education advocacy associations in place in many communities, and these associations have already done the basic spadework. Typically, they provide a range of services, as well as acting as repositories of useful information. They support parents of special needs learners by creating connections among those who have similar concerns, needs, questions, and interests, and by organizing social and resource-sharing networks and gatherings. There are also national and international advocacy groups, such as the National Association for Gifted Children (NAGC) in both the U.S. and the U.K., and the Association for Bright Children (ABC) in Canada.[9]

Here's another true story, this one about advocacy. It's from a father who's working hard to support his child's learning needs. The situation he describes illustrates the limitations, challenges, and power of advocacy.

Felix was going mad in kindergarten because he was so bored. His teacher asked us, "What can I give him so he's

interested?" We mentioned he'd been really excited the eve-
ning before when we played a little game. Without showing him what we were doing, we'd printed out a sentence
("Tomorrow Miss Christine will be playing with the puppets in the school"), cut the paper between the words, and
challenged him to make the longest possible sentence with
the pile of shuffled words. After quickly placing the puzzle pieces into a sentence, he was delighted and shouted,
"Another one!"

Instead of thinking about how she could use this information in the classroom, the teacher reacted, eyes wide with
horror: "That's impossible! I can't do that! That's not sup-
posed to happen until grade 2!"

Two months later, after many similarly thwarted attempts
to help the teacher challenge Felix, we switched schools. He's
now at a school that welcomes parent involvement, and
where teachers strive to address individual learning needs.
Through our advocacy efforts, his mother and I have been
part of that process. We've strengthened our understandings
of high-level development, and made a concerted push to
share the information with others—via a web site, in regular conversation, in professional development sessions with
educators, and in dialogue with politicians, writers, and
researchers. All of this has helped us become more aware of
what's important, and how to make a difference for our son
and other youngsters.

I've seen up close how parent advocates are at the fore-
front of a changing dynamic for helping children who require
educational adjustments. I believe it's a parent's responsibility to search for the most appropriate academic environment
for a child, and to stay involved with the school. At present
Felix is very content. He's learning and growing, and the
principal tells us our advocacy has been instrumental in that
happening, not only for him but for other high-ability learners as well.[10]

CHECKLIST:
ADVOCACY STRATEGIES FOR PARENTS

We've pulled together some advocacy-oriented strategies for parents who want to make changes in educational policies and practices, in the interest of supporting their children's optimal development:

- *Look for like-minded others.* Advocacy is easier, more effective, and more congenial when working with others.
- *Strive to nurture a climate of trust.* Change is always emotion-laden, and a school community is a complex and interdependent workplace. A climate of trust is essential to healthy and productive long-term change.
- *Get the facts straight.* Gather the necessary information about the situation or concern. Make sure your facts are up to date and accurate.
- *Prioritize.* Identify the core of the issue. Discern exactly what needs to be addressed, and why—from the start, throughout the advocacy process, and when making recommendations.
- *Make a plan.* Define a reasonable goal, a sensible timeline, and fair responsibilities.
- *Be specific and practical.* Put the ideas in writing, then discuss them with others. Make sure your suggestions are specific, practical, and clearly communicated.
- *Think broadly.* Consider community resources—sectors of society not normally associated with education, including business, volunteer groups, industry, media, seniors, and professionals.
- *Foster productive working relationships.* When encountering people who want to obstruct change you believe to be necessary, listen thoughtfully. Do your best to understand their perspectives and concerns. Maintain open communication channels, and aim for mutually respectful dialogue.

- *Stay committed.* Try to retain a sense of optimism—even when the advocacy process gets bogged down—and strive to regenerate forward momentum.
- *Encourage children to engage in self-advocacy.* Assist them in learning to identify and communicate their own learning needs, as appropriate to their age and maturity level.[11]

Our final thought on advocacy and working collaboratively with your child's school: no one can change everything at once. Start small, go slowly, and be patient.

A HOME AND SCHOOL QUIZ

What are the ten most important things parents can do to support schools in fostering children's intelligence? Here are some yes/no questions to ask yourself:

1. Do I listen actively and attentively to my child when she talks about school? (Y/N)
2. Do I respond thoughtfully to her questions and concerns? (Y/N)
3. Do I have a growth mindset about the ups and downs that occur at my child's school? That is, do I see obstacles as opportunities for learning, and trust that change happens one step at a time, with effort? (Y/N)
4. Do I stay attuned to my child's learning needs? (Y/N)
5. Do I pay attention to his emotional, social, and physical functioning, in addition to how well he's doing at school? (Y/N)
6. Do I maintain a positive connection with the school? (Y/N)
7. Do I avoid making assumptions about my child, including about his learning, preferences, or capabilities? (Y/N)
8. Do I clarify my expectations about my child's learning, keeping them well-defined, realistic, and fair? (Y/N)
9. Do I consult as needed with medical, educational, and psychological professionals? (Y/N)

10. Do I advocate for my child as needed, building bridges from home to school, community, and parent organizations, and back again? (Y/N)

You can use this quiz as an aid to problem-solving if you're not happy about what's happening in your child's education. Your "no" answers may provide clues about how to get started on improvements. If things are going well right now, you might want to review this quiz from time to time, just to make sure everything stays on track.

Our Secrets: Parents' Roles at School

1. Educational leaders have identified three factors leading to students' high academic achievement: (i) hard work, (ii) encouragement from respected adults, and (iii) patience on the part of teachers and parents.
2. Informed parents can make a big difference in their children's educational outcomes, particularly if they see teachers as allies with whom to work collaboratively.
3. Most teachers are professionals who are committed to children's academic success and overall development. They're operating under many constraints, and parents may not be aware of these. Voice your concerns about your child's education with the teacher, but do so respectfully. Be open to dialogue, suggestions, new approaches, and teamwork in problem-solving.
4. When working with the teacher to address an issue relating to your child's schooling, start informally.
5. Parents can contribute to their child's educational success by reinforcing habits of self-discipline and hard work at home, and also by ensuring that the child takes responsibility for his own engagement in learning and doesn't feel entitled to constant entertainment.
6. When figuring out what's important, parents can use our

A-list to think about what needs attention: authenticity, augmentation, autonomy, achievement, affirmation,
accountability, attitude, activities, assumptions, advocacy.

7. Try to determine if your own (and others') assumptions
   might be interfering with perceptions of what's happening at school. Work to eliminate any such interference.

8. Intelligence-building possibilities can be found by parents willing to search them out—and they don't have to
   cost a lot of money.

9. If you see a need for changes in your child's schooling,
   consider working together with others to engage in
   advocacy efforts.

We've shared stories of several children in this chapter, including
Felix, Lena, Caryn, and Paula, whose parents took initiatives that
led to beneficial changes in their schooling. Before we consider
some additional complications and concerns that kids and their
families sometimes experience (which we do in chapters 8 and
9), we'd like to focus on the nuts and bolts of education. It's helpful for parents to know what teachers have in their toolboxes—or
what they can acquire—to enable them to work effectively to foster children's ability. And, equally important, what else informed
parents can do to help teachers support those processes.

CHAPTER 6

Education:
Teachers' Roles,
Responsibilities,
and Requirements

*"Perhaps educators are not so different from their students—
learners who have their own starting points, and who need
to measure their success according to essential goals . . .
persistent effort, and progress toward their goals."*

– CAROL ANN TOMLINSON[1]

I N OUR EXPERIENCE, most teachers are serious professionals who want to do a good job with every child who comes
into the classroom. Parents who understand something about
teachers' professional responsibilities and constraints are well
positioned to be effective advocates for their children's learning.

In this chapter, we share information parents can use to
become more knowledgeable about what happens in their
children's schools. What are the essential tools, resources, and
supports that teachers require in order to be strong partners
in developing children's abilities? How can parents tell if their
children's classrooms and schools are capacity-building learning
environments? What can parents expect and request from their

children's teachers? And how can parents support teachers in their shared agenda of nurturing kids' strengths?

Classroom Essentials for Teachers

Teachers are trained professionals with a working knowledge of teaching and learning processes. Teacher education doesn't always include a focus on current findings concerning capacity-building, however. Parents who know about the educational essentials of building kids' intelligence, creativity, resilience, resourcefulness, and other important strengths are better prepared to support teachers in nurturing the development of their children's abilities.

> *"Some children study the rhythm of the tides. Others want to work out lengthy equations, ponder great novels, or think about the significance of historical events. So many possibilities!"*
>
> – JULIE[2]

The first essential for teachers is *appreciation of children's remarkable differences from each other*. Teachers with backgrounds in special education know that one size doesn't begin to fit all when it comes to children's learning, but kids who aren't identified as having special learning needs also vary tremendously from each other. There are differences in timing: some kids have advanced learning needs in preschool, whereas others discover their interests and abilities later on. There are also differences in focus: some children have special learning needs in mathematics—whether because they're advanced compared to their classmates, or struggling—whereas others need special attention in language, literature, science, or geography. As we discuss in chapter 1, there are many kinds of intelligences, and children have varying levels of competence in different areas. There are big differences in children's social and emotional maturation, too. And, of course, in kids' temperament, behaviour, motivation, experience, and other factors that affect their capacity to lead happily productive lives.

Thoughtful attention to what fits a given individual in a particular situation is the second essential factor in teachers' supporting children's abilities. This involves assessing the child's learning needs and interests in different areas, and attending to what makes him unique. It also involves assessing the nature and extent of his current strengths, as well as his learning challenges or possible problems. The more exceptional the learner, the more important it is that adjustments be made to his classroom experiences.

The third essential concerns teachers deciding for creativity. This involves *a willingness to stretch their boundaries, try new techniques, and go beyond teach-to-the-test curriculum guidelines.* Teachers take advantage of a broad range of teaching and assessment options. Erich Fromm said, "Creativity requires the courage to let go of certainties."[3] We've seen that when a creative spirit enhances an appreciation of individual differences, it invigorates teaching, enhances learning, and enlivens the entire dynamic of a school.

The fourth essential for teachers is *administrative support for the application of best practice.* Some educators find exciting ways to apply creativity in appreciating kids' individual differences, ensuring that every child has learning experiences that challenge and motivate his learning. When administrators do what they can to support teachers' autonomy and strengths, they create a school culture that motivates learning and capacity-building for everyone.

The fifth essential requirement for teachers is *well-planned, challenging professional development opportunities.* Children's abilities fluctuate from subject to subject, and over time. Multiply these individual differences by a whole class (or grade, or school) and it becomes clear that teachers' responsibilities are hugely demanding. Professional development is not a perk but a necessity.

Consider, for example, what carpenters know. They need large, medium, and small flat-tips, square shanks, Phillips, stubbies, and crosspoints. Sure, they're all screwdrivers, but every carpenter has learned to recognize that each one works well in certain situations, and not at all well in others. In a perfect world, teachers' toolboxes would contain a comprehensive set of approaches to working with a range of learners, including those who are having difficulty with school work and those who are exceptionally advanced in one or more areas.

Good educators appreciate that if one approach doesn't work with a given child, they have to reassess the situation and carefully select another. Of course, this requires solid teacher training and professional development opportunities. Carpenters don't just pick up a toolkit one day and call themselves master cabinetmakers. In addition to having all the right tools, it takes years of training—including skill development, apprenticeships, practice, practice, practice, and learning about standards of design and craftsmanship—before they can craft a few pieces of wood into a beautiful piece of furniture.

Like woodworkers in their areas of expertise, teachers require years of training, learning, and experience to become experts. They also need collaborative partnerships with colleagues; support from special education and other resource teachers, consultants, educational administrators, and parents; an understanding of professional standards of practice; and access to a wide range of real and online resources.

CHECKLIST:
PROFESSIONAL DEVELOPMENT
OPTIONS FOR TEACHERS

Suggestions for professional development include the following:

- continuing education and additional qualifications courses;
- collaboration with university-based researchers on different approaches to teaching, learning, and assessment;
- consultations with special education, social work, and psychological resources as needed;

- mentoring relationships with colleagues, both as mentor and mentee;
- attendance and presentations at conferences and workshops;
- self-study groups, using videos and peer discussion to develop stronger skills, and consider different approaches to teaching and learning;
- technology-based projects (e.g., exploring how computer applications can apply to different areas of study); and
- resource-sharing with other teachers.[4]

Communities that provide teachers with rich opportunities for professional development reap valuable rewards. The Program for International Student Assessment (PISA) compares how students and schools achieve across academic areas (including mathematics, reading, and writing) in sixty-five countries. Andreas Schleicher, who co-ordinates the international testing and analyses, reported that the highest performing PISA schools have "ownership" cultures. As Thomas Friedman wrote in a *New York Times* article when the 2012 results were released, this implies "a high degree of professional autonomy for teachers in the classrooms, where teachers get to participate in shaping standards and curriculum, and have ample time for continuous professional development."[5]

Benefits of teachers having this kind of autonomy and opportunities for professional growth include increased numbers of children engaging in meaningful learning; a more vibrant school experience for teachers, principals, students and others; and better learning outcomes across subject areas. Over time, this translates into more people having higher levels of expertise in a number of different areas, which in turn leads to increased engagement in lifelong learning, invention, and discovery. Everyone benefits when we ensure that teachers have the supports they need to encourage the fullest possible development of children's abilities.

CHECKLIST: WHAT DO TEACHERS NEED FOR INTELLIGENCE-BUILDING?

Here's a quick overview of five essentials for building children's capacities:

- appreciation of children's remarkable differences from each other
- thoughtful attention to what fits a given individual in a particular situation
- a willingness to be creative; to stretch boundaries, try new techniques, and go beyond teach-to-the-test curriculum guidelines
- administrative support for the application of best practices
- well-planned, challenging professional development opportunities

Classroom Ideas That Work

People just entering the field of teaching often bring thoughtful new perspectives on schools and education—seeing afresh what works, and also identifying what needs to be changed.

> *"Discontent is the first necessity of progress."*
> – THOMAS EDISON

We asked several teacher candidates some questions about their experiences after their first teaching practicum.

What did you notice about the way children learn?
- No two kids are alike.
- I saw students who were really bored. There was nothing for them to do!

- There were kids who just needed to talk, and have someone listen.
- Lots of students were curious, and asked great questions.
- One little guy was very intelligent, but shy. He seemed to
  know about so many things, but he didn't know how to
  interact with anybody. I'm sure there are loads of kids like
  that!

What options are available for advanced learners?
- The teacher I worked with had a policy of pre-testing kids
  before she started a unit of study. Then she made a point
  of chatting with the ones who already knew the material
  so they could help design and extend their learning experiences.
- The school had a special program at 7 a.m. for kids who
  wanted to learn more.
- There were no enrichment programs of any kind that I
  could see. Nothing!
- There were dozens of extracurricular activities that kids
  could choose from, and a resource teacher who ran an
  "inquiry club" in the library during lunchtime three days
  a week.
- The teacher assigned independent work—and then more,
  and more, and more of it.

These teachers-in-training made some excellent observations.
Some saw that children's learning needs can differ enormously.
Some saw excellent teachers doing great work in classrooms, and
others saw some pretty questionable situations. (A special program at 7 a.m.? A mountain of independent work? Not too many
children will see these as desirable options.)

We also asked these aspiring educators for their suggestions
for change. Here, too, their answers were insightful:

What do you think has to be done to ensure all children get the best possible education?

- Teachers need more information about how to work with individual learners.
- Targeted professional development opportunities, resource material, access to collaborative networks, consultants, and more.
- Principals are key. Administrative buy-in generates two things: funding and a culture of support for improving the standard of education. Both can improve the teaching and learning that occur within a school.
- Schools should offer more leadership opportunities for students.
- Teachers have to be open to all students—not just those who might, at first, appear to be superstars. You never know who can do what until they're actually given a chance to shine.

Interestingly, the observations and concerns shared by these novice teachers are very similar to what we hear from their more seasoned colleagues. Here's a story shared by experienced teacher Susan Miller about a moment of illumination she translated into action:

I ran into problems with one of my tenth graders, a bright, articulate boy named Ivor. Toward the end of second semester, he started missing assignments, and his marks really slipped. When I discussed the situation with him, he told me he was bored with school—and had been for many years! I asked Ivor if he would've done better in my course if I'd kicked up the assignments for him. He grinned and said, "Yes! I would've proven to you I could do it."

I thought about his response, and approached a guidance counsellor to see what could be done for Ivor (and maybe others) during third semester. She spoke with the science and math teachers to see how they could motivate him, and they were willing to investigate a wide range of options. Ivor began enjoying school. He wasn't bored because he was being challenged to think critically and creatively.

As delighted as I am about how things turned out for Ivor, I can't help but wonder how many other students are declining academically and maybe psychologically—appearing to be behaviour problems, or invisible, or labelled "lazy" because of their lack of effort—because nobody recognizes or addresses their abilities.[6]

"Differentiation" is a blanket term used to describe the many ways that teachers like Susan and her colleagues change their teaching practice in response to the needs of individual students. It's not something most teachers immediately welcome. Not surprisingly, teachers often perceive differentiation to be a great deal of extra work, perhaps even impossible, given the weight of responsibilities for student learning, assessment, and administrative paperwork they already carry.[7]

However, strong research evidence supports the effectiveness of differentiation, and many professional development efforts have been made over the past decade to help teachers acquire the necessary knowledge and skills to do it well. Differentiated instruction is built on knowing children, and responding to their individual learning needs, something that Lannie Kanevsky describes as "deferential differentiation."[8] It involves understanding that every child enters the classroom with a unique set of competencies and concerns—and it allows teachers to put the emphasis on moving forward from there to develop children's many and varied intelligences.

Here are three differentiation experiences that teachers with strong track records have shared with us:

- I teach one of three grade four classes in my school. During the reading period, I teach all those who are reading at grade level, while one of my colleagues takes the children who are having difficulty, and the other teacher works with the advanced readers. Every child is challenged at his own level, and no teacher is trying to cover the whole spectrum, or short-changing any of the learners.

- A parent volunteer is helping our school with some extra resources. She organized a field trip to the museum, arranged for a scientist to come into our class as a special guest, and planned an artist-in-the-schools project.

- Students who get 85 percent or more on a pre-test are able to use class time to work with our school librarian to select and participate in online learning activities. So far, they've studied topics like trigonometry, magic, and the culture of the countries where their grandparents lived. Currently there's a group investigating how to save beached whales and the kids have been e-communicating with a marine biologist. The students get super-engaged, and share their enthusiasm and what they learn with others.

These teachers have discovered some of the many options that can help them respond to children's individual learning needs. These options include flexible grouping, parent involvement, collaborations with colleagues, inquiry-based and problem-based learning, and choice. However, teachers usually need some help mastering the various techniques involved in effective differentiation.

Educational researchers and advocates have long argued for improved teacher training in special education, including giftedness.[9] Most student teachers receive general courses in child development, and many teachers learn at least a few differentiation techniques for some of the more prevalent learning exceptionalities, such as specific kinds of learning disabilities. The extent of differentiation training is highly variable from one school district to the next, and even where teachers learn about it, attention to advanced learning needs tends to be minimal.

There are many reasons for this widespread disregard for the special learning needs of advanced students. One of these is the common misconception that smart kids will do just fine without extra attention. Another is the political view that concerns about high-level development are trivial in the light of numerous competing issues, and growing demands for limited educational funding allocations.

When teachers avail themselves of opportunities to develop solid approaches for working with *all* learners—and when they're supported by their administrators in doing so—it's to everyone's advantage. Parents can be instrumental in this process by recognizing that too few teachers are given what they need by way of training in special education and differentiation. Parents who advocate for school-wide teacher development opportunities in these practices, including those best suited for advanced learners, can make a big difference for their own children, and many others, too.

So, how can teachers learn about differentiation practices? They can participate in study groups, enroll in courses, join professional networks, and take part in conferences and distance education programs. These learning opportunities address the topics covered in this book, including how to tailor programming for specific areas of strength (linguistic, mathematical, scientific, musical, etc.), how to address social/emotional concerns, and how to adapt curriculum, assessment procedures, and more.

A Four-Part Framework for Teaching Kids: Planning, Assessment, Activities, and Learning Environment

A workable framework for teachers who want to differentiate curriculum for children's learning differences consists of four elements: planning, assessment, activities, and learning environment. Parents who understand this process are in a better position to be informed advocates for addressing any gaps that might exist in their children's learning.

Thorough *planning* is important for teachers working with a wide range of learning needs. That includes in classrooms where every student has been formally identified as gifted, as well as in general education classrooms where some children work at advanced levels and others don't, and in special education classes for kids who experience learning problems.

Planning involves thinking about the goals and objectives of what's being taught, investigating available resources and supports so they're in place when needed, and helping students become better planners themselves. It also means figuring out how learning can be extended to provide challenges for children who have already mastered material.

Effective planning strategies help teachers respond more effectively to children's interests, learning needs, and academic levels. Parents who know about the importance of this aspect of the teaching/learning process can help teachers acquire the support and resources they need.[10]

As we note in chapter 4, *assessment* is a complicated business, and even experienced teachers can have questions about how to implement best practices. No wonder so many parents find it confusing. Nevertheless, they can meet with teachers to discuss assessment approaches, and come to understand them better.

CHECKLIST: GOOD ASSESSMENT PRACTICES

Here are some questions for parents to think about:

- *Elastic?* Are the assessment processes flexible enough to show children's strengths across a wide range of levels? (Think of Roberto, for example, who is several years ahead of the rest of the class in math; as well as students like Alexander, who get anxious or perhaps even belligerent when questions are too difficult.)

- *Diverse and multi-faceted?* Is there a variety of assessment formats in place, so that all students are given opportunities both to identify their areas of weakness and to demonstrate their strengths?
- *Educationally meaningful?* Do students take part in assessment tasks in a way that increases their learning?
- *Fair?* Are assessment practices fair, unbiased, and reasonable?

Assessment can be woven seamlessly into the learning process, enabling steady increases in challenge levels. There are many forms of assessment, from norm-referenced standardized tests of academic achievement through to a teacher observing a child while she completes an assignment. Some of the more interesting assessment formats include debates, student blogs, co-created rubrics, concept drawings, historic dramatizations, and student-designed portfolios.

Which assessment option is right depends on why the teacher needs the information. For example, brainstorming can be a good preliminary assessment in order to start the process of seeing who knows what about a topic before it's taught, providing good information for designing and differentiating curriculum. Portfolios and concept mapping are better for formative assessments, enabling a teacher (with the help of students) to fine-tune the focus of teaching along the way. Options like standardized tests work well for summative assessments, where the objective is to find out how much a child has learned at the end of a unit of study.

Careful planning and meaningful assessment prepare the way for effective *learning activities*—the third element of our framework for teaching kids.

CHECKLIST:
OPTIONS TO CHALLENGE LEARNERS

Here's a list of recommendations educators can use to support children's high-level development:[11]

- daily challenge in areas of advancement
- high standards in all subject areas
- attention to concepts, issues, problems, principles, generalizations
- faster pacing in math and science, as needed
- elimination of excess drill and practice
- opportunities for academic credit for prior learning
- opportunities to work independently and be unique
- exposure to content beyond grade level in areas of talent
- shortening the number of years spent in the K–12 system
- opportunities to socialize and learn with like-ability peers

There are many programming models that incorporate three or more of these recommendations. Some require extensive teacher training, so we don't include them here.[12] However, there are other approaches parents can use at home, or to inform their advocacy efforts, and some may be seen in their children's homework assignments or completed work. Over the next few pages we pull together several ideas for learning activities, including some we introduced briefly in other chapters (such as multiple intelligences). We also discuss the practical implications of each of these suggestions.

Bloom's Taxonomy is a tried-and-true approach to differentiating teaching for different kinds of learners. Benjamin Bloom devised a list of six educational objectives: knowledge, comprehension, analysis, application, evaluation, and synthesis.[13] This framework can be used to enrich children's learning experiences in any subject area. When used effectively, it offers children meaningful choice and challenge, supporting them in becoming better at creative and critical thinking, and more engaged in the learning process.

Bloom and many others have developed practical activities to accompany this taxonomy.[14] Although some learners move faster than their age peers to the higher-order thinking skills (analyzing, evaluating, and creating), it's essential that, like everyone, they master the lower levels as well (remembering, understanding, and applying). For example, you can't evaluate the relative merits of different perspectives on Renaissance painting until you have some knowledge and understanding of basic components such as colour, form, line, and perspective.

The *multiple intelligences (MI)*[15] *approach* is a method of expanding the range of what is considered to be intelligence. (We discuss this in chapter 1.) MI liberates parents' and teachers' imaginations, opening windows of possibility for teaching and learning. The big caveat with this approach to intelligence-building is that it can be applied in ways that trivialize or distort knowledge and concepts. We've seen it artificially applied to teaching mathematics, for example: instead of learning to multiply and divide, students sing songs, draw pictures, or do stretching exercises using numbers. Roberto, who loves a mathematical challenge and is highly advanced compared to the other children in his class, hated the assignment he was given to create a poster board using toothpicks to illustrate Roman numerals I to L. "That's not math!" he said in exasperation. "That's just BORING!"

The *triarchic intelligences approach* separates intelligence into three components: analytical, practical, and creative.[16] As we mention in chapter 1, analytical intelligence is the intelligence most emphasized through elementary and secondary schooling, and is reasonably well measured by IQ. In his careful attention to detail and logical deductions, Sherlock Holmes is a good example of analytical intelligence in action. Children who are great at solving puzzles and enjoy comparing and contrasting ideas are developing their analytical intelligence.

Practical intelligence is sometimes called "street smarts" or "common sense." It refers to the ability to adapt to changes in personal, social, and professional contexts, and can be seen in people like Oprah Winfrey, whose business successes reflect her extraordinary practical intelligence, quite independently of what her IQ score or academic achievement might be.

Experiential or creative intelligence is the ability that's used in inventing or designing. You might remember Caryn, who enjoyed making up dramatic scenes and plays, and hated wasting time on activities that had no connection to a product or performance in the real world. Although she wasn't a particularly good test-taker, from a triarchic intelligences perspective, her less-than-stellar scores reflect the IQ test's limitation, and not Caryn's.

Affirming diverse ways of being smart and expressing one's intelligence expands a child's sense of possibility. An approach like the triarchic framework enables children to discover their preferred ways of thinking, and also helps them develop their capabilities more broadly. For example, this approach could help Caryn learn to value her analytical and practical/experiential abilities in addition to her creativity, and also give her parents a structure for understanding the kinds of abilities she might want to explore further as she matures.

However, the triarchic approach can also be used to subvert important learning objectives. Sometimes teachers create assignments that allow students to work in an uncritical "creative" or "practical" mode, despite the fact that there is some important analytical learning that must be done first, as a foundation for creativity or practical application. For example, it's hard for a child to write a good poem about a mongoose if she has little or no idea what a mongoose is.

Problem-based learning begins with problem-finding, where children or adolescents work together with each other, their parents, teachers, or other mentors to identify a real-world problem or question of interest. It works best when the issue is authentic and challenging. Choice and collaboration are important aspects of this process, as is the feeling of accomplishing something important and relevant.

CHECKLIST:
PROBLEM-BASED LEARNING

Here's what problem-based learning boils down to, whether pursued at home or school:

- *problem-finding:* identifying what needs changing
- *investigating:* asking questions and working out possible answers
- *problem-solving:* arriving at one or more viable solutions
- *implementing:* making it happen

How does this concept translate into a learning activity? Once a juicy problem has been identified—one that engages children's interests and feels important—the next step is to understand the background issues, obstacles, opportunities, and complicating factors as thoroughly as possible. From there, learners move to the problem-solving process, where they work together to identify ways forward, and come up with recommendations for action. They might make predictions, design experiments, conduct research, draw conclusions, organize information, communicate with others, and ultimately hone their higher-order thinking skills. They may try to implement their ideas, evaluating their impact on the identified problem, and making suggestions for future efforts.

One secondary school teacher we spoke with shared this story about problem-based learning:

Over the past few years, my students have identified various interesting local and large-scale problems, and have worked at solving them. For example, one group decided that a neighbourhood elementary school needed better playground equipment. They worked together and investigated state-of-the-art designs and environmentally friendly materials, and scouted volunteers to help them create a plan. Then they got community and corporate support, permits, and top-notch construction assistance, and actually built it!

This kind of productive activity can be motivating and fun, and at the same time foster high-level outcomes for diverse kinds of learners. For those who want to explore this approach further, we suggest checking out Joseph Renzulli's enrichment triad model.[17]

Potential pitfalls of problem-based learning include that busy parents or teachers who are stretched in too many directions can send children off to do projects on their own, with insufficient guidance. Alternatively, they may provide or accept trivial "problems" for investigation, or accept uncritical "solutions," thereby robbing the process of any lasting significance.

No matter what learning approaches or activities are used, effective differentiation is built on and enhances solid teaching practices. In every classroom there are certain non-negotiables that encourage high-level learning outcomes. We've characterized this approach as the five R's: being resourceful, reasonable, receptive to change, respectful of students' feelings and abilities, and responsive to their questions. The best activities are those that are designed or adapted for children's learning interests and levels of readiness. Expectations and goals should be clear, and aligned with children's areas of strength and weakness in different domains.[18]

When it's well understood and implemented, differentiation does not present an insurmountable challenge. Quite simply, it can be viewed as a way of thinking that should pervade what teachers do in the classroom all day long, and every day. It means being attentive to children's individual levels of competence, and being amenable to change. It means adopting a flexible range-of-options approach to pretty much everything. It also means opening channels of communication, thinking creatively, and adjusting learning experiences in accordance with differences in how children learn. In a nutshell, it's what good teaching is all about.[19]

Elenora has taught grades four through six for the past twelve years. Like many teachers, her initial reaction was to resist the suggestion to differentiate programming in her classroom. She wrote to us about what changed her mind:

> I had an aversion to the idea of differentiation. Why draw attention to students' differences? I don't believe children should get used to special treatment. The world is simply not like that.
>
> Every time we had a professional development workshop the word "differentiation" lay beneath the surface like a rotting onion slowly decaying in a vegetable bin, and I didn't like it. I thought, "Who has time to modify materials, alter instruction, change assessment practices, and tailor the curriculum for every single child?" I was already doing plenty. In addition to all the usual classroom preparation, test design, and administrative paperwork I had to take care of, I sometimes offered my students choice that deviated from my normal curriculum and routine. For instance, they could choose their books for their reports, and they could be creative if they wanted. I also assigned a self-directed learning activity every other week.
>
> Then I took part in a three-day seminar. I realized the onion was not rotten, and that differentiation is actually a planned, consistent, and daily approach to teaching and learning—that it might even be something that could help my teaching, not bog it down. I saw that it's not just a "sometimes" thing; that it's not only doable, it's necessary.
>
> Now my students help me locate resources, and we learn together. As long as I monitor what's going on, they evaluate much of their own work. I ask open-ended questions, and

students analyze, interpret, and use concrete and abstract thinking. I still believe teachers shouldn't draw attention to students' differences, but *everyone* is different, so it actually makes sense to have lots of things happening in the classroom. It's true that the world is not always accommodating, but that doesn't mean I should follow suit. In fact, maybe it's all the more reason I shouldn't . . .

Administrators (and parents) should encourage teachers to take advantage of as many learning opportunities as possible. There are countless workshops similar to the one Elenora attended that are available to teachers throughout the year. These can be found in professional journals, associations, and online.[20]

It works to everyone's benefit when parents feel they're integral to the school culture, and actively contribute to what's happening there. Administrators—head teachers, principals, vice-principals, superintendents, and others in charge of organizing schools—play an important role in ensuring that children experience meaningful learning activities. Those in administrative positions can facilitate useful collaborations within a school and outside of it. They can also spearhead professional development opportunities for teachers. This might include networking with other schools locally and internationally, as well as with neighbourhood organizations and businesses.

Having considered various demands and possibilities involved with *planning, assessment,* and *activities,* we now consider the final cornerstone in our four-part framework for teaching kids, the *learning environment.*

CHECKLIST:
SUCCESSFUL LEARNING ENVIRONMENTS

What are the key aspects of a successful learning environment? Parents should keep their eyes open for the following:

- a network of professionals (teachers, mentors, specialists) who share ideas and resources, and work co-operatively
- programs that mesh well (e.g., general and special education, cross-grade or cross-subject offerings)
- a continuum or range of services that provide ample opportunities for growth and intelligence-building, enabling students' interests to develop and their strengths to emerge at their own pace
- ongoing support and commitments from administrators, such as principals, superintendents, and district policy-makers

A school culture that includes these factors is conducive to productive learning for every participant—teachers, parents, administrators, and children, all of whom are engaged in dynamic community development. This leads to increased vitality, excitement, and intelligence, as teaching and learning unfold in surprising directions.

> *"Our school does not offer any kind of advanced programming, and the special education co-ordinator also told me they don't recognize gifted-level abilities on Individual Education Plans because if they did, there would have to be appropriate programming available. And there isn't. He said, 'Those kids can go to another school for that.'"*
>
> – COLLETTE[21]

Thought-Provoking Questions

There are many schools and school boards that don't offer any kind of advanced programming. The attitude that advanced learners can do just fine on their own without any special educational provisions shows a callous disregard for individual developmental differences. Attitudes like this are reminiscent of the days before special education was seen as a necessity rather than a luxury, before most jurisdictions had legislation in place protecting the rights of special needs learners to an education commensurate with their abilities. Lack of attention to children's learning needs reflects a recklessness bordering on negligence. Yet sadly, these situations continue to exist, and in fact are all too prevalent.

Many teachers work hard to circumvent or change policies that are unfair, rigid, outdated, or too narrowly focused. In fact, the above quote comes from a teacher who was incensed by the situation in which she found herself working. She decided to do something about it. She enrolled in a course in gifted education so she could learn more about meeting children's advanced learning needs, and maybe even someday change the culture of the school where she taught. She's gone on to do just that.

In any one district, educational planning, assessment, activities, and learning environments can vary greatly across schools, and even across classrooms within a given school. Wise parents think carefully about whether or not children's capacities are encouraged within their child's classroom or school. To that end, we provide below ten questions for parents to consider. Although the questions are posed in a yes/no format, the situation is usually more nuanced than that, and the answer will be somewhere along the spectrum between "excellence really valued" and "excellence means a kid's a pariah." When parents aren't sure about the answers, they should talk about them with their kids. If they're still not sure, it may be time to visit the school, engage in a little inquiry, and find out what's happening there.

QUIZ: YOUR CHILD'S SCHOOL

1. *School culture:* Is it cool to be smart?[22] Is capacity-building a priority? Is academic excellence a goal, and is it held in esteem? (Y/N)
2. *Administrative attitude:* Is there administrative flexibility and support for teachers who engage in and share differentiation practices? (Y/N)

3. *Teacher development opportunities:* Is there an active schedule of professional development, with a focus on meeting various kinds of learning needs? (Y/N)

4. *Respect for individual developmental differences:* Are students' diverse strengths, weaknesses, and interests identified and taken into account by means of well-planned teaching and thoughtfully designed activities? (Y/N)

5. *Level of work and quality of outcomes:* Are expectations appropriate? Are children given high-quality work, with an emphasis on conceptual mastery and deep understanding? (Y/N)

6. *Depth and breadth of learning experiences:* Are students encouraged to explore ideas on a broad scale? (Y/N)

7. *Ability-fair assessments:* Are there many different ways for children to demonstrate what they know and understand? (Y/N)

8. *Spontaneity and flexibility:* Are unexpected events and students' contributions used as opportunities to build on children's existing knowledge? (Y/N)

9. *Home and school connections:* Are communication channels open, honest, and reciprocal? Are parents welcome, and are their viewpoints considered? (Y/N)

10. *School milieu:* Are students excited about learning? Is the school safe, inviting, spirited, and encouraging of diversity? (Y/N)

Parents who reflect on the ten questions in the quiz are better able to help teachers do the work they want to do. Even when the answers are mostly no, parents have a solid starting point for thinking about how they can become advocates for change, and support teachers in their day-to-day work. Once educators have the essential tools, and begin to use them wisely, the rest is a matter of ongoing professional development, constructive practice, collaborative effort, experience, and support. A tall order perhaps, but certainly doable.

Our Secrets: Teachers' Roles, Responsibilities, and Requirements

Teachers can foster the development of children's abilities by appreciating their individual differences, implementing a range of teaching and assessment options, deciding for creativity in their teaching practice, experiencing administrative support, and engaging in rich and plentiful opportunities for ongoing professional development. This means being resourceful, reasonable, receptive to change, respectful of students' feelings and abilities, and responsive to their questions.

To understand teachers' roles, responsibilities, and requirements, parents can keep in mind the following points.

1. Teachers' work is infinitely more complex and demanding than it might appear to an outsider.
2. Differentiating for individual developmental differences is a key factor in creating a capacity-building educational setting.
3. Four areas where differentiation can occur are planning, assessment, activities, and learning environment.
4. Administrators play an important role in ensuring that children experience productive learning opportunities at school.
5. The Your Child's School quiz is a tool to assess whether a child's school experience is as productive as it can be.

A child's school experience makes an enormous difference to her education and well-being, but that's not always enough. Sometimes decisions, issues, and problems arise that require careful consideration. That's what we think about in chapter 7.

CHAPTER 7

Decision-Making about Schooling

"Fortune favours the prepared mind."
– LOUIS PASTEUR

PUBLIC SCHOOL, private school, charter school, or home-schooling? Arts focus, science program, gifted education, or sports? Neighbourhood school, alternative school, magnet school, or online learning? So many options and possibilities, each one with advantages and disadvantages. No one can know the complex context of another person's life, and no one can tell someone else what's best for their child's education. In this chapter, we discuss the pros and cons of many possible educational choices, consider different kinds of evidence, and share some of the decision-making processes that have helped other families when they've been faced with difficult choices about their children, learning needs, and schools.

Before we get into the details of school decision-making, however, we'd like to mention recent research findings comparing home and school factors. In a study of academic achievement in more than 10,000 students, plus parents, teachers, and school administrators, researchers compared what they called "family social capital" and "school social capital."[1] Family social capital includes trust, communication, and engagement in academic life. School social capital includes learning environment, extracurricular activities, teacher morale, and teachers' ability to meet the needs of individual children.

The results showed that school quality matters, but not as much as family support and connection. This is very encouraging news for parents who worry about not sending their children to expensive private schools, or think they have to move into a higher priced neighbourhood for better public schools.

Ideally, of course, parents want to provide their kids with optimal home *and* school environments. It can be confusing to decide which school or program is the best one, and whether it's worth a disruption to make a change.

Noreen, for example, is fully engaged in her extracurricular music and second-language lessons, and seems happy at the local elementary school, but her teacher recommends she go into a part-time enrichment program. Michael's parents would rather he receive a public school education, but their friends tell them a private school will do a better job of challenging his intellect. Javon's been accepted into an advanced program. Should his parents sign him up even though he'll have to change schools, leave his friends, and take the school bus instead of walking? What should these families do? What should they be thinking about in order to make the best possible decisions? We discuss situations like this, and more, in the pages that follow.

> *"The key to good decision-making is not knowledge.*
> *It is understanding. We are swimming in the former.*
> *We are desperately lacking in the latter."*
>
> – MALCOLM GLADWELL[2]

Much of our work with parents, children, and educators has been done in Toronto, London (UK), and New York, richly textured urban settings where there are countless schooling options and learning possibilities: public, private, parochial, online, and

more. Not all urban options are good ones, of course, but there are
a lot of them. At the same time, some of the most creative solutions we've found to support children's development have been in
remote communities. We've observed first-hand that every situation has its own constraints, advantages, and challenges. We've
also seen that when parents have more choices, their decision-
making can be more agonizing.

Where there are fewer schools to choose from, there are still
important decisions to be made. Parents in rural or suburban
communities—or other situations where there are limited schooling options for a given age or ability level—can take an active
advocacy role, or homeschool their children, or consider a move
to a community with different schools, or supplement their children's education with any number of challenging learning experiences. These might include online learning, summer programs,
extracurricular activities, travel and adventure, and other creative
possibilities.

The Good, the Bad, and the Mediocre

Schools should be places where children develop their literacy,
numeracy, technological skills, and other capacities. Schools
should also be places where kids learn about inquiry, strengthen
their character, feel comfortable, learn to appreciate the value of
reflection, and experience the rewards of effort and perseverance.
What does a good school look like? How can parents assess that?

International comparisons of educational outcomes demonstrate that teacher quality matters a lot more than variables parents
often pay attention to when they're choosing schools—variables
like class size, sports programs, field trips, or technological enrich-
ments. In *The Smartest Kids in the World and How They Got That
Way,* Amanda Ripley writes, "The smartest countries prioritize
teacher pay and equity (channeling more resources to the neediest
students). When looking for a world-class education, remember
that people always matter more than props."[3]

CHECKLIST:
ELEMENTS OF A GOOD SCHOOL

Educational psychologist and researcher Marcia Gentry[4] writes that a good school, which she describes as a "quality" school, is a place where students

- learn to think and apply knowledge to new situations;
- are involved in and excited about learning;
- make individual gains in process and knowledge;
- experience adults who know and care about them;
- develop "I can" attitudes and efficacy about learning; and
- are prepared for success after school.

We shared this description with 200 parents who attended an education forum for a large urban school district, and asked if they thought their children attended a good school, using these criteria. We were disheartened to find that only 15 percent responded in the affirmative. We asked several other groups of parents the same question, and the results were sadly similar.

These findings spurred us on to ask hundreds more parents, teachers, principals, and students about the factors they think are important for supporting children's development. Putting their responses into the context of the research literature on effective schools,[5] we developed a quiz for parents to help them consider each potential school or program in their school decision-making process:[6]

QUIZ: DOES THIS SCHOOL SUPPORT CHILDREN'S OPTIMAL DEVELOPMENT?

Please answer no, mostly, or yes.

1. Do children feel safe and secure? (N/M/Y)
2. Do all students experience challenge in many different subject areas? (N/M/Y)

3. Are students offered a wide range of possibilities for meaningful learning? (N/M/Y)
4. Do teachers reinforce their students' efforts and intellectual risk-taking? (N/M/Y)
5. Is success measured according to clear and attainable goals? (N/M/Y)
6. Are grouping practices developed, monitored, and adjusted as needed, recognizing that children's learning rates are dynamic, not static? (N/M/Y)
7. Are teachers well trained (including in differentiation strategies), and encouraged to engage in high-level professional development? (N/M/Y)
8. Do teachers respect and understand diversity, including high-level development? (N/M/Y)
9. Are parents, children, teachers, and administrators all welcome to participate in open communication? (N/M/Y)
10. Do the stakeholders share responsibility for co-creating a school climate that's inclusive and collaborative? (N/M/Y)

By assigning your response to each item a score of one to three (one for "no," two for "mostly," and three for "yes"), it's possible to get a preliminary sense of how a school measures up. Recognizing that very few schools will satisfy all these criteria and get a perfect score, parents can use this list as a starting point for thinking about whether a certain school supports children's optimal growth.

Excellent schools do exist. We've seen them in action. Unfortunately, however, it's been our observation that this kind of learning environment tends to be more the exception than the rule. That said, it's possible to move toward achieving these factors, thereby creating a quality school. Informed parents greatly increase the likelihood of that happening.

Parents can make their own list of factors, or arrange the ones on our list according to their own priorities, based on their child's learning needs. If top priorities aren't met, it's time to consider whether some kind of action is called for, like getting involved in advocacy efforts, or changing schools.

Considering the Possibilities

Frank Lloyd Wright said, "The truth is more important than the facts." While some learning environments really are better than others, the most important truth about school choice is that a good school is one that's right for a particular child at a particular time in his development. That may or may not be the school that aligns with other people's perceptions of the "facts" or what matters most—such as the highest academic standards, the best-maintained building and grounds, the most celebrated sports teams, or the best reputation in the community. There's no universal answer, no single slam-dunk choice that works for everyone.

Here's an account of one family's deliberations:

> Tim was twelve years old and in grade 7. He was recently tested, and his English teacher said he did well enough to go into an advanced language arts program at a neighbouring school. Some of his teachers put pressure on his parents to send him there, but they wondered if this was wise. They told us that Tim can't expect to be intellectually stimulated all the time, and he has to learn how to handle this reality.
>
> They said, "We live in a world where being an all-round learner is important. If he's bored at school, we can help him find extracurricular activities that will keep him challenged and learning. An advanced language arts school might make him think he's something special, or undervalue other important subjects like math and science."

People often have strong opinions on these matters, but our experience suggests there's no right answer for Tim's parents, and no wrong answer, either. Given their focus on his long-term well-being, on his developing academic competency, and on helping him acquire good habits of mind, we think this family will make it work, whatever option they choose.

Decision-making requires careful thought and attention to individual personalities, interests, abilities, and learning requirements. No two children are the same. Some thrive in relaxed environments where they're given latitude about what courses to take, and when to show up for class, and whether or not to do their homework. Others only do well when the rules are strictly enforced, and adults take responsibility for setting and reinforcing expectations. These preferences change over time across a child's development, and can vary among children in the same family.

> From early on, Robin was a passionate reader and a keen student, but she was insulted when teachers attempted to control her learning. She felt respected—and learned well—when she was allowed to make choices, follow her own interests, and study intellectually challenging material. She wanted to be responsible for establishing her own schedule and curriculum, and functioned best when she was able to negotiate attendance, assignments, and course credits.
>
> Robin's sister, Erin, on the other hand, liked to know the rules, and have them dependably enforced. She realized that when guidelines were lax, so was she. At one point in her schooling, Erin chose a school that required a uniform and provided little leeway in course choice or other decisions. It worked well for her, but Robin would've rebelled.[7]

Two girls in the same family, two entirely different experiences, illustrating that whether a school is "good" depends on the nature of the student and her learning, as well as other needs at that point in her development.

Choosing among placements (like whether to go into a special program), or among possible schools (such as public, private, or charter), should be considered on a case-by-case basis, keeping individual circumstances in mind. School choice is at its best when parents and children work together, carefully thinking through the pluses and minuses of each of the options, as they apply to a particular child in a particular context at a particular point in time.

One of the most important jobs parents have is helping their children develop solid decision-making skills. When children are young, they need their parents to make the big decisions, like school choice. As kids get older, however, parents can solicit their children's thoughts and feelings, and use them as an integral component of the decision-making process. As children move into adolescence, it's time to give them more of the decision-making power. By the time they reach the later years of high school, they should be playing a big role in any decisions about their schooling. No matter the age of the child, or how academically capable he may be, decision-making is a skill and, like other skills, it has to be learned.[8]

What Are the Choices?

Parents are all too aware that their children's lives will be affected by the choices they make. Although very few school choices are irrevocable—and parents or kids can walk right back through most doors if a decision proves to be a mistake—school choice does matter. No one wants to risk their child feeling miserable, or go through the trouble of reversing a decision and starting all over again.

> *"Choices are the hinges of destiny."*
>
> – PYTHAGORAS

For easy reference, and in order to help with decision-making processes, we include here thumbnail sketches of some of the schooling options available in many communities.[9] It's important to remember that no option is "good" or "bad" in itself. Whether or not a given choice is appropriate for a child depends on her personality, age, areas of strength and interest, the location of the school relative to home, and much, much more.

Public school teachers are more likely than their private school counterparts to have some knowledge of special education, to have access to a broad range of professional learning and network opportunities, and to know how to adapt their teaching to meet children's unique learning needs. This leads to a school environment that can be friendlier to individual differences than is found in most private schools. Because of this, the more exceptional a child's development (whether advanced or other), the more consideration a family should give to public school options.[10] On the other side of the ledger, however, public school teachers are more likely than others to be held to rigid curriculum guidelines and union constraints that prevent them from differentiating kids' learning opportunities.

Private schools often do an excellent job of supporting the development of children's intellectual abilities, emphasizing high-level achievement across a wide variety of subject areas. There are many private schools that cater well to specific learning needs, and certain independent schools provide highly competitive learning environments, which can appeal to academically advanced and motivated children. Elite private schools often offer excellent athletic opportunities that are only available on an extracurricular basis to kids in public schools.[11]

Charter schools sometimes exemplify the best of both public and private schools. They're publicly funded, and therefore may be more inclusive than most independent schools. They also tend to be free of many of the burdens imposed by public system regulations and union rules, allowing for more teacher initiative and educational innovation. Charter schools vary more than others, though. Each one has its own unique approach and establishes its own unique culture, so these have to be considered more carefully than most other school options.

Gifted education ranges from entire schools for identified-gifted learners, through full-time programs for high-ability learners that are housed in schools with other kinds of classes, to one-hour-a-week or other part-time programs. What happens by way of instruction is highly variable, too, ranging from students being asked to do the usual grade-level work, but more of it, all the way to radically different curriculum that's disconnected from the usual grade-level requirements.[12] For some kids in some situations, gifted programming is a lifesaver. For others, it's seriously problematic. We discuss this topic more fully in *Being Smart about Gifted Education*.[13]

Acceleration is more than just grade-skipping, although that's certainly one form of it. Other forms include subject-specific acceleration (e.g., acceleration only in mathematics), and early entrance to elementary, middle, or high school. When done well, acceleration is a viable and cost-effective way to give advanced learners the challenge they need.[14]

In *language immersion and dual track* programs, students are taught two or more languages over several years. Typically, some or all of the basic academic subjects (mathematics, geography, history, etc.) are taught in a language other than English. Because of the challenges of compressing the academic program to allow for the extra language focus, there's usually little time or opportunity for enriching or accelerating subject areas other than languages. As a result, these programs can be problematic for kids who are more interested in other subjects. For children whose interests lie in languages, however, these programs can be beneficial, expanding their worlds and possible futures.

Specialty subject focus schools work to develop talent in non-academic subjects such as music, visual arts, athletics, leadership, or dramatic arts. As with the dual track and language immersion programs, they can be wonderful when they match a child's areas of strength and interest, but seriously problematic when they're not a good fit for a particular individual.

Magnet schools and programs are typically focused on one or more subject areas, such as performing arts, science, technology, or mathematics. Students are usually required to satisfy entry requirements, often by audition or some other demonstration of ability and motivation. Magnet programs can address advanced learning needs when the student's areas of interest and ability align well with the school's offerings.

Alternative schools are public or private schools that attempt to meet a demand for teaching methods or learning requirements not met in conventional schools. As with charter schools, there tends to be more autonomy granted to administrators and teachers, and this leads to enormous variation from one alternative school to the next. More than most school options, alternative schools require careful consideration and due diligence.

The *International Baccalaureate* (IB) is an internationally administered course of studies. It's offered for the last two years of high school, and some schools begin IB preparation as early as kindergarten. It's an academically demanding inquiry-based program that can provide an enriched learning experience. Providing an internationally recognized university entrance credential, IB can be a cost-effective option for high-ability learners.[15] Its drawbacks include a tendency to be too rigid and constrained for students who are intellectually advanced, independent, and spirited in their desire to choose their own areas of learning focus.

Advanced placement courses are another option to consider, consisting of college-level courses offered to high school students. Program options range from mathematics, physics, and arts through to philosophy, psychology, and others. These courses vary enormously in level of challenge and method of instruction from one school to another, and—as is the case with any educational option—are only as good as the teachers who teach them.

Montessori schools are designed to ensure that children's individual learning needs are well met so that each child experiences continuous challenge in his areas of interest. When the programming follows a true Montessori philosophy, or is adapted in a way that is consistent with this approach, it nurtures children's developing independence, autonomy, competence, and self-confidence.

Because of their responsiveness to individual learning needs and interests, Montessori schools can be particularly good for highly capable young children.

Homeschooling can work well for those who have exceptional learning needs that make it difficult to find a suitable school fit.[16] Homeschooling can also work well for a few months or years when a child is going through a transition or vulnerable period, or is intensely engaged in some kind of learning exploration that the parents deem productive, but that interferes with the child's schooling.

> When Andy was nearing his last year of high school, he wanted to research, design, and develop a vehicle from scratch. He and his parents decided this was doable, and so Andy spent a year full of learning by carefully researching automobile engineering and technology, and then building a car in the garage instead of going to school. Sometimes neighbourhood kids would come by to see the work in progress and assist him. Andy loved the combined autonomy and interaction with others, but mostly he relished his chance to take a hands-on creative approach to learning about something that intrigued him, combining serious study with inventiveness. He ultimately sold the car, and learned a lot from that experience, too.

Sometimes a child is homeschooled for part of the day, and then attends a local school for one or more subjects. Homeschooling advocates generally recommend connecting with a network of other parents before getting started, and maintaining those supportive connections throughout the homeschooling process.[17]

What's the Evidence?

There's so much information about schools and educational programs—in books, articles, online, and from well-meaning others—

that it can be difficult for parents to discern what to pay attention to, what to believe, and how to make a selection. For potentially high-stakes decisions like school choice, personal biases and experience should be supplemented by solid evidence when at all possible.

> *"As a rule . . . he who has the most information will have the greatest success."*
>
> – BENJAMIN DISRAELI

When in the throes of decision-making, it can be helpful to recognize four general categories of evidence.[18]

The first type of evidence is *anecdotal*, which is based on one's own or others' personal experience. Our stories of Andy and his car-designing venture, of Tim's school-related decision-making, and all the other accounts of children, parents, and teachers that we share throughout this book, are examples of anecdotal evidence. Stories like these can illustrate points being made, heighten awareness of issues, and trigger pertinent questions. Although this kind of evidence can be quite compelling (which is why so many journalists and politicians rely on it so heavily), on its own it isn't strong enough for valid generalizations, and is rarely enough for wise decision-making.

The second category of evidence is *theoretical*. This type of evidence pulls together knowledge from one or more fields of study such as education, neurology, psychology, and so on. For example, Howard Gardner's multiple intelligences theory proposes that each person has a profile of abilities in several different areas, in contrast with the view that a person is intelligent (or not) across all domains. Consider Roberto's difficult school placement experience (he was extremely advanced in mathematics but not other subjects), and Caryn's need to have her language-oriented and theatrical passions addressed. When multiple intelligences theory was applied to each of these cases, it helped to ensure that the child's learning needs were met.

Theoretical evidence is more abstract and complex than anecdotal evidence. It's not as easily understood, and not as obvious in its practical implications. However, it can be useful in enabling parents to think more objectively, creatively, and critically about educational decision-making for their children.

The third evidence category is *empirical*. This kind of evidence is derived from a systematic effort to collect information about a clearly defined research question. The evidence, once gathered, analyzed, and interpreted, is used either to confirm or refute prior knowledge about the question of interest. For example, research on the effect of caffeine, Ritalin, or fish oil on brain functioning can reveal how dietary habits, medication, or supplements might affect a child's learning. Good empirical evidence is essential in making sound decisions for children, particularly when it comes to specific details of their development. We refer to empirical evidence when we talk about best practices at home and at school, like providing a language-rich environment in the early years, or paying more attention to acceleration as an option for supporting high-level development.

The fourth kind of evidence is the strongest of all, *empirically validated theory*. It's a synthesis of theoretical and empirical evidence, and is usually illustrated with anecdotes. For example, Carol Dweck and her colleagues conducted dozens of empirical studies over three decades. This led to their developing a theory about mindsets. In her book, *Mindset*, Dweck then described the applications of this theory with anecdotes about real people. The mindset theory has important implications for parents in supporting high-level development, and we've introduced it here in many ways, including illustrating it with Paula, whose growth mindset was eroded by a fixed-mindset school situation, and Alexander, who suffered from fixed mindset–induced fear of failure.

These four categories of evidence can be found to different degrees across information sources. The more anecdotal the information source, the less robust the evidence is likely to be.

Possible information sources for educational decision-making range from schoolyard chats with other parents, to daily newspaper and parenting blogs, how-to references, magazine features, and scholarly books, all the way to peer-reviewed articles and detailed research reports in academic journals. It's also useful to talk to school personnel—the principal, a teacher, a secretary—and have a look at the school's literature. With these sources, as with all others, parents are wise to think about what kinds of evidence they're dealing with, and be skeptical but open-minded.

School Is Not Enough

Sir Arthur Conan Doyle once wrote, "Give me problems, give me work, give me the most abstruse cryptogram, or the most intricate analysis, and I am in my own proper atmosphere. . . . But I abhor the dull routine of existence. I crave for mental exaltation."[19] For those who share Sherlock Holmes's creator's need for intellectual challenge, school alone will never be enough. No school can satisfy that kind of insatiable need for intense intellectual engagement. For children like the young Arthur Conan Doyle, and for others whose schools are adequate but not stellar, parents must look further. Extracurricular activities can complement what happens in school, giving children a place to develop their talents, broaden their interests, challenge their minds, and extend their love of learning.[20]

Life beyond the classroom links the real world of experience, achievement, and meaningful ideas to children's academic learning, and makes that learning relevant. Play, extracurricular experiences, visits to theatres and sporting events, family gatherings, community-based involvement, and leadership roles can supplement what happens at school. Extracurricular activities can stimulate increased engagement in school, and make up for some of what might otherwise be missing.

Learning opportunities can be cultivated in any field: the arts, entrepreneurial activities, social action, athletics, academics, recreation—you name it. Parents and kids can find endless possibilities by searching online, or in community newspapers, or school bulletin boards, and by networking with family, friends, corporate and political entities, and social circles. Children can enjoy doing something different, innovative, or challenging, while at the same time sharing their excitement and building relationships with others with similar interests, enthusiasms, or talents.

The possibilities are boundless when parents and kids think creatively about education, outreach, and learning.

High school students Mathew and Asad read an article about sending a balloon into space. They spent evenings and weekends designing and constructing their own version of this—with a handmade parachute, a mounted camera, and a Lego man (holding a Canadian flag) firmly attached to the surface. They checked atmospheric conditions and, when the conditions were right, they launched their creation. It flew three times higher than commercial airplanes, and the pictures transmitted from that height were breathtaking! The curve of the earth was clearly visible, and the panoramic views and cloud formations were stunning. They were able to retrieve the camera, chute, and Lego man from a distant field a few days later.

Not only did Mathew and Asad learn a great deal over the many months it took them to complete this project, they felt enormously fulfilled by their accomplishment. They generated considerable media excitement, and were asked to display their photos at the University of Toronto. They were also invited to give a presentation to the board of directors of Bombardier, a large aircraft manufacturer.

The Lego man mission became an inspiration to others. Mathew and Asad now mentor other kids so they, too, can experience the exhilaration of seeing a challenge through to unimaginable heights.[21]

Mentorships can provide excellent opportunities for children and adolescents to develop supportive relationships with others in areas of shared interest. Mentors can offer guidance, inspiration, intellectual challenge, and practical know-how in business, politics, science, the arts, or whatever it is that a young person is keen to learn. There are many mentorship models, and mentors can come from all walks of life.[22]

Making smart decisions about participating in online learning can also be beneficial. For example, consider what Andy did during his homeschooling year. He was computer-savvy and studied car-building specs online. When he wasn't designing, building, and marketing his one-of-a kind car, he ran a business where he did computer troubleshooting, and developed web sites for individuals and small corporations. Since then, he's travelled halfway around the globe to nurture entrepreneurial connections he made through proactive networking, sold an online business he developed, and joined a think tank group based in South America.

Resourceful parents can sometimes find ways to help their children explore and develop their areas of interest, and translate their dreams into reality. Consider the following two stories that illustrate innovative and inexpensive decisions to support children's passions.

One mother helped catapult her daughter's interest in the performing arts into an exciting learning experience.

> Marta's always been interested in drama. When I saw she was intrigued by a poster for a play, I called to inquire about student tours and backstage learning. I discovered that local theatres offer inexpensive last-minute student tickets, as well as pre-show questionnaires, character studies, and basic script-writing exercises. Marta enjoyed exploring staging and design elements, and learning how drama can be used to delve into issues relevant to her life.

Not too long ago, Marta was inspired by a play dealing with racial issues and violence among inner-city youth. She wrote two short scripts concerning these issues, and submitted them to a local radio station. They asked her to record them, and she invited her classmates to perform the pieces with her. The entire school listened. Marta is now heading a Youth Forum committee that's creating an original production dealing with violence in our city.

Not only is Marta challenging herself, she's also becoming more socially conscious and compassionate. She's developing useful skills, and sharing her knowledge with other kids. I hope she'll continue to explore directions for future growth, artistic and otherwise.[23]

Lee's father describes how his son's extracurricular activities have led to enriched learning, personal growth, and leadership development:

Lee is fascinated by the natural world. When our family first began visiting the zoo, he was captivated by the Himalayan tahr. It was only possible to view this exotic goat from a distant vantage point while riding the Zoomobile, and in the winter, the vehicle didn't operate because the paths were too treacherous, so the Himalayan tahr was not well known to zoo visitors.

When he was eleven, Lee e-mailed the zoo to find out what could be done about this situation. He thought more people should know about this interesting animal. The director invited our whole family to a personalized behind-the-scenes tour, so we could all view the Himalayan tahr and his goat buddies more closely.

The staff at the Education Centre offered Lee a volunteer placement where mentoring opportunities could occur naturally. He's been volunteering ever since. He comes home with fascinating tidbits about the animals—orangutans love bubble gum, pregnant gorillas like herbal tea, and giraffes and elephants eat onions.

Last year, Lee became concerned because people were tossing things into cages, and endangering the well-being of animals. He's now helping train the primates to take these thrown items to the handlers in exchange for a treat. He laughed as he described Daisy's antics. Someone dropped a wallet into the orangutan cage, and she picked it up. Instead of delivering the entire wallet to the handler she took the contents out one by one to exchange for treats.

Lee's experiences at the zoo have inspired him to start a club at school affiliated with the World Wildlife Education Fund, and he's also fundraising for a winterized Zoomobile. Not surprisingly, he's also looking at a possible career in animal psychology.[24]

Community-based experiences like those embraced by Marta and Lee have enriched lives—their own and those of others—in unexpected ways.

CHECKLIST: COMMUNITY-BASED LEARNING OPTIONS

Community-oriented learning options are plentiful. They include, but are certainly not limited to

- *music:* playing an instrument, or participating in a choir, band, festival gathering, or other musical ensemble;
- *physical activity:* dancing, gymnastics, team and individual sports, martial arts, swimming, skating, running, walking, yoga;
- *cultural institutions:* museums of every type, zoos, historical centres, archives;
- *theatre:* costume design, makeup, clowning, script writing, lighting, set design and construction, puppetry, and performance;

- *art:* painting, sculpting, photography, mosaics, visiting art galleries;
- *crafts:* woodworking, pottery, quilting, model-building, jewellery design, origami;
- *writing:* stories, poems, articles for local newspapers, journals, contests, web sites, or bookstores;
- *robotics:* studying, designing, and building, for contests and science centres;
- *leadership:* coaching; tutoring; leadership roles for religious, cultural, sports-based or other community organizations;
- *clubs:* chess, astronomy, cooking, debating, computers, book groups, at local community centres and libraries;
- *community service:* local, political, or global causes;
- *camps:* kayaking, archery, soccer, hockey, or horseback riding; and
- *competitions:* local to international; writing, geography, math, arts, athletics, science, technology, design, engineering.

Dilemmas and Decisions

Robert Frost wrote, "We dance in a ring and suppose, but the secret sits in the middle and knows."[25] To the best of our knowledge, there isn't really a secret who sits in the middle and knows. Parents have to figure out for themselves, and with their children, how to make the right decisions about programs and schools. But how do parents finally decide which school is the most promising for their child? When you're caught up trying to balance your child's academic, intellectual, motivational, social, physical, and emotional needs—as well as the issues of time and money that are involved in these types of decisions—how do you make the best decision?

Once choice is narrowed down to a few promising options, it's time to look more closely at the culture of individual schools. Some schools put a high priority on supporting kids' intellectual development, and some don't. Some schools emphasize social and emotional well-being, while others reward athletic prowess. What matters most in making a good decision for your child is the match between your child and that culture.

A good place to start the final screening is with the principal or head teacher. The principal typically hires the teachers, oversees spending and management priorities, and provides support for vibrant professional development and collaboration—or not.[26] What a principal thinks about providing extra challenge for kids who need that is a good preliminary indicator of how well the school will accommodate a child's advanced learning needs.

Wise parents realize that educational decision-making is tough because it's so complex and multi-faceted. What parents *can* do is find out all they can about the available possibilities; sift carefully through the relevant evidence; think about their children's learning needs, in addition to their psychological, social, physical, and emotional development; consult with people who really matter (including the child); and then take a deep breath and make a choice—together. After that, they have to trust that they and their children have what it takes to move forward. And if for some reason the decision doesn't work out well, they can always re-evaluate the situation, reflect upon what they've learned from the experience, reconsider the evidence, and redirect their energies anew.

Our Secrets: Decision-Making about Schooling

1. The calibre of schools varies in many ways. See our School Support quiz to consider how well a school measures up as an intelligence-building environment.
2. No one school choice works well for every child. Children's personalities, social and emotional development, interests, and abilities should be taken into account when deciding on a school.
3. A placement that's excellent now may not be quite so good as a child's interests and abilities develop, or as the

school changes. Keep your eyes open, and be responsive to change over time.

4. Decision-making is a skill that's best learned early. Give children more responsibility for decision-making as they mature.

5. Schooling options include public, private, charter, gifted programs, acceleration, language immersion, dual track programs, specialty subject focus, magnet schools, alternative schools, International Baccalaureate programs, advanced placement courses, Montessori, homeschooling, and more.

6. Each type of evidence—anecdotal, theoretical, empirical, and empirically validated theory—can shed light on what parents need or want to know about educational options for their children. Each evidence type is valuable but limited, and they work best used in concert with each other.

7. A school cannot always supply all the challenge and education that a child needs. There are unlimited learning opportunities beyond the traditional classroom.

8. In making a decision about a school, pull all the evidence sources together; consider the school culture, including the administrative leader; take into account the child's interests and abilities, and the family, financial, geographic, and educational constraints; and trust that you'll be able to change your decision when and if necessary.

Finding a great school situation—one where there's a good fit between an individual child and the learning culture—is only one factor in a child's development, of course. In the next chapter, we discuss some of the complications that can be associated with high ability.

CHAPTER 8

Possible Complications

"I recently bumped into one of my children's former teachers. She inquired about my son, reminiscing about how he'd been such a behaviour problem in her class. 'Oh, really?' I replied. 'He's at Harvard Law School now.'"

— RENATA[1]

GENERALLY SPEAKING, there's no connection between intelligence and the risk of social and emotional problems. That said, being different than others—including doing better academically, or understanding intellectual concepts more thoroughly—does bring certain social and emotional challenges.

Parents whose children are ahead of their age peers often have questions about social and emotional well-being. Questions like "What if my child doesn't fit in?" "How can I make sure she's not bored?" "Why does he procrastinate?" "Why does she always take the easy way out?" In this chapter we think about issues that can be troubling to children and their parents, and offer strategies to help parents address the ongoing challenges of raising kids to thrive intellectually.

Inferences, Assumptions, and Truth

Some complications are caused by faulty inferences and assumptions people make about children based on their behaviour. Here are five examples from our case files:

1. *Sam is an excellent student but he resists doing his homework.* Is he arrogant? Is he lazy? Or is he choosing to invest his time differently?
2. *Collin insists on forging ahead of his reading group, so he always knows more than everyone else about what's happening in the story.* Is he a show-off? Does he want to be seen as superior to others? Or is he a keen learner who's fully engaged in his reading?
3. *Shelby won't allow any digressions or interruptions while she's doing her school work.* Is she too intent on control? Is she anxious? Or is she a conscientious child who likes to concentrate on whatever she's doing?
4. *Tula has four different research topics on the go at once.* Is she scatterbrained? Is she distractible? Or is she a versatile Renaissance girl—intensely curious about a lot of things?
5. *Anil prefers to work alone, and avoids doing classroom activities with others.* Is he shy? Is he disdainful? Or is he choosing to spend his time productively, knowing he can complete things faster and better when he does them on his own?

Any and all of these inferences can be valid, but we can't know whether a given explanation applies to a certain situation without further investigation.

Sometimes not doing homework does come from arrogance. Other times it's due to laziness, or not wanting to appear too clever. Or maybe the work's too hard and the child has no one to assist him, or he's reluctant to ask for help. Some kids don't have a quiet space in which to do their work at home. And then there are those who don't do their homework because it's insufferably boring, and they have more useful, interesting, or compelling things to do with their time.

> *"The least questioned assumptions are often the most questionable."*
>
> – PAUL BROCA[2]

Children and adolescents who are different than others in some way, including those who are well ahead of their classmates academically, are more likely to be misunderstood. Even when their behaviour is "normal," like avoiding homework, their motivations and concerns can be unusual. Parents can help their children by checking out their own inferences, assumptions, and perceptions, and by doing their best to figure out the truth that underlies their children's behaviour.

CHECKLIST: FIVE QUESTIONS TO ASK WHEN KIDS HAVE PROBLEMS

Parents with concerns about children who are experiencing difficulties can start moving toward a solution by asking themselves some simple but important questions:

1. "What is the problem, exactly?"
2. "Is that really a problem?"
3. "If yes, whose problem is it?"
4. "How can we help?"
5. "Is it time to look for professional help?"

Because a problem can't be solved until it's clearly identified and well understood, the first three questions focus on problem-finding, on discovering the precise nature of the problem. Very often, the answers to these three questions expose people's biases—their unexamined inferences, assumptions, and potentially flawed perceptions—thus allowing a clearer understanding of the problem at hand.

The two remaining questions focus on problem-solving. The best answers to the fourth question (about how parents can help) are practical, specific, and respectful of a child's developing individuality, as well as the family's circumstances.

Once the first four questions have been addressed, and parents understand the nature of the problem and what they can do to help, they have a better sense of whether or not they need to call in professional assistance. Depending on the circumstance, that assistance might take the form of an educational psychologist, a learning specialist, a tutor, a psychiatrist, a social worker, or someone else with the expertise to assess and address the issues at hand.

With these five basic questions in mind, we look at key issues relating to children's emotional development as this intersects with high-level ability. We pay particular attention to the role of parents in preventing and solving the problems that can arise.

Being Different

The most obvious problem for exceptional learners—including those who are intellectually advanced—is the sense of being different than others. This can be painful at any age, but tends to be most troubling at early adolescence (age eleven to fourteen), when acceptance by peers is critically important to self-esteem. This is the time when young people are working out who they are. They're intensely focused on their uniqueness, and equally concerned about fitting in. They want to be noticed as individuals, but they also want to be like others. Those who are different in some way have an advantage on the distinctiveness side of the ledger, but a big strike against them in the "fitting in" department.

> *"If you ever need people to interview, I'd be happy to share with you my harrowing experiences of life in the ninety-ninth percentile."*
>
> – KARLA[3]

Sometimes kids will try to hide whatever it is that sets them apart.

Janette is a curious twelve-year-old. She enjoys science activities and mystery books. She's concerned about environmental issues and animal welfare, but she rarely discusses her interests with anyone. According to her teacher, she avoids leadership roles and contributes little to class discussions. She works on sounding less knowledgeable than she is. She gets top marks, but quickly packs away her papers in her knapsack rather than disclosing that information to her classmates.

Sometimes kids don't want to let on that they're smart. They may feel embarrassed about being different, or think it's just not cool. Smart girls, in particular, often undergo a difficult transition as they move into adolescence.[4] Their self-esteem can drop, and some children and teenagers, like Janette, make a point of concealing their strengths and talents in order to blend in with their age peers, and avoid being perceived as different.

Other than the self-acceptance that comes with healthy maturity, there's no simple solution to the problem of feeling different because of one's abilities. The more exceptional the ability level, the truer this is. One option is to look for intellectual peers who are the same age, which is one of the reasons to support congregated high-ability programs. Many parents describe such programs as lifesavers for their children.

Sadly, however, gifted programs serve to underline some highly capable kids' feelings of differentness. Because the ability range in a typical gifted program is as wide as the range in most other classrooms (starting at a higher level, but continuing to a higher level than in most classrooms), those who are markedly advanced relative to their age peers can find they still don't have the intellectual peers they'd hoped for. In every advanced-ability program, there are kids who are well ahead of their classmates in one subject or another.

No matter the degree of advancement, good places to find intellectual peers include extracurricular interest groups, and activities that are focused on children's areas of enthusiasm. Online learning activities, summer academies, international contests, and talent searches greatly increase the likelihood of kids finding people they can really talk to about their interests and passions.

In addition to looking for intellectual peers, parents can address young people's sense of being uncomfortably different by helping them understand that everyone is unique, with personal patterns of strengths and weaknesses. This solution can emerge from considering the problem-finding question "Is that really a problem?"

A feeling of being ostracized because of individual interests and strengths is not trivial. Its power to devastate a child—particularly at early adolescence—shouldn't be underestimated. Parents have important roles in guiding their children, so they come to have positive perspectives on their ways of being different. It helps when youngsters understand that intellectual ability is a long-term strength: although high intelligence can sometimes feel like an albatross, that's usually temporary.

Strengthening Emotional Intelligence

Emotional intelligence is what enables children (and their parents) to deal with the many ups and downs of life, including setbacks, moods, and relationships. Emotional literacy is at least as important for success and fulfillment as other kinds of literacy.[5] It involves perceiving emotions accurately, expressing them effectively, and understanding and regulating one's feelings and behaviours.

> *"Our emotional capacities are not a given; with the right learning they can be improved."*
>
> – DANIEL GOLEMAN[6]

High academic intelligence is no guarantee of high emotional intelligence, and all children—no matter how smart they are—need help learning to cope with the complexity and intensity of their feelings.

How can parents support the development of their children's emotional intelligence? They can model good coping mechanisms like relaxation techniques, stress management, conflict resolution, and resilience. They can also help their children acquire self-regulation skills by encouraging them to take time to reflect on their own experiences, and to focus on effective communication with others, including listening. They can show kids through their own examples the power of being positive. Displaying optimism can be mood-lifting and infectious. It's important to demonstrate a growth mindset, including having positive attitudes toward failure, change, and challenge. Other good habits that parents can model include pacing oneself, and eating and sleeping well.

Stuart Shanker has developed a highly effective approach to helping parents and teachers support kids in acquiring self-regulation habits.[7] In his Calm, Alert, and Ready to Learn program, Dr. Shanker emphasizes the importance of establishing routines for sleeping, eating, and exercise. He provides tools that help young people—starting as early as two or three—engage in assessing, monitoring, and addressing their own physical needs. When a child recognizes his need for something to eat or for physical exercise, he's beginning to gain the self-regulation tools that will serve him in good stead for his lifetime, enhancing his learning, relationships, health, enjoyment, and achievement in every area.

QUIZ: DO YOU FOSTER YOUR CHILD'S EMOTIONAL INTELLIGENCE?

Here are some questions to consider if you're wondering what else you might do to support your child's emotional intelligence. Answer "yes," "usually," "I'm working on that," or "no."

1. Do you cultivate a safe and accepting home environment?
2. Do you model emotional awareness and self-regulation? Do you attend (as well as possible) to your own needs for food, sleep, quiet time, stimulation, and exercise?
3. Do you handle well your reactions to provocative, aggressive, or threatening situations? If not, are you open about that, and actively working on it?
4. Are you available to offer reassurance and encouragement as needed?
5. Do you engage your child in conversations about your personal belief systems, feelings, and attitudes? Do you welcome his responses and opinions?
6. Do you help your child identify and understand feelings such as happiness, sadness, anger, surprise, fear, love, disgust, shame?
7. Do you help your child understand the power of emotion in guiding her decisions, perceptions, and efforts?
8. Do you share stories about friends, family, and others who have grappled successfully with change, potentially stressful issues, or emotional challenges?
9. Do you teach your child to empathize with others?
10. Do you watch television and movies together, and discuss the emotion-related issues that arise (e.g., ethics, con-

flicts, relationships, trauma, and character)? Do you read stories about people who prevail over adversity, and talk about why and how they've done that?

11. Do you introduce your child to people who have experienced problems, and learned how to manage their emotions successfully?

12. Do you provide access to professional counselling if necessary?

If you can answer a resounding "yes!" to a question, you get 3 points. If it's "usually," you get 2 points. If your answer is "I'm working on that," you get 1 point, and if your honest answer to a question is "no," then that's a zero. If you've got mostly 2's and 3's, you're providing your child with a rich environment for his emotional intelligence. The questions where you get 1 or no points can give you ideas for possible action.

Parents who want to advocate for changes at the school level can introduce Stuart Shanker's Calm, Alert, and Ready to Learn program. Another option, which is more directly connected to educational curriculum, is called Teaching for Intellectual and Emotional Learning (TIEL). It's a program that helps teachers, parents, and children integrate their thinking and feeling by emphasizing the connections among the cognitive and social/emotional dimensions of the teaching/learning process.[8] TIEL can help children understand things on deeper levels, whether it's literature, science, or geography, and also use their thinking skills for real-world social benefits.

Many children who show early signs of academic advancement—like Alexander, who was praised for his intelligence but worried he wasn't as smart as people thought—find it hard to connect their thinking with their emotions. TIEL is a straightforward approach that can be used at home as well as at school to help children like Alexander make conscious intellectual connections to their feelings, and learn to manage their emotions more productively.

Some schools employ the Tools of the Mind curriculum, which was designed to promote self-regulation.[9] The teacher's role is emphasized in scaffolding children's learning experiences, ensuring that each child receives the right combination of support and challenge in each area of learning, as well as plentiful opportunities for productive interaction with peers. Tightly following the school's prescribed curriculum takes second place to the teacher's professional judgement about meeting each child's learning needs at a given point in time. Research findings comparing the Tools of the Mind approach to standard teaching methods show large gains in learning outcomes across all areas, as well as improved emotional intelligence.

Similar to Tools of the Mind in many ways, the Montessori approach is another research-validated method for supporting children's self-regulation skills. Montessori methods focus on ensuring that each child develops at her own pace, following her interests with active learning opportunities, in a supportive climate that cultivates joy, pride, and self-confidence. There's a strong emphasis on constructive social interactions.[10]

Even when parents do their utmost to provide love and support, children can nevertheless experience problems. These include difficulty coping with challenging situations, boredom, fear of failure, fear of success, perfectionism, laziness, and procrastination. Intellectually advanced children are no more likely than other kids to have these issues. When they do experience them, however, high-level development can be a troublesome complication, and that's what we consider here.

Developing Resilience and Coping Skills

While we were writing this book, a huge hurricane devastated the American northeast. It reminded us that preparing for disaster is about more than making sure you've got enough fresh water, batteries, candles, and non-perishable food to last several days without power. It's also about having effective coping skills and, for parents, knowing how to help your child weather the storms that life brings. These may occur in the form of crises like hurricanes, floods, or fire, or in the form of family or personal problems such as illness or the death of loved ones.

> *"When you come to the end of your rope, tie a knot, and hang on."*
>
> — FRANKLIN D. ROOSEVELT

It's tempting to think that once the trouble has passed, children will be over it. But long after the disruption, some children will continue to need reassurance. What can parents do to help their child manage a current situation, and also develop the coping skills he'll need to be resilient in the future, as he faces the inevitable problems that come along—both the small-scale challenges of growing up, and the larger-scale problems as well?

To begin with, it's good to remember that it's normal for children to worry. How could it be otherwise, when they depend on others for their well-being and survival? But normal worries can be made worse if the adults in their lives have concerns, and don't include their children in conversations about what's happening.

Some children with well-developed emotional and communication skills are able to verbalize their worries clearly. Until children reach the age of ten or eleven, however, when the capacity for self-awareness usually begins to develop, that's more the exception than the rule. Some children exhibit anger when they're worried; some become difficult, irritable, or resentful; and other children appear to be sad or lethargic. Still others become unusually helpful, clingy, or affectionate. Worried kids can act out, distance themselves, seek attention, or become distraught.[11] Children who are more emotionally sensitive will usually react to a troubling situation more intensely than others.

Parents can help a child deal with her fears by modelling effective coping skills during troubling times, listening carefully to her concerns, providing a dependable environment, and encouraging her to take appropriate action. These four key components of an effective response to adversity can help a child develop the resilience she'll need to deal with other troubles she might encounter as time goes by. Adults can soothe their child's worries, prevent deeper distress, and foster resilience—but only if they're paying attention to what their child is saying, asking, and doing.

One way to help kids take appropriate action is to give them opportunities to talk things over with others, such as grandparents, extended family members, and teachers. The child's ability to cope is strengthened when all the adults in her life are on the same page, receptive to her concerns, and providing similar messages about the nature of the problem and how best to proceed.

Sarah Chana Radcliffe is a counsellor who works with kids and families. She has written a book about dealing with children's fears, from the normal everyday fears of the dark and doing something new, to bigger fears occasioned by major changes or legitimate traumas like a death in the family. Radcliffe suggests that parents practise emotional coaching, a method of welcoming, naming, and accepting a child's feelings, before beginning any kind of problem-solving about the fears. She includes scripts showing parents what not to do, like underplaying a child's worries ("There's nothing to be afraid of here!"), or providing quick solutions ("Why don't you give it a start?"). Instead, by listening deeply and reflecting the child's feelings back to him, the parent validates those feelings. Radcliffe writes, "The child must be encouraged to feel all of his fear in order to release it fully."[12]

Reflecting the worries can be a useful starting point for "fixing" fears, but Radcliffe also reviews several action strategies for parents to use with children who are more seriously worried. Strategies for emotional healing include journaling, breathing exercises, and other focusing techniques.

The child who observes others coping well, who feels safe and reassured, and who learns how to deal with his fears or take action to address problems is much better able to move on from adversity. He's also acquiring important skills that'll make him more resilient the next time hardship strikes. We've developed a three-pronged list of practical suggestions for parents of children who may be struggling with difficulties of one sort or another.[13] The suggestions apply to children of all ages, from toddlerhood through adolescence, although there will be obvious differences depending on a child's age. Younger children (and those who are more sensitive, no matter their age) usually need more reassurance, whereas older children (or those who have an advanced grasp of issues) can participate in more sophisticated problem-solving activities.

CHECKLIST:
RESILIENCE AND COPING SKILLS:
HELPING KIDS DEAL WITH CHALLENGES

Model Effective Coping Skills

1. Take stock of your own feelings before attempting to address your child's concerns.
2. Try to model a positive problem-solving attitude to the issues at hand, so your child can see what that looks like in action.
3. Strengthen your social support networks. Talk to friends, family, and others about issues that might be unsettling.
4. Security and predictability matter more than usual in times of trouble. Be as available to your child as you can be, and make sure you're there when you say you will be. Try to stick to normal daily routines if you can.
5. When possible, choose a quiet, comfortable place for discussion, when there's ample time to chat, and when you're feeling relatively relaxed. This is always a good idea, but it's especially important at high-stress times.

6. Be as calm and responsive as you can be. Give yourself permission (as always) not to do everything perfectly.

Reassure

1. Listen, really listen, to your child's questions. Pay attention to the words, hear what she's saying, and also what she's *not* saying but might want to know.

2. Ask your child what he wants to know more about, and what other concerns he might have.

3. Be particularly attentive if your child has experienced other traumatic events, has a history of emotional problems, lacks friends with whom to share ideas, or shows signs of undue stress. (This might include sleeplessness, changes in eating habits, mood swings, academic decline, changes in activity level, substance abuse, or behaviour that's markedly different than usual, or out of step compared with age peers.)

4. Deal with issues one by one, as they arise.

5. Be honest, but provide only as much detail as the child is able to handle. Children's abilities to process emotionally loaded information differ with age, development, and personal experience.

6. Talk about the ways relationship-building can help in overcoming difficulties.

7. Kids don't always feel like talking, and that needs to be respected, too. Whether or not your child feels like talking about what's happening—and some kids won't—a warm hug or a few quiet moments together can provide comfort when it's needed.

8. Help your child steer clear of excessive exposure to conflict, violence, or human suffering in the media. Acknowledge that there are problems, but explain that it doesn't help to focus on them too much.

9. Focus on the positives. Describe how the troubling circumstances are being productively addressed by experts, professionals, and volunteers. Do some research with your

child on what's happening by way of relief efforts, plans for rebuilding, the roles of first responders, and so on.

10. Help your child realize and accept her limitations, including recognizing that despite her best intentions, she's too young to fix major or global problems.

11. Remember that parents can't always do it alone, especially in times of unusual peril. If your child is deeply troubled and cannot be calmed, it's important to consider consulting a professional with expertise in children's emotional well-being.

Support Your Child in Taking Action

1. Encourage your child to express his ideas and feelings through the arts. Drawing, music, journal writing, and other forms of expression can be good emotional outlets, and also serve as springboards for discussion if your child chooses to share their efforts with you.

2. If a child has fun, it doesn't mean she's insensitive to the misfortune of others. Encourage her to play, to continue to be active, and to maintain balance in her life.

3. Find stories (fact or fiction) about people who've been affected by unsettling events (such as earthquakes, tornadoes, violence, etc.). Help your child see how it's possible to be persistent, or find courageous ways to confront challenge, suffering, or loss. Focus on the strengths and resilience of the people in the stories.

4. Help your child fortify existing family ties and friendships. During times of trouble, a strong social support system can make a big difference.

5. If your child wants to contribute to relief efforts, you can help him look for volunteer opportunities at levels he can manage. Information is available from associations that deal with disaster preparedness, health centres, food banks, youth groups, and charitable organizations such as UNICEF, the Red Cross, the Salvation Army, and many others.

By providing a safe environment, and being calm and attentive—and seeking professional assistance when it's needed—parents can alleviate the fear children experience during chaotic times. Parents cannot and should not shelter their children from all adversity, but they can use challenging times as opportunities to help their children explore and understand their feelings, respond effectively to adversity, and acquire resilience.

Boredom

As with pretty much everything else to do with human development, each case of boredom has its own history, causes, and solutions. George Bernard Shaw wrote, "I want to be thoroughly used up when I die, for the harder I work, the more I live." This is a great attitude toward life and an antidote to boredom.

We discuss basic parenting approaches to boredom in chapter 5, including ways parents can ensure children take responsibility for their own playing and learning—the best possible boredom prevention technique. Sometimes, however, boredom moves up a notch and constitutes a bigger and more complicated issue. We illustrate some of the more serious problems with boredom by sharing a few examples.

> Jonas is intense, sensitive, and emotional. People have made comments through the years about his outstanding showmanship, writing skills, and sense of humour. He also demonstrates creativity, musicality, and athletic ability. In spite of all these strengths and interests, he's always described himself as "dead bored" at school. He finishes his work quickly, and has no patience waiting for his classmates to catch up. He hates sitting around or doing what he calls "time-filler crap."
>
> Lately, his teachers have voiced serious problems with his attitude. Although Jonas still has bursts of outstanding achievement, his academic standing has been declining steadily. He's acquired a class clown reputation, which

he considers a badge of honour. Teachers usually refer to him as "disruptive," and that's when they're being polite. He describes himself as "exuberant," and is always on the look-out for creative ways to avoid doing assignments and distract others from working on theirs.

Boredom can be the logical consequence of work that's too easy. Ensuring there's a good match between a child's learning needs and the academic curriculum is a sensible starting point for tackling boredom at school, no matter what the cause turns out to be. In this case, Jonas's parents worked with Jonas and the school to create a better match between his ability level and what he was being asked to do. (That's the focus of chapters 6 and 7, and the essence of differentiated education.)

Once Jonas's parents determined this mismatch was the problem (question #1 from earlier in this chapter), realized that yes, it was a problem (question #2), and identified the problem as Jonas's and the school's, together (question #3), it proved relatively straightforward to address. Similarly to the problems Ivor was experiencing, as described in chapter 6, the solution was to find learning activities that were better matched to Jonas's ability and areas of interest.

Boredom isn't always about work that's too easy, though. Sometimes it's the opposite.

Riva didn't mention boredom until grade 9. Before that, she loved going to school, and would stay up late to finish her homework. When she started high school, however, she started talking about being bored. "School is too easy, Mom." Her parents weren't shocked when she brought home a report card with more C's than A's. They attributed it to the boredom she'd been complaining about, and asked the teachers to give her harder work. The teachers complied, but found Riva couldn't handle the heavier load. Instead, she appeared even more stressed and unhappy.

People sometimes describe themselves as bored when they're having trouble managing their assignments. Children who lack the necessary skills to do the assigned work can tune out, then misinterpret their frustration and unhappiness as boredom. Boredom can feel more acceptable than their own lack of ability, effort, or knowledge. Claiming boredom can serve to distance a child from the source of her frustration, and allow her to think that, with a bit of luck, something easier and more enjoyable will come along.

The solution in a case like Riva's is similar to that for Jonas: an assessment of learning needs and abilities, with the aim of ensuring the child has the skills she needs to succeed academically. The necessary skills include organization and time management, as well as good study habits.

And boredom is not always about school-work mismatches.

Chloe's parents are both busy professionals who wish they had more time to spend with their daughter. When she complains of boredom, one of her parents leaps into action and helps her find something that's fun to do. They take her on an outing, or buy her an electronic gadget or some new clothes. Lately, she's been complaining of boredom quite a lot.

Sometimes parents respond to their children's boredom claims by taking them places, purchasing items, or offering more entertaining—and less effortful—activities. Parents who feel responsible for fixing things if their children aren't happy hear a child's cry of boredom as a call to action—for them. Although some people might see a child like Chloe as manipulative and demanding, we put the blame for that kind of "boredom" squarely on the parents' cleverly manipulated shoulders. Chloe's parents will be more successful in addressing their daughter's boredom if they help her discover some productive interests, and encourage her to pursue them.

Boredom can have psychological causes, too.

Bogdan is in a grade eight enrichment program. He used to be actively involved in several sports, and was an avid Boy Scout. Now he comes home from school, gets himself something to eat, plops in front of the television, and watches it until bedtime. Since his parents' divorce, he's dropped all his extracurricular activities, gained twenty pounds, and isn't doing well at school. When anyone asks him why he's failing, he replies angrily, "School is boring."

The most troubling boredom is the kind that masks more serious psychological problems, including depression, frustration, helplessness, sadness, loss, or anger. Bogdan's feelings and behaviour suggest deeper problems that need to be addressed before he can re-engage with academic achievement and other activities. In cases like this, we refer the child and his parents to a family counsellor.

When a child describes himself as bored, we suggest that parents ask themselves the questions listed at the outset of this chapter: "What is the problem?" "Is that really a problem?" "If yes, whose problem is it?" and then think about how they can help. This might mean working with teachers toward assessing academic challenges, and setting expectations that match the child's ability level. Such was the case with Jonas and Riva. It might mean working on parenting skills, as with Chloe's situation. And it might mean engaging with the child in some family therapy, as in Bogdan's case. Boredom can be an urgent call for help, but the nature of that help varies considerably from one situation to another.

Fear of Failure and Fear of Success

Frequently, people who are afraid of tackling tough challenges are suffering from a fear that they'll fail. They worry that failure will show them up as incompetent, that it'll open them to criticism and rejection, and so they develop habits of staying within their comfort zone. A fear of failure can severely limit a person's achievements.

Querobin was in the process of switching professions, to teaching from engineering, when he provided this candid perspective:

> In my career as a consulting engineer, I work alongside people in many positions, from presidents and vice presidents of leading companies to factory workers. I have to initiate change and work through it, and I've learned that I'm most successful when I can create a positive learning environment for the teams I lead.
>
> In the companies I work with, people are afraid of looking foolish, of failing in one way or another. I help them see that failures are just setbacks that remind us we're making mistakes that have to be fixed. If we can avoid repeating the same mistakes, we can be successful and move on. As with athletes, I've found that the greatest success comes to people who have this kind of mastery-oriented approach to learning. They're not afraid of using their mistakes to direct them in putting more effort into their training. They thrive on challenge and learn from their blunders. I think their success becomes evident on the field of play, whatever that field might be.[14]

Not everyone recognizes as Querobin does that a mastery orientation to learning is usually the best antidote to a fear of failure. Those who avoid challenge because they're afraid of failing can become energized when they realize that every kind of ability grows incrementally, step by step.

> *"Nothing in life is to be feared. It is only to be understood."*
>
> — MARIE CURIE

In every field, whether business, music, science, athletics, or something else, people learn and grow by making mistakes. When failures are understood as learning opportunities, they can be the best possible stepping stones to growth. This realization can help people persist through the setbacks that are an inevitable part of learning in every area of life.

Parents can model this positive attitude to problems, and they can also discuss its value with their children. They can share their own experiences of surmounting obstacles, and talk about the merits of getting to the finish line a little more slowly if necessary. They can look for real-life role models, and biographies of people who've learned to overcome setbacks, and gone on to find fulfillment in achievement.

We don't want to understate the potential problems that can be associated with a fear of failure. Like any fear, it can be serious and debilitating, and getting past a deeply embedded fear of failure isn't as simple as changing a sweater. Working toward a growth mindset (which we discuss in chapter 1) can help a child who's suffering from a pronounced fear of making mistakes. However, as with other problems, whether they're medical, academic, or psychological, there are times when parents' best course of action includes calling in an expert.

As counterintuitive as it might seem, some children avoid challenging circumstances because they're afraid of succeeding. It's relatively easy to understand a fear of failure, but people can also experience its opposite, a fear of success. That can be just as debilitating. Fear of success is almost always unconscious, and therefore difficult to identify, but it can be powerful nonetheless. As with fear of failure, if ignored, fear of success can derail a young person's academic and career trajectories.

Jay was a strong student until he discovered theatre. He started attending acting and improvisation classes on weekends, and made new friends who shared his love of musical

theatre. Although he'd participated in advanced-level programs for several years, and excelled in math and science, he
suddenly became intent on attending the district arts high
school. He started handing in late and incomplete assignments. His teachers were concerned about his attitude and
lack of interest in anything other than the arts.

Jay's parents wanted him to explore and develop his
interests, but they were worried. They'd seen too many of
his passions come and go through the years, and didn't want
him to forfeit a good academic education for what might
prove to be one more temporary enthusiasm. It seemed that
every time he got close to real proficiency at something, he
put his energy into something else.

When a person excels, he's achieving at a high standard. If Jay
stays with his current strengths in math and science, his parents
and teachers will almost certainly have increasingly high expectations for him. He may be worried there's a limit to his ability
in those subjects. As it stands now, by moving into another area
entirely, he can appear to be a smart young man who's decided to
put his energy elsewhere.

There are many possible reasons for a fear of success. People
can be afraid that once they reach their goal and accomplish all
they set out to accomplish, they won't be happy: "I love law school,
but what if I hate being a lawyer?" They can worry that others
won't like them as well if they're successful: "Everyone likes the
underdog." They might think that others will expect too much of
them when they see how capable they are: "As I get better [at
writing, sports, whatever], everyone demands more and more
from me." Some believe they don't deserve the recognition that
can result from success, and so forestall the embarrassment of
unearned rewards: "There are so many kids who are smarter than
I'll ever be. If I make it, they'll see I'm a fraud."

Some people fear the burden of responsibility they think comes
with success. Others fear that any success they might achieve will

disappear; they don't want to achieve it only to suffer its loss. Others believe success will bring a loss of enthusiasm; they think they'll lose more than they'll gain by working hard enough to succeed.

Changing focus to pre-empt success (as we saw in the case of Jay) is one sign parents can watch for. Other kinds of self-sabotage that can indicate a child is afraid of success are procrastination, pessimism, forgetting essential tools for an important presentation, and not getting a good night's rest before a big day. Sometimes fear of success looks like laziness. Always, it interferes with people doing as well as they otherwise could.

At its root, fear of success is an unconscious fear of future possible changes. What happens when your dreams come true? You lose those dreams. So, for some people, it's easier to relinquish dreams before they come true.

One of the most effective ways for parents to prevent or combat a fear of success is to help their children see they can manage any future changes that might accompany high-level accomplishment. Jay's parents talked with him about what might happen if he chose to develop his math and science interests further. They encouraged him to talk about his fears and his aspirations. They reassured him that his real friends liked him for himself, and wouldn't disappear.

His parents talked about their own experiences, and those of others, demonstrating that once a person achieves his current dreams, he usually finds other worthwhile dreams. They also helped Jay explore how he could satisfy his interests in musical theatre without compromising his academic achievement possibilities. He decided to stay with his math/science focus at school, and to continue with the local community theatre on an extracurricular basis. In this way he was able to keep several options open, including the possibility of mathematical or scientific achievement.

Perfectionism

We wanted to use just the right quote about perfectionism here. We really liked this one, from an unknown author: "Use what talent you possess: the woods would be silent if no birds sang except those that sang best." But then we found this one from Salvador Dali: "Have no fear of perfection—you'll never reach it." We thought that was perfect until we encountered Hugh Prather's words: "Unless I accept my faults, I will most certainly doubt my virtues." And then we had to think again when we discovered this one, from Vince Lombardi: "Perfection is not attainable. But if we chase perfection, we can catch excellence."

Such a dilemma! We couldn't decide which quote was best.

Then we relaxed, realizing that sometimes the best course of action is to lighten up, and step back a bit from the task at hand. When people believe that everything they do must be perfect, it can interfere with their pleasure in what they're doing, and ultimately with their achievement.

Here's another story from our case files:

Sheila used to be a keen student with lots of friends, and glowing reports from her teachers. Now that she's in high school, however, there's fiercer academic competition, and she finds it hard if she doesn't know the right answer immediately. Last week, her teacher handed back an assignment, along with some suggestions for improvements. Sheila burst into tears. She asked to be excused, and stayed in the bathroom until the class ended.

The assignments Sheila hands in are accurate, but apparently they lack creativity and "stretch." Her teachers say that she resists doing anything that challenges her mind or her imagination. Over the last few weeks, she's been spending a great deal of time in her bedroom, designing and trying out different studying techniques. She refuses to submit an assignment until she thinks it's perfect. She's staying up way too late, and asking for extensions even on small assignments.

It's wonderful when children strive to excel. However, it's not healthy when a keenness to achieve morphs into a burden of overwhelming expectations, as happened with Sheila. Perfectionism can lead to over-commitment, procrastination, reduced initiative, unhappiness, challenge-avoidance, and underachievement. In more serious cases, children can exhibit anxiety, eating disorders, performance paralysis, and other psychological and medical concerns.

The origin of perfectionistic behaviour differs from one person to the next. Perfectionism can result from problems with decision-making, organization, work habits, or risk-taking, as well as worries about substandard performance like those Sheila seemed to be experiencing. Living up to a gifted label can also be part of a problem with perfectionism: it's daunting to think you have to be impressively intelligent all the time.[15]

So what can parents do to help children who are showing signs of perfectionism? In Sheila's case, her parents worked with their daughter to help her set more realistic expectations for herself. They helped her see that every assignment didn't have to represent her very best work, because learning is actually *about* making mistakes. They persuaded her to work at intentionally submitting less than her best in one or two weekly assignments, to see what might happen. They told her about an Indian folklore belief that leaving a flaw in the weaving of a blanket lets the soul out.[16] It was therapeutic. Her grades didn't change—she was still an excellent student—but her teachers commended her for an easier writing style, and for the creative ideas that began to enliven her work. She learned that she didn't have to spend four hours on a rough draft of a paragraph for an English assignment, and that she might have time for some of the hobbies she'd given up.

Stories, quotes, and parental support helped Sheila overcome her need to be perfect in her school work. Her parents talked to her about their own setbacks and imperfections, and modelled out loud their thought processes as they reacted to mistakes and disappointments in their own lives, showing Sheila that mistakes can be great opportunities to learn.

Parents can help prevent or solve problems with perfectionism by reassuring their children about their weaknesses as well as their strengths. They can encourage them to strive for improvement—as opposed to absolute accuracy—in their school assignments or other tasks. They can emphasize the value of learning for the sake of learning.

Another practical strategy is to help children learn to pace themselves. This involves the child developing reasonable timelines, taking on only as much as he can handle, and setting priorities. It's also smart to keep evaluation processes in healthy perspective. Even highly perfectionistic Tiger Mother Amy Chua learned that not every assignment or test has to be done to as high a standard as possible.[17] A sense of humour helps, as does modelling the effective use of relaxation strategies. Most importantly, perhaps, parents should demonstrate that their love and support aren't conditional upon their children's achievement.

And, as with all of the issues and concerns we cover here, if problems with perfectionism get unwieldy, and aren't solved by the thoughtful application of these recommendations, it's time to think about calling in a professional.

Laziness

As with boredom, low academic achievement, perfectionism, and many other complications of children's development, what looks like laziness has many possible roots. Parents sometimes describe to us a child who was once a positive, energetic participant in school, home, and other activities, who has become lazy, unproductive, and difficult.

> When Oren was fourteen, his parents began to worry. His grades had slipped, he was barely passing, and his teachers were complaining that he wasn't doing any homework. He'd lost his love of sports, too. All he wanted to do was play computer games, hang out with his friends, and listen to music. His parents said he'd become insolent with them, and they described how their home had become a battleground. They

wanted their son to change back into the happy, respectful, and motivated person he'd been before.

In Oren's case, it happens that he was going through a normal developmental phase. As a child, he'd acquired good work habits and self-discipline skills, but now he was in the early stages of that tricky adolescent process of figuring out his identity. As we discuss in chapter 3, with so many changes going on all at once during adolescence, it can take a lot of energy just to be a fourteen-year-old.

For children who've been high achievers until they reach early adolescence, it can actually be healthy to become something of a lazy do-nothing, at least for a while.

> "The early bird gets the worm,
> but the second mouse gets the cheese."
>
> – ANONYMOUS

This attitude can drive parents crazy, of course, but it's only by experimenting with opting out that kids can decide to opt back in. After the lazy period ends, they can decide to recommit to hard work, persistence, and productive efforts. It will then be their own choosing, as opposed to complying with the wishes of their parents, teachers, or others. Parents may have to suffer through a child's period of apparent laziness, waiting until he decides to connect, or reconnect, with the drive and ambition that will stand him in good stead for his lifetime.

Sometimes kids at early adolescence appear lazy to their parents, when in fact they're intensely engaged in alternative areas of learning. Girls in particular can go through a stage when all they want to do is shop, experiment with their image, watch television, listen to music, surf the Internet, or talk to their friends (whether in person, on the phone, by Twitter, or by other electronic means).

Even very smart girls can appear to be gripped by a bout of idle-minded empty-headedness when what they're actually doing is the important work of deciding how they want to present themselves to others, and interact in the world. This involves studying societal norms, learning about relationships, and discovering who they are. No easy task!

Laziness isn't always a good sign, though. If parents want to understand their child's apparent laziness, they can start by stepping back from being overly critical. It's usually more productive to spend some time thinking about what might underlie the behaviour that looks like laziness.

Sometimes, what's needed is higher expectations from parents—requirements of hard work and real responsibilities which provide opportunities to learn the value of sustained periods of engaged time, and task commitment. Ideally, this starts in early childhood, with parents expecting their young children to pick up their toys. As we discuss in chapter 3 in connection with household chores, responsibilities for other household and family tasks can increase appropriate to the child's age, maturity, and strength. With all that's going on during adolescence, however, that isn't the easiest time to have to begin to learn about self-discipline.

As with boredom and other behaviours we discuss here, laziness can be a lot more complicated than it seems, and is not always easily resolved. It can reflect health problems, issues with friends, or a fear of failure or success. Laziness can mask anger, bullying issues, depression, or other problems that we discuss elsewhere in this book. Parents who aren't sure what's going on and are worried about it should consider consulting a professional.

Procrastination

Motivated learners are productive. They show initiative, and are keen to complete tasks at a high standard. In other words, they're go-getters. And they don't procrastinate.

Or do they?

Here are brief profiles of five elementary school students. What do they have in common?

- Damon likes to consider his options carefully. He weighs the pro and cons, ponders alternatives, and doesn't begin anything until he feels satisfied about where he's heading.
- Experience has shown Mallory that she always manages to get things done and score an A. So what's the rush?
- Jacinta puts off assignments that don't interest her and spends her time more productively on her real passion— chess.
- There are so many things that intrigue Maury. He always has people to meet, places to visit, things to do. Homework takes a back seat to more exciting activities.
- When asked to complete a task, Emma makes it her own. She designs a visual framework, creates extensions, and decides on a timeline. This rarely coincides with the teacher's deadline.

Each of these children is capable and motivated to learn. Each has also been labelled a procrastinator by parents and teachers. As far as the kids are concerned, though, their behaviour makes perfectly good sense.

Timelines and punctuality can seem critically important to adults.

> *"Intelligence without ambition is like a bird without wings."*
>
> – SALVADOR DALI

The word *procrastination* (which by definition means putting forward until tomorrow) tends to have negative connotations, like the word *sloth*. It implies avoidance, opting out, and sabotaging one's own efforts.

As with laziness, when children procrastinate, they almost always have a reason. Perhaps they're overwhelmed, under-challenged, distracted, or low on energy, or sleep, or nutrition. Maybe they enjoy the rush of last-minute hustle and bustle. Or they lack a necessary skill, or have trouble focusing, getting organized, or developing a framework for action

Children may, in fact, want to succeed, but find themselves unable to proceed for one reason or another. They might be afraid of starting something for fear of making mistakes, and might require help to get going. Advanced learners, in particular, could be in the throes of formulating complex concepts, or working through different approaches before embarking on a given task. Children may also see their parents, family members, or teachers procrastinating, and decide it's fine to do likewise.[18]

Kids do need to learn that a disregard for deadlines can have consequences. Parents can do some problem-solving with a procrastination-prone child to figure out what's behind the behaviour. They can think together about what might work better, while taking into account the child's needs and preferences. Parents can model decisive and plan-oriented attitudes in their own lives. That's usually the best way to show children how to manage their time and hone their organizational skills.

Each person chooses what to strive for, what to settle on, what to delay, and what to avoid. Parents can encourage their children to think intelligently about what they will put off until tomorrow, and hopefully they'll learn to choose wisely and proceed with confidence.[19]

Self-Confidence

It's been said that the greatest gift a parent can give a child is self-confidence.[20]

While we agree that self-confidence is a worthwhile goal for parents to hold for their kids, there are two widespread misconceptions that can stand in the way. The first is that confidence is a global attribute—meaning that people are either confident or insecure. In reality, very few people feel good (or bad) about themselves in every area of life. Like with intelligence and creativity, confidence varies across different areas within the same person. Someone might have strong confidence about her social abilities, for example, but feel insecure about her athletic or musical ability. It doesn't really make sense to talk about someone as confident or insecure, except as that relates to a particular area of life.

> *"I am not afraid of storms for I am learning how to sail my ship."*
>
> – LOUISA MAY ALCOTT

Academic or intellectual self-confidence can come from academic achievement, and social confidence comes from experiences of social success. Healthy all-round self-confidence is usually built on achievement in several important domains, including intellectual, physical, social, behavioural, and emotional.

The second misconception about self-confidence is that praise helps people feel confident. In fact, hollow praise actually diminishes self-esteem.[21] A strong sense of self is built on succeeding in areas that matter to the individual, whether it's sports, academics, social popularity, or something else.

Parents who are worried about their child's self-confidence can help her find activities in an area of interest—perhaps painting, creative writing, or some other pursuit.

> *"If you hear a voice within you say 'you cannot paint,' then by all means paint, and that voice will be silenced."*
>
> – VINCENT VAN GOGH

Luis, now a teacher, shares this story, thinking back to when he was fifteen.

> I never had lots of friends, and other kids may have thought I was kind of weird. Winning all those academic awards didn't help. I was shy, and not interested in team sports. But something at our community centre captured my attention: a martial arts teacher was giving Aikido lessons. It seemed a bit scary, but I wanted to know more, so I decided to go to a class.
>
> I enjoyed that first session, and stayed with it. I've actually learned a lot about life from Aikido, not just the moves. We were taught how to relax in confrontational situations. Understanding humility and proper etiquette are also part of the training. I worked toward the rank of Nikyu (two levels below black belt), and then beyond.
>
> I remember doing a presentation on Aikido for my English class. Everyone thought it was so cool. The other kids started asking me about it. I didn't mind answering their questions. Even now, I feel like Aikido has given me confidence in myself.[22]

Luis's involvement in Aikido took him into a whole new realm of activity and interaction. He found himself succeeding at something that made him feel good about himself, and gave him something to talk about with others.

By branching out beyond academics into Aikido, Luis cultivated important dimensions of social intelligence, such as collaboration, negotiation, and conflict resolution. Aikido led to him having something to share with his classmates, and over time to greater ease in other kinds of conversation, too. All these newly strengthened abilities helped him as he moved forward in his academic, personal, and career pursuits.

Confidence emerges from experiences of competence in areas that a person values. Not everyone is competent at everything they do, of course, and certainly not right at the beginning.

Sometimes what's required is more effort, guidance, or assistance. A child's lack of self-confidence can indicate problems with goal-setting—figuring out what he wants to invest his energy in—or persistence—staying engaged with a pursuit long enough to experience fulfilling and confidence-building experiences.

Parents can help a child develop self-confidence by celebrating the small steps that lead to achievement. They can show him how to face setbacks with a positive mindset, seeing difficulties as ways to learn, not as insurmountable obstacles, and then taking pride in overcoming hurdles. By being available to encourage their child as he investigates options, reviews goals, and adjusts his efforts to adapt to changing demands and circumstances, parents can bolster his self-confidence—and this will stand him in good stead through the years.

Our Secrets: Addressing Possible Complications

1. Being different than others brings challenges. Children who are distinctive in some way—including those who are intellectually advanced—can be misunderstood or have trouble with social acceptance. This is particularly troubling at early adolescence, and the more exceptional the child's ability, the truer this is.

2. When emotional concerns arise, parents can consider these three problem-finding questions: What is the problem? Is that really a problem? If yes, whose problem is it? These questions can be followed by two problem-solving questions: How can we help? Is it time to call in some professional help?

3. Finding intellectual peers can help advanced learners feel better about their differentness from others. Look for interest groups and activities in their areas of enthusiasm.

4. Encourage your child to appreciate her uniqueness, and to understand that everyone has different strengths and weaknesses.

5. Emotional intelligence involves perceiving one's own and others' emotions accurately, expressing feelings effectively, and understanding and regulating one's own emotional reactions.

6. There are strategies parents can use to help their children develop emotional coping skills. Some of these are focus on pacing; talk together about personal belief systems, feelings, and attitudes; share stories of those who have overcome challenges or stressful situations and who have managed their emotions successfully; and offer reassurance as necessary.

7. Kids with intellectual strengths can experience problems with boredom, fear of failure and success, perfectionism, laziness, procrastination, and lack of self-confidence. We discuss in this chapter many ways parents can prevent and reduce each of these problems.

8. If things become complicated or can't be resolved by the thoughtful application of parenting strategies, consider calling in professional help.

We've considered how parents can help their children understand and manage their feelings, and also deal with other complications that can accompany their intellectual growth. In the next chapter, we think about how parents can support and strengthen their children's social intelligence.

CHAPTER 9

The
Social Context:
Friends and
Others

*"Each friend represents a world in us, a world
possibly not born until they arrive, and it is only
by this meeting that a new world is born."*

— ANAIS NIN

FRIENDSHIPS serve an important function in children's lives, helping them learn about collaboration, conflict resolution, affection, compassion, trust, courtesy, and a whole host of other qualities that are central to living and learning. In this chapter we explore social issues including friendships, belonging, social contexts, resiliency, and siblings. We also think about difficulties kids sometimes have, and strategies for addressing these difficulties. We consider parents' concerns about their children's social development, such as "How can we help our child make friends?" "What should we do if our child is bullied?" and "How do we maintain family harmony when each of our kids is so different?" We offer suggestions for parents so they can empower kids to strengthen their friendship networks and build their social intelligence.

Why Do Friendships Matter?

People differ in what they look for in a friendship, but the need to be accepted as part of a social network is something everyone shares. Relationships are important to all aspects of health and well-being, and people with strong social networks do better than others when dealing with illness, poverty, and trauma. For children as well as adults, "Close friends are emotional resources. Children draw on their friends for the security they need to strike out into new territory. Close friends act as buffers against negative events."[1] Across ages, cultures, and socio-economic status, the single most important resiliency factor for every category of risk is social support.[2]

> *"Walking with a friend in the dark is better than walking alone in the light."*
>
> – HELEN KELLER

Children vary in their friendship-building abilities. Some are sociable and extroverted, and make friends easily; others are introverted, and prefer time alone. Some are popular with their peers, others are tolerated, some are neglected, and then there are those who are pointedly rejected. And acceptance can vary across settings, too. The most popular child at summer camp may be ignored by kids at school, or vice versa.

Social navigation can feel like driving along a twisting mountain highway in uncertain weather conditions. It requires care, composure, a sense of direction, and the patience to work through the sudden surprises, traffic jams, and ever-shifting road conditions. Having good social skills is akin to having good driving skills. When the going gets complicated, strong social skills can make all the difference to a child's experience of life.

When kids are little, they're interested in buddies, people with whom they can play, talk, and giggle: Suki and Leila are elbows-deep at the water table, and merrily splash themselves and their kindergarten classmates. As children get older they become better able to understand the perspectives of others, and to take that into account in their interactions. With increasing age, friendships become more reciprocal, and also more supportive: Jeff knows that Greg is interested in playing the drums, and invites him to help form a band after school.

Maturity brings more sophisticated forms of friendships, deeper relationships that incorporate trust, acceptance, disclosure, and a desire to safeguard the connection. Francesca and Hannah will be heading off to college soon to study languages. They plan to travel during the summers, as they study to become interpreters. They'll spend time together and time apart, and they'll rely on one another as they each adjust to the routines, challenges, and complexities of life abroad.

In a recent study, 283 high school and college students were asked what qualities they value in their friends.[3] Points mentioned most frequently included being comfortable with each other; being able to share confidences without judgement; having fun together; feeling that the other person cares and is interested in their successes; and having a sense of trust, knowing the other person will support and listen to them. Students were also asked to indicate the principal benefit they felt they gained from friendship. The number one answer? Positive emotional support.

Optimally, friends have many points of connection with each other, and this is where high-level abilities can be a liability. When a child's intellectual development outstrips his emotional or social development, it can be hard for him to find someone with whom he enjoys talking, and who's also at the same level, both emotionally and physically.

Ten-year-old Damien is an excellent student. If you ask him about his friends, he'll tell you he doesn't have any. His

intellectual peers are more socially, emotionally, and physically mature than he is, and his age peers aren't interested
in the same ideas at the same level of intensity. "I don't fit in
anywhere," Damien says.

When intellectual development is advanced, it doesn't mean
other areas are also advanced. Asynchrony across areas of development like Damien experiences is not uncommon. Children
who are intellectually exceptional still need friends their own age
if they're to experience a social, emotional, and physical match,
and healthy development in all of these important areas.

There are children who are both cognitively and socially
advanced, but that doesn't necessarily make it easier for them
to find friends. Although they may relate better with older kids
than some of their same-age intellectual peers do, because of their
physical immaturity they may have a hard time really belonging.
At the same time, however, their social and intellectual advancement makes it difficult for them to have meaningful interactions
with their age peers. It can be socially isolating to be outside the
circle of classroom, lunchroom, and schoolyard friendships.

How Can Parents Help?

Children's and adolescents' social experiences, needs, and abilities
are enormously variable, but there are a few basic principles for
parents to consider that can help kids with friendship problems.
The first is to avoid imposing adult-defined sociability requirements on a child.

Samantha is eleven years old. She enjoys spending time on
her own, reading science fiction, and working out baseball
statistics. When her parents have people over for dinner
(which is quite often), Sammy joins in the conversation,
and usually the adults are surprised at her knowledge and
insight.

Samantha's friends in the neighbourhood are mostly older kids. She has a big extended family, and loves playing with her cousins of all ages. She says she usually finds spending time with children her own age boring, and at recess she prefers sitting under a tree with a book. She's rarely invited to classmates' parties, but that doesn't seem to bother her.

Samantha's teacher, Ms. Elkind, became concerned when she saw Sammy sitting on her own in the playground day after day. She tried a "buddy" approach and paired her with Anna, a talkative little girl who needed help with her school work. Samantha ended up doing all the work, and found Anna's constant chatter annoying. Neither child learned very much, and neither of them enjoyed it.

Ms. Elkind decided Samantha needed social skills train ing, and signed her up for the Interactive Fun Group organized by the school's visiting social worker. The other kids in the group had problems with bullying or rejection. Sammy hated it. She began to worry there was something seriously wrong with her. She became too self-conscious to read by herself under a tree, and began to ask her teacher if she could just stay inside at recess.

Well-meaning parents, family members, and educators sometimes exert pressure on children to be more social, or to go out and make friends. Sometimes they go as far as Sammy's teacher did, and enroll kids in social skills courses, whether they want them or not. It's not usually a good idea, however, to push children to be more socially active than they want to be. What parents can do is create friend-friendly home environments, facilitate activities with other kids, address their children's social and emotional concerns as they arise, and model close, warm friendships in their own lives.

Some children are perfectly content without too many friends. Social skills training is needed only if a child is aggressive, demonstrates behaviour problems, or requests help learning how to interact with others. Special training is not needed just because a child prefers sitting with a book to playing a noisy game at recess.

Another basic friendship principle for parents to keep in mind is that every classroom should be a place of acceptance and respect for diversity. School should provide kids with a haven of sorts, where labels don't define people or marginalize them, and where every child experiences learning in a safe and welcoming environment. Parents can take an advocacy role at their child's school, helping to ensure that all children feel safe, comfortable, and connected. Effective initiatives include conflict resolution, parent-support groups, peer mediation training, and professional development for teachers in social and emotional development.[4]

A third basic friendship principle is that people can't be expected to get along swimmingly with everyone they encounter. Of course, children should be taught about respect and courtesy. However, like adults, they have to be able to select those with whom they'd like to interact. They'll be drawn to some people and not to others. Generally speaking, kids connect well with those with whom they have something in common—a shared interest, goal, or experience. Not being chummy with everyone in the schoolyard is okay. Rudeness, disdain, and bullying are not.

When kids want more friends, or have trouble connecting with their classmates, parents can encourage them to make social contacts through extracurricular activities they enjoy (like Luis's Aikido lessons in chapter 8). This can happen through sports teams, community service, or other activities in the neighbourhood, or cultural or religious circles.[5]

Parents can also help their kids learn the basics of making friends. This includes openness to others, greeting people and responding to their greetings in a friendly manner, maintaining eye contact, speaking loudly enough to be heard (but not so loudly as to be obnoxious), and many other nuances of the greeting process that can be learned. Parents can role-play games with their child, practising how to initiate a greeting, and how to respond so they show an interest in being friends.[6]

Parents can help their child learn that treating someone with kindness and respect will gain that person's positive attention. It's best when this is learned from the earliest days by observing the day-to-day interactions among family members, but some kids take longer to learn how to put these attitudes into practice, or need explicit help with it.

One misconception that some kids hold that interferes with the friendship process is the idea that they have to be super-amazing in order to win friends. That can lead to bragging and class clown behaviour, both of which can be counterproductive in the popularity stakes. Parents can help their child realize that other kids will be more interested if they see how they're alike, not how they're different. The best approach to finding friends is to be oneself, to be good to others, and to discover the ways you're like others. Unless you're a rock star (in which case friendships are sometimes fleeting and superficial), you don't make friends by impressing people by how special and different you are.

What else can parents do? Make sure your home is friend-friendly. Encourage your child to invite other kids over, and do what you can to welcome them. Check with the other parents ahead of time. Be kind to the children your child invites home, offer good snacks, and ensure that your child and the others are comfortable, safe, and happy. Don't hover or try to direct the playtime, but be available as needed to ensure a harmonious experience.

One last suggestion for parents interested in helping their kids make and keep friends: children's friendships are usually built around having fun together. Popular kids are fun to be around. Do what you can to help your child learn how to enjoy time spent with others. That's not always instinctive. Some kids need to learn how to find out what other kids like doing, and accommodate those interests. Other kids need to learn how to share decision-making, or lose gracefully, or be a good winner.

Bullying

Bullying is a more serious and prevalent problem for kids than many adults realize. In a published report on bullying, the authors wrote:

> Bullying happens to about 10 per cent of children every day at school. About 30 per cent of students are involved as witnesses or as fellow aggressors. Peers, teachers, and other adults rarely intervene to help a child who is being victimized—they either fail to recognize the problem or they turn a blind eye.... Being bullied can lead to physical and mental health problems—and in extreme cases, suicide. At its core, bullying is a relationship problem. It is about an imbalance of power with repeated aggression, with harm as its intent. It takes many forms—social, verbal, physical, cyber.[7]

Anyone can be a target for bullying, but a child or adolescent who is different than others—such as being advanced intellectually—can become a magnet for bullies. Being advanced can increase a child's feelings of isolation. It can also trigger rejection, envy, or aggression by age peers. Patrick is now an adult, but his story still resonates.

> As my intellectual development raced ahead, my emotional development did not, and I don't believe this was recognized by anybody. I might've been reading at university level in grade seven, but my ability to deal with conflict was that of a twelve-year-old.
>
> One afternoon during a baseball-like game that my friends and I had invented, I got caught out by the same trick everyone else had been fooled by at some point previously. I stormed away from the group, hurt by my friends' laughter and unable to laugh at myself.

No one else had stayed away sulking when they were tricked. After an emotional exchange the next day (I was still angry about the incident), my ex-friends spent the rest of the spring semester ostracizing me, then picking on me. I wanted out of that school in the worst way, and convinced my parents to send me somewhere else the next year. I didn't have the emotional tools to handle the increasingly negative situation. In re-examining that period of my life, I realize the bullying only became such a big problem because of my reaction to the inciting incident.

Managing feelings does not come naturally, even to people who are very smart in other ways.[8] Children who are caught up in bullying, whether as victim or bully, usually need help learning to stop taking offence or going on the offensive so quickly.

CHECKLIST:
FOUR PRACTICES PARENTS CAN
TEACH KIDS TO PREVENT BULLYING

Parents can teach their children four useful practices:[9]

1. To carefully think through the issues and alternative responses to others' comments and behaviour before reacting;

2. To be tolerant, learning to think positively rather than suspiciously about what others say or do, asking themselves, "What's the best possible way to view the other person's words or actions?";

3. To question their inferences, learning to separate their perceptions of the issues from the actual facts of the situation; and

4. To become aware of the possible consequences of their own actions.[10]

Had someone helped Patrick and his friends with these skills before the baseball incident, or at some point before it had escalated too far, his story might have turned out quite differently.

"Everyone who doesn't like Seth, put up your hands."[11] It's hard to believe, but these words were actually spoken by a grade eight teacher about a student in his class. Yes, the teacher probably had reason to be frustrated with the young man in question, but this remark conveyed the message to every child in the classroom that it was acceptable to marginalize and humiliate others, especially Seth. Flash forward several years and the sting still lingers for Seth. Hurtful episodes have a way of staying with people.

Imagine, then, an incident that isn't a single occurrence in a classroom, but instead occurs in a much larger forum, and takes on an uncontrollable life of its own. Kids can readily goad other kids using social media. "Everyone who hates Quinn, post something." Sadly, this kind of bullying happens far too often, sometimes with tragic consequences. And as social networking platforms and devices proliferate, the sting is increasingly potent. Online messages can circulate widely, quickly, and unchecked. Targeted children can become demoralized, depressed, or even suicidal.

More and more kids have easy access to online venues, and many participate in a digital life that includes extensive social networking. Adults may have little or no knowledge of the vast technological landscape their kids engage with. Even parents who are tech savvy and actively part of social media milieux themselves may not know what their kids are up to. This can make it difficult for caring adults to identify, prevent, or stop what has become a very real and increasingly dangerous problem: cyberbullying.

Parents' Questions about Cyberbullying

We address here some of the questions we hear most often from parents:

- *What is cyberbullying?* A prevalent and malicious form of harassment,[12] cyberbullying has been called a "virtual lynch mob."[13] It includes, but is not confined to (1) hacking—intruding into someone else's e-mail account or web site, and sending harmful messages or pictures; (2) smearing—spreading rumours on social networking sites, or creating hate groups, web pages, or embarrassing profiles; and (3) damaging—sending out computer viruses that compromise others' computers, causing them to crash, transmit, or delete information.

  Although face-to-face and cyberbullying are both abusive, the latter can be particularly disturbing. Because cyberbullies can hide behind pseudonyms or have multiple and anonymous e-mail addresses, it can be extremely difficult to find, communicate, or reason with them. A cyber attack can involve a large number of people in no time at all—just as long as it takes to strike a few letters on a keyboard. Moreover, because the cruel result of a cyber assault is not immediately discernible to bullies, they can avoid seeing the serious harm they're inflicting. The bully remains sheltered while the hurtful action escalates, and the menacing continues.

  The role of bystanders can't be overstated. Whether with face-to-face bullying or cyberbullying, bystanders who don't intervene empower the bully, and are part of the problem. Anyone who condones bullying behaviour by laughing, contributing negative comments of their own, forwarding information, just being silent, or even walking away is complicit in the abuse.

- *How do parents know if their child is being cyberbullied?* If a child begins to act in an unusual manner when using technological devices, it's important to find out what's going on. Parents should be alert if a child or adolescent suddenly stops using the computer or cellphone; is nervous when messages appear; seems ill at ease when going out;

appears angry, anxious, or withdrawn; or shuns conversations with friends and family.

- *How do parents know if their child is cyberbullying others?* The more technologically adept a child is, the more ways she can find to be an undetected bully by cyber disgracing or technologically assaulting someone. Someone who's involved in bullying others may suddenly switch activities to avoid detection, abhor restrictions to Internet access, avoid discussing her online activities, or open multiple accounts. Any kind of unusual, avoidant, or obsessive tech-related behaviour merits parental attention.

- *What's the connection between cyberbullying and high-level ability?* There are two aspects of cyberbullying of particular importance to parents of academically advanced children. The first is the fact that technological expertise can be used either for positive or for destructive purposes. While most kids who are exceptionally talented with computers apply their skills constructively, others are tempted to involve themselves in mischief. Another concern—as with any kind of bullying—is that children can be targets of abuse because of their exceptionality. Kids who are advanced relative to others can be victims of jealousy, envy, or ridicule because of their high-level abilities.

- *How can parents prevent bullying, and support their kids if they're targeted or involved?* Protecting kids against all forms of bullying, including cyberbullying, means focusing on social connections. As noted earlier, "At its core, bullying is a relationship problem."[14] Parents can help by ensuring their kids learn about conflict resolution, engage in healthy friendship-building, develop coping mechanisms in advance of an attack, and realize the terrible damage that even playful online "teasing" of others can cause.[15]

Parents who are concerned about bullying can advocate for teacher training in creating safer classroom environments. Strategies for teachers include creating communication forums (both virtual and face-to-face) that are open to teachers, parents, and students interested in making improvements to the school climate, and training children to become peer mediators who are available to help resolve conflicts when they arise. Teachers can discuss with their students the roles of bystanders and defenders in bullying situations. They can work with parents to ensure strong home and school links so that messages are strong and consistent.

> *"When people hurt you over and over, think of them like sand paper. They may scratch and hurt you a bit, but in the end, you're the one who ends up polished."*
>
> CHRIS COLFER[16]

There's also a role for proactive law enforcement. Police officers can be invited to schools to help educate kids about the issues, including the potential seriousness of bullying; the impact of online offences; provisions of the law; how and where to report offences such as stalking, harassment or threats; and how to engage in safe day-to-day and online behaviour to pre-empt bullying or prevent it from getting out of hand. As awareness of the seriousness of bullying gains momentum, legal action is being taken. In Canada, the province of Nova Scotia has taken the lead with its legislation designed to curtail cyberbullying,[17] and more jurisdictions are following suit.

CHECKLIST: SCHOOL-BASED STRATEGIES TO REDUCE BULLYING

Parent advocacy at school can make a big difference to children's experiences of bullying. Strategies for reducing bullying at the school level, including cyberbullying, follow:

- increasing awareness of the need for bystanders, parents, and teachers to step in early;
- highlighting links to mental health services, for both the bully and the victim;
- emphasizing the need for adults to model anti-bullying behaviour, including intervening when bystanders;
- supporting kids in building healthy relationships; and
- working collaboratively, for example by reinventing the PTA, and creating twenty-four-hour support networks of kids, parents, and teachers, on-call as needed.[18]

Children need to know there are people who will assist them if they experience bullying, including concerned adults who will make every effort to stop the cruelty or embarrassment. No child should have to deal with abuse single-handedly.

Social Context Matters

Where in the world a person lives and the people he connects with have a tremendous impact on his experiences and intellectual growth. Intelligence is increasingly being thought of not as a "lump of something that's in our heads, but as a transaction among people."[19]

Children learn best when there's a network of social support that encourages them to work hard, and when there's a real-world reason for their learning. Consider this story shared by sixteen-year-old Heidi, who wanted to spend a summer in Italy as an exchange student:

> I explained to my parents that if a person lives in an English-speaking community and tries to learn Italian by taking classes, it'll probably feel like work, and require loads of discipline. If, let's say, that person spent some time in Italy, she would be *so* motivated. She could take some classes, and also find opportunities to talk to shopkeepers, waiters, and other people. She could spend time learning the language all day,

every day. She could read the labels and packages in super-markets, go to Italian films with English subtitles (or English films with Italian subtitles), and make new friends and then they could speak Italian together.

Heidi was not only astute, she was also persuasive. Her parents were somewhat hesitant at first, but with the assistance of the school guidance counsellor, Heidi was able to put a sensible plan in place. (For the record, she prevailed with her language learning while in Italy, and did establish a good foundation in Italian that summer, which she built upon over the next few years.) As this determined teenager so convincingly indicated, being in a social milieu where it really matters that you speak the language is a powerful motivator, and is likely to accelerate the learning process. And, just as she predicted, a person generally ends up knowing a lot more after time spent productively abroad than if she'd stayed home and taken lessons.

Social context—including opportunities for interaction and collaboration with others, and real-world inquiry and consequences—makes an enormous difference in what and how much is learned, and how quickly that happens. Teachers believe implicitly in the value of education, yet they sometimes forget how important contextual relevance is. Parents, who may be focused on their children's grades or on other concerns, sometimes forget the importance of social context, too. People thrive with the right sorts of interaction and support, and that doesn't occur in a vacuum.

> *"Great intellectual breakthroughs often have as much to do with context, collaboration, and good fortune as they do with the person as a unique individual."*
>
> – BARRY HYMER, JACK WHITEHEAD, AND MARIE HUXTABLE[20]

The European Renaissance, which started in fifteenth-century Florence, provides a great illustration of the power of social context, collaboration, and authentic relevance in the development of intelligence. The Renaissance resulted in extraordinary achievements and discoveries in banking, art, architecture, science, literature, politics, and more. Political historian Robert Putnam analyzed this fertile period and found that it wasn't individual genius that created the Renaissance, but rather the nature of the social milieu that made possible the genius of the achievements. He concluded it was the history of investments in social capital, reciprocity, and networks of engagement that enabled the creative flowering of people like Leonardo da Vinci, Machiavelli, and Michelangelo.[21]

A modern illustration of the ways these collaborative factors foster intelligence can be found in the social milieu that led to the extraordinary creative productivity associated with Silicon Valley. Luis Alvarez and William Shockley—both of whom were tested, and neither of whom made the IQ cut for Lewis Terman's landmark study of giftedness—went on to win Nobel prizes for their invention of the transistor and their work in elementary particle physics.[22] As with the Renaissance, the Silicon Valley story is interesting here not so much for the genius of individual contributions, but rather for the nature of the social milieu that happened to coalesce, and that nurtured creative collaborations, enhancing communication possibilities around the world.

For many years, Joseph Renzulli and his colleagues[23] have been showing how to foster high-level development more broadly across the population by creating a social context where children can strive together, with the help of caring adults, to identify and solve authentic problems. When people live or work in a milieu where social interaction is positive and nurturing, there's no end to what can evolve. For example, when Sidney Crosby, captain of the 2014 Canadian Olympic men's hockey team, was asked about winning Olympic gold, he said, "We played together the whole time. . . . We all believed in one another and the way we needed to play, and stuck with it."[24]

From Strength to Strength

In a perfect world (as we see it), each child's well-being is paramount. He aspires to achievement and fulfillment, and he gets the guidance, nurturing, and support he needs to realize his aspirations. He grows up surrounded by a positive peer group, and learns to manage negative influences and difficult feelings. He experiences challenges and learning opportunities in a range of areas, sometimes working collaboratively with others. His knowledge continues to grow, and his interests continue to deepen. He works on the edge of his comfort zone, constantly stretching his mind in directions he finds exciting. His confidence develops as he sees himself achieving success in areas that he values.

"It is not the mountain we conquer, but ourselves."

– EDMUND HILLARY

What are the social strengths and resiliencies parents can foster in their children to help them aspire to goals like these, and to meet the challenges they will inevitably experience?

In previous chapters, we discuss the importance to children, especially in the early years, of exposure to many kinds of opportunities for playful exploration, both on their own and with others. As young people develop increasing competence, they need greater challenge, higher levels of instruction, continued interaction with others with similar interests, and many more hours of disciplined practice. In the course of maturing and moving from competency to real expertise, their psychosocial skills (such as resilience, emotional self-regulation, relationship-building, capacity to deal with setbacks, and grace under fire) become more and more important.[25]

Proactive parenting for long-term success includes modelling effective social skills, and helping kids develop a sense of their areas of strength and weakness, recognizing that others have them, too. Parents can talk candidly about individual differences, demonstrating how to restore self-confidence in those inevitable circumstances when a child's confidence is threatened or compromised.[26]

While "playing the game" may sound to teenagers like the social conformity they abhor, and a cowardly retreat from being true to themselves, it's actually a critical component of success in any field. Learning to play the game means finding out how things are done in a given field in order to communicate effectively with others, and succeed. A young musician, for example, needs to learn how to get along with conductors, marketing people, studio technicians, and other musicians if he wants to get steady work. Just like a young child needs to respect the turn-taking and toy-sharing ethos of the playground if he wants to be invited to join in games with other kids. Parents who help their children pay attention to the rules of engagement, and the way those rules change from one social context to another, are giving their kids an essential tool for success.[27]

In order for children to be at ease with others—that is, to develop relationships and make connections comfortably and meaningfully—it helps if they feel at ease with themselves. Self-acceptance is built on a foundation of knowledge of one's own way of being, including attitudes, abilities, and liabilities. It also has a lot to do with ease with one's personal identity (age, sex, gender identity, cultural background, and so on) and values (such as integrity and responsibility). Healthy self-acceptance provides the most solid foundation for social intelligence and, ultimately, wisdom. Achieving the kind of self-acceptance that underpins wisdom can take a lifetime. Throughout this book we've offered strategies to help parents give their kids a head start on that exciting and worthwhile endeavour.

Siblings

Every parent who has more than one child will tell you that each one is unique. Whether it's attitude, temperament, talent, appearance, or something else entirely, variations run through every family. These differences can be appreciated, but they can also be a source of conflict.

> *"Comparison is a death knell to sibling harmony."*
>
> – ELIZABETH FISHEL[28]

Thoughtful parents consider the ways their children's needs vary, and attempt to meet them, both individually and, where possible, collectively. In order to nurture their children's individuality and support their growth, parents have to find ways to let each of their children discover and become himself, while providing the steering assistance each one needs when the road gets twisty or there are unexpected detours. Even though two or more children may share both parents and the same home environment, they'll learn differently because of differences in motivation, interest, or personal attributes. They'll behave, mature, and think about things very differently, too. As the eldest in a family of nine siblings, each of whom is taking a distinct pathway through life, Dona can tell you about this first-hand.

Each child needs many and various chances to explore who she is uniquely, and who she wants to become. She'll do best if at least one of her parents values her efforts as she finds her way. For example, if one child in a family is learning piano concertos, another is a community soccer star, a third is interested in astrophysics, a fourth loves to read mystery novels, and a fifth wants to become a master chef, the parents should try to ensure that they *all* get opportunities to develop their interests. It can be an enormous juggling act, but is ultimately worth the effort.

What about a situation where there's one child who appears to be unusually intelligent in one or more domains? Others in the family circle, such as siblings, grandparents, and extended family members, may not understand or appreciate his particular needs, inclinations, or capacities. They may not realize that a child who's intellectually advanced may experience academic, social, or emotional turmoil just like any other child, and may require guidance in some areas and not others, again just like any other child. Families function well when the different members work together toward valuing each other for their uniqueness, understanding that intellectual ability is only one facet.

In the same way that effective teachers differentiate for learners in the classroom, so should parents try to differentiate their parenting. Although sometimes the entire family can enjoy doing things together, different opportunities and activities are needed for different members of the family based on what each individual is keen to develop at a given point in time. Consider these scenarios:

- "Every time my brother opens his mouth to give his opinion, my father listens attentively and replies as if my brother just said something brilliant. Even if it's stupid. When I say something, no matter how important, it's a big yawn. Nobody listens."
- "My sister is some kind of piano genius. Our family revolves around her practising schedule, her rehearsals, her concerts. My mother never drives me anywhere, because she's always driving Sophie somewhere. We can't afford the science experiment stuff I want because all our money is going into Sophie's lessons and her grand piano."

One of the concerns we've frequently heard from people who've grown up with superstar siblings—whether academic, athletic, musical, or something else—is their sense of having been overshadowed by their exceptional sibling. In an attempt to ensure that one child's talent is nurtured as far as possible, some parents lose sight of the needs of the other children in the family, or invest so heavily—money, attention, emotion, or time—in the child who has demonstrated exceptional talent that there's little left over for the others. We've encountered parents who overbalance the other way, too, downplaying one child's talent so the others don't feel left out or inferior.

This isn't an easy balancing act, so parents should try to stay attuned to each of their children's needs by watching, listening, and redirecting their time and attention as required. It's important to make sure each child feels respected and valued.

On the other side of the equation, a child who exhibits unusual or very high-level ability can sometimes try to minimize it. She may not want to show anyone up or drain more than her share of the family's resources.

And if things weren't complicated enough, something else to consider is that parents can undermine their kids' confidence in the areas where their siblings excel. In a family, for example, where one child is designated "the smart one" and another "the athletic one," "the smart one" may think he's not athletic, and "the athletic one" may feel insecure about her intelligence. Yes, it's great for kids to be celebrated for their individual strengths, but parents have to try to balance this with a nuanced appreciation for each child's many abilities and interests.

Competition among siblings takes many forms, and sibling rivalry can be particularly fierce in families where one or more members are centred out for unusual recognition. Parents can watch for—and attempt to moderate—the much-recognized child underplaying or bragging about his achievements, or the less-recognized child disparaging or overemphasizing the remarkable sibling's achievements, or depreciating his own. Things go best in families where each member feels stronger for being connected to the others.

Author Joyce Maynard writes, "It's not only children who grow. Parents do too. As much as we watch to see what our children do with their lives, they are watching us to see what we do with ours. I can't tell my children to reach for the sun. All I can do is reach for it myself."[29] By doing so, and by valuing their own strengths, parents can help each of their children get the best possible shot at becoming proud of their abilities and achievements.

The attributes that make families work—mutual respect, generous enthusiasm for others' strengths, patient tolerance for others' weaknesses, sensitivity, honesty, and so on—serve children well in their social interactions in playgrounds, schools, extracurricular activities, and later, in colleges and work places.

Our Secrets: The Social Context

1. Children's friendships matter. Social connections are people's biggest single resiliency factor.
2. Sharing points of connection with others can be challenging for kids when their intellectual development · outstrips their emotional and social development. Parents can help children find opportunities to interact with age peers who share interests.
3. Three principles for parents to keep in mind if they think their kids have friendship problems: (i) avoid imposing adult-defined sociability requirements on children; (ii) every classroom should be a place of acceptance and respect for diversity; and (iii) children (like adults) should be able to select as friends those with whom they have something in common.
4. Although children who are intellectually advanced are no more or less likely to have social problems than others, just the fact of being different than others can trigger rejection, envy, or aggression. Parents should watch for this, and be available for guidance as needed.
5. Children who are caught up in bullying, whether as victim or bully, can be helped when parents teach them to (i) carefully think through the issues, (ii) be tolerant of others, (iii) question their inferences, and (iv) become aware of the possible consequences of their own actions.

6. Celebrate children's individuality, efforts, and accomplishments. Children who feel good about themselves are more likely to be self-confident. They're also less likely to be victimized by bullies or to participate in bullying activities.

7. Parents can help kids deal with cyberbullying. Teach them to resolve conflicts harmoniously and engage in safe and responsible networking; familiarize them with strategies to cope with attacks; and help them realize the damage that apparently light-hearted online teasing can cause.

8. Children learn best with real-world social reasons for their learning, including a network of support, and ample opportunities for engagement and collaboration.

9. Learning how to interact successfully with different groups of people is an essential social skill for success in relationships, careers, and life. Parents can model this, and talk about it with their kids.

10. Siblings usually have different strengths. In a healthy family environment, each person feels good about her own abilities, and values the abilities of others.

In these last two chapters, we've considered some of the emotional and social challenges associated with raising kids to thrive, along with strategies for helping children become more successful at managing difficulties, feelings, and relationships. It's time now to turn our attention to tying together all the threads within this book. In chapter 10 we look at how to raise kids who are not only intelligent, but who are fulfilled, resilient, and happily productive in a rapidly changing world.

CHAPTER 10

Raising Children to Thrive

*"If you would take, you must first give,
this is the beginning of intelligence."*

— LAO TZU

I N THIS CHAPTER, we reconsider some of the ideas we've shared throughout the book, and also present additional ideas for moving forward. We present our top seven parenting practices, and address some further questions, including "How can I teach my child to be more reflective?" "How can I help my child become wise, with a strong character?" and "What if my child isn't so intelligent?" And, finally, we look toward the future, thinking about parents' long-term goals, with a final quiz where we review strategies you can use to increase the likelihood of your children living successful, happily productive lives.

Going Beyond Intelligence

Reflectivity—or mindfulness—helps people apply their intelligence thoughtfully. It enables them to understand what matters to themselves and others, providing a foundation for deeper insight and empathy, healthy self-awareness, relationships, decisions, and leadership ability.

Jim Higley, a columnist who writes about family life, has written about mindful parenting, and advocates that parents follow three simple rules. The first is "put it on ice," which means giving yourself time to think before responding to a child's problem, behaviour, or question. The second is the "thirty-second rule," which reflects his observation that kids hate being lectured to, so when a parent thinks a lecture is absolutely necessary, he should confine it to thirty seconds maximum. And the third rule is "stop solving everything," which reflects Higley's discovery that kids sharing problems usually just want to feel heard, and be respected enough to solve their own problems.[1]

> *"Most people who attain success in their lives, however defined, are people who figure out who they are—what they have to offer themselves, others, and the world at large."*
>
> – ROBERT STERNBERG[2]

As with so much else we discuss in these pages, reflective habits of mind can be taught. Mindfulness is increasingly being studied in schools, but it can be learned at home, too. Teaching mindfulness to your child means paying attention to the ongoing experience of daily life, becoming fully aware of the here-and-nowness of each moment. It means moving beyond habitual or impulsive responses to situations, people, and events by learning to process experience thoughtfully before reacting to it, creating a gap between perceiving something and responding to it.[3] It means turning away from all distractions—phones, friends, electronic devices—for at least a few minutes every day, and turning inward, taking notice of one's own thoughts, feelings, and reactions. When a mindful approach to daily life is modelled by their parents, kids are more likely to practise it for themselves.

Martin Luther King Jr. said, "The function of education is to teach one to think intensively and to think critically. Intelligence plus character—that is the goal of true education." Children who reflect wisely upon what they know can contribute to the larger good.

Parents and teachers can work together to help children develop both local and global awareness through meaningful discussions, role-playing activities, and hands-on investigations into topics that relate to current challenges. Children can learn about the use (and misuse) of natural resources, progress (and regressions) in social justice, or other areas of particular interest to kids. Community-based projects can engage kids and inspire them. For example, Me to We is an action movement for young people, created by Canadians Craig and Marc Kielburger. They've translated their work with Free the Children into a network of local to global activities that attempt to engage young people in initiating and sustaining social change.[4]

Scientist David Suzuki hits the mark when he says, "An educational system isn't worth a great deal if it teaches young people how to make a living but doesn't teach them how to make a life." To that end, in addition to supporting the development of their children's intelligence and creativity, parents can foster basic virtues, such as respect, honesty, kindness, integrity, responsibility, and patience. They can also ask that these virtues, which build character and lead to wisdom, be respected and modelled at school.

Wisdom can't be reliably quantified, and it's not easy to define. It may help to think about what it looks like in the real world. Here's one perspective, from researchers interested in understanding the interactions of intelligence, creativity, and wisdom, on what it means to be wise: "Wise people do not look out just for their own interests, nor do they ignore these interests. Rather, they skillfully balance interests of varying kinds, including their own, and [others']. . . . Wise individuals realize that what may appear to be a prudent course of action in the short term does not necessarily appear so over the long term."[5]

For us, wisdom means going beyond intelligence. It involves acquiring knowledge, thinking about the effects on the environment of one's actions, and making choices that leave the world a better place. It means treating others the way one would like to be treated, and making a habit of reflecting upon daily actions, including asking, "What would happen if everyone behaved as I do?"

We also like the way Madeline Levine incorporates reflectivity, wisdom, and character into her thinking about what it means to teach children well: "While we all hope our children will do well in school, we hope with even greater fervour that they will do well in life. Our job is to help them to know and appreciate themselves deeply; to approach the world with zest; to find work that is exciting and satisfying; friends and spouses who are loving and loyal; and to hold a deep belief that they have something meaningful to contribute to our society."[6]

Andrea Nair writes with humour and verve about the very real challenges inherent in parenting in today's world, and makes practical experience-based suggestions. In one recent column, she provided a step-by-step parents' guide to being calm and empathetic, even in times of impatience and stress. Nair broke it down into seven essential steps: (1) notice your negative thoughts, (2) hit the pause button, (3) release the pause button slowly, (4) create an alternative thought to the negative one, (5) act on the new thought, (6) adjust your tuning to the "empathetic station," and (7) repeat. Nair writes, "With continued awareness and practice things will improve."[7]

Reflective habits of mind provide a starting point for the development of character and wisdom. Parents can help their children go beyond intelligence and live more thoughtful lives by modelling a mindful and caring approach to everyday life.

Tracy Dennis is both a mother and a developmental psychologist who blogs about a relatively new challenge for parents: the impact of digital media on human development.[8] Dr. Dennis does not recommend against digital multi-tasking around children, but she does think it's important to keep it in perspective, and keep it to a minimum: "Multi-tasking on our devices all the time is a sure-fire way to interfere with our ability to look our children in the eye, hear what they have to say, sensitively pick up on their feelings, and transmit that sparkle in the eye. The multi-tasking mode is the opposite of mirroring and of being present."[9]

Catherine Steiner-Adair is another eminent psychologist who has written about the challenges of parenting in an age of encroaching technology. She writes movingly about the eternal basics of child development, including the fact that children need their parents' time and attention, and thrive best with strong, healthy, familial relationships. Dr. Steiner-Adair cautions that this reality can be lost when people "are lured away by the siren call of the virtual world."[10] In the final chapter of her book *The Big Disconnect*, the author advises parents how to turn technology into "an ally for closeness, creativity, and community."[11]

What If My Child Is Not So Intelligent?

Intelligence is something that children build for themselves, with support from their parents and others. So sometimes parents ask us, "What if my child isn't particularly smart? Does that mean I haven't done a good job?" Our answer, clearly and strongly, is "No, it doesn't mean that at all!" Although intelligence is something that parents can foster, many aspects of a child's development, such as her interests and temperament, are predominantly outside parents' influence. What parents can create are environments that support the likelihood of talent developing.

> *"It's not that I'm so smart, it's just that I stay with problems longer."*
>
> – ALBERT EINSTEIN

Parents have an important role in shaping their children's habits, attitudes, learning opportunities, and coping skills, but the rest is up to the child, and to circumstance.

It helps to realize that being identified as highly intelligent or creative in childhood does not predict success over the long haul. Retrospective research starting with adult high achievers, and going backward in time to consider early developmental factors and environments, shows that subsequent eminence has little or no connection with gifted identification in childhood. Areas where childhood virtuosity is more likely to lead to adult eminence include violin playing, gymnastics, and ballet, but for most areas of adult achievement, gifted identification is not part of the pattern.[12]

Technological advances are providing new kinds of learning opportunities for those who can take advantage of them. New devices, software, and applications are being used to help kids with learning problems. Digital tools can enhance opportunities for collaboration, both locally and globally. They can also increase the engagement of kids who might be uncomfortable participating in face-to-face encounters. Although there's certainly a time and place for technology (and around the dinner table may not be one of them), children with strong digital skills have an advantage in a world where people rely more and more on technology.

Timing is another important variable to keep in mind when considering the factors that lead to a child's eventual achievement. People who become great novelists, philosophers, or experts in other fields often look unremarkable or even awkward in childhood. A report card for a young Winston Churchill, from St. George's School, dated April 1884, shows that Sir Winston wasn't noted for his intelligence in his early years, or for anything else that might have predicted all that he subsequently attained. Quite the contrary. According to this report card, he was ranked sixth out of the eleven boys in his class. He was described as "a constant trouble to everybody, always in some scrape or other . . . cannot be trusted to do any one thing . . . disgraceful."[12]

A more recent illustration of how eventual demonstrations of exceptional ability aren't necessarily recognized in childhood can be seen in John Gurdon's story. He won the 2012 Nobel Prize in

Medicine, and this is what his high school biology teacher wrote on his report card: "His work has been far from satisfactory. . . . Several times he has been in trouble, because he will not listen, but will insist on doing work in his own way. I believe he has ideas about becoming a Scientist; on his present showing this is quite ridiculous . . . it would be a sheer waste of time, both on his part and of those who have to teach him."[14]

The take-home message for parents is that children's potential can't be accurately measured by anyone. As we say in chapter 1: if someone takes out a crystal ball and foretells limits on your child's future, smash that crystal ball. (And a note to teachers: be careful what you write about the kids in your class!)

Just as there are many ways parents can foster children's intelligence, creativity, and other strengths, there are also ways they can delay or obstruct high-level development. We haven't made a not-to-do list for parents, but if we were to do so, it would include inculcating a fixed mindset; discouraging children from finding their interests and following their passions; not being available to them; over-programming their activities; and restricting their opportunities for learning.

We could go on with this not-to-do list, but rather than cataloguing the negative, we'd like to emphasize the positive: by understanding how your children develop, and doing the best you can to support and encourage that development, you maximize the likelihood that their abilities will emerge in their own time. Whether that's in childhood, adolescence, or adulthood doesn't really matter. We suggest that parents be as compassionate, patient, and understanding with themselves as they try to be with their children.

Putting It All Together

There are many ideas we hope you'll take from this book, but perhaps the most important is that intelligence is neither innate nor fixed. It's not an attribute owned exclusively by some people, and not by others. The pathways to exceptional achievement are complex, diverse, and socially constructed, varying across individuals, developmental periods, contexts, and cultures. Intelligence and, perhaps just as importantly, creativity, develop over time, and can be influenced by many factors.

> *"We must have perseverance and above all confidence in ourselves."*
>
> – MARIE CURIE

There's still much to learn about how the brain develops, but enough is known now to say that Marie Curie was right to emphasize perseverance as critical to the behaviour that leads to achievement, and from there to self-confidence. A "yes we can!" attitude takes parents and children a long way toward making the best possible lives for themselves.

QUIZ: ARE YOU RAISING YOUR CHILD TO THRIVE?

Our final quiz includes a brief recap of seven of the most important ideas we've covered.

1. *Do you pay attention to your child, really listen to what he's saying, and observe what he's doing, with his interests in mind?*
   Parenting for happy productivity starts with being attuned to a baby's individual personality, interests, and needs. Parents who are attentive and responsive, from infancy right through to adulthood, give their child a strong appreciation for curiosity, exploration, and persistence. This is the foundation upon which intelligence, creativity, success, and fulfillment are built.

2. *Do you nurture your child's abilities, interests, and creativity?*
    Intelligence and creativity are both active choices people
    can learn to make. They develop over time, with the right
    opportunities, support, and challenges. Do you provide as
    many different kinds of experience as you can think of,
    encouraging your child to find pursuits she wants to fol-
    low? Do you support her with the resources and reinforce-
    ment she needs? And do you model a love of learning,
    an engagement with your own interests and enthusiasms?
    Parents are most successful at teaching their children to
    behave intelligently and creatively when they decide for
    intelligence and creativity in their own lives.

3. *Do you cultivate a growth mindset for yourself, and sup-
    port its development in your child?*
    Learning happens step by step. Children don't start off
    smart, but become that way with experiences that inter-
    est them, and that provide enough challenge at the right
    points in the learning process. Parents can help their
    children welcome setbacks as useful information about
    directions for improvement. A growth mindset leads to
    greater confidence, risk-taking, motivation, and success
    over time, both for parents and for their children. Having a
    growth mindset is certainly useful for parents in confront-
    ing the inevitable challenges of parenting.

4. *Do you keep your focus on creating an educational match
    for your child?*
    Helping your child get a good education is not about getting
    him into the best school; it's about finding and maintain-
    ing the best educational fit for him. By thinking carefully
    about your child's interests and abilities, taking into con-
    sideration challenges he might experience, you become
    better informed about his learning needs, as well as other
    academic, social, or emotional supports that might be

required. It's good to know at least the basics of assessment and other educational processes so you can be an informed advocate for your child's education.

5. *Do you foster your child's emotional and social intelligence?*
All kids—no matter how academically capable—are happier if they acquire the self-regulation and relationship-building skills upon which fulfilling lives are built. Sometimes intellectual ability leads to feelings of being different, problems with friendships, or other difficulties. Parents can work with their children, getting help from others as needed, to prevent, minimize, or address possible problems.

6. *Are you willing to collaborate with others?*
It really does take a village to provide the best possible supports for a child.[15] The more exceptional your child, the more important it is that you find others with whom to interact, in order to ensure your child continues to engage in meaningful learning. Sometimes that means getting professional advice, but more frequently, it means talking to other parents, teachers, friends, and family members, thinking together about how to support the best possible outcomes. Collaborative activity—including involvement in advocacy efforts—leads to a richer continuum of challenging learning opportunities for your child, and more pathways for her to develop her diverse abilities as fully as she can.

7. *Do you recognize what's central to your child's well-being?*
The essential thread that runs through the pages of this book is that parents recognize what matters most with respect to their child. This means taking into account all the contextual factors, including the child's temperament, preferences, and interests; family dynamics; and circumstances such as health, financial considerations, and

available support systems. Also important are school provisions, community possibilities, and cultural values. And,
parents who model mindfulness, strength of character,
and wisdom help their children develop and harness these
and other important capacities.

Because each child's developmental path is unique and changes
over time, and because each family's circumstance is individual,
some of these ideas are more important in some circumstances,
and at some points in time, and other ideas apply better in other
circumstances, and at other times. For example:

Josh was a lively and curious little boy. He loved learning,
but hated sitting still. The problems started when he was in
kindergarten and repeatedly refused to leave the building
block centre for story time. He told his teacher he could listen to the story just fine if he continued working on whatever he was making that day.

Things got worse in grade 1, where he was expected to
stay at his desk for long chunks of time, completing paperwork the teacher assigned instead of the hands-on, mind-
stretching activities he so eagerly wanted to do. By grade
3, he'd been identified as a behaviour problem. By grade 6
he was getting into serious trouble in the classroom, playground, and elsewhere.

When his parents came to us, he was in grade 8, an
unhappy loner who wanted to drop out of school. "Where's
the little boy who used to get up in the morning with tons of
energy, bursting with enthusiasm for his latest project?" his
mother asked.

"How will he ever succeed at life when he's failing school
at thirteen?" his father wondered.

We helped Josh's parents reframe the problem, and understand
that their son was indeed a highly capable child who'd experienced

an unfortunate mismatch with the demands of his schooling. We talked together with Josh about what he was interested in learning more about, and how to seek opportunities that would enable him to experience the happiness that comes from productive engagement, and we suggested his parents meet with the teacher to discuss this. His interest in building had matured from Legos to real housing for real people. We helped him find an extracurricular position with Habitat for Humanity, where he could participate in building projects and contribute to the community while gaining an academic credit. The head of Habitat took on a mentorship role, and for the first time in a long time, Josh felt productive and successful.

Josh is doing well in high school now, focusing intently on math and arts courses but balancing several others, while also enjoying volunteering with an experienced draftsman. Josh is looking forward to attending a community college where he can learn about energy-efficient building.

There are no rigid rules that work for every child, every family, and every situation. Sometimes what's needed is more listening and attention; sometimes what's needed is more stimulation and challenge; and sometimes—as in Josh's situation—it's a matter of fine-tuning the match between the child and the school by tapping into community-based resources. Each child's situation is unique, but the seven core ideas we discuss here—paying attention to your child, nurturing his interests and abilities, cultivating a growth mindset, creating an educational match, fostering his emotional and social intelligence, collaborating with others, and recognizing what is central to your child's well-being—can help you see your child building his intelligence, and his creativity, too.

Over the course of this book, we've presented many vignettes from our case files to illustrate how different parenting and teaching approaches can have an impact on children's development. In most cases, we provide only a snapshot in order to make a certain point, but sometimes—where we know how the child is doing now and think it's relevant to this book—we've included that information along with the story. There are some additional generalizations, however, that apply to the children's lives collectively—Nicholas, Tony, Paula, Caryn, Alexander, Roberto, and the others.

Each of the individuals whose lives we've followed, some into young adulthood, has followed a unique developmental trajectory. As you might expect, they're each experiencing and will continue to experience their own changes, challenges, opportunities, and achievements as they write their own life stories and advance their own intelligences. What we can generalize from their experiences, and those of their parents, is that a foundation of love and caring—coupled with supports and nudges in (mostly) the right directions at (mostly) the right times—empowers young people, while providing them with the best possible chances for intellectual, creative, social, and emotional fulfillment.

Realizing the Promise of Ability

And so, as we look forward, we also come full circle, revisiting the topic of change that we address in the introduction.

> *"It is not the strongest of the species that survive, nor the most intelligent, but the ones most responsive to change."*
>
> – CHARLES DARWIN

Throughout this book, we've considered how parents can empower their children to accept and even welcome change, learning that what evolves can add spice, intrigue, and vibrancy to life. We've focused on ways to help children maximize their abilities, and learn to adapt to the many challenges they're bound to encounter.

Parents can support this process by staying attuned to their children as they establish and reach higher goals, invest effort, learn from setbacks, and develop faith in their own abilities. They can demonstrate these attributes in their own actions and attitudes. Parents can encourage their kids to ask for guidance when it's needed, and to stretch themselves in many directions. Things go best for kids when their parents are available and responsive—but not controlling—and engaged in their own intellectual and creative fulfillment.

Although one can never know what lies ahead, most parents hope their children will be well prepared for our rapidly changing world. Howard Gardner wrote about education at a crossroad: "We cannot anticipate what future schools and education will be like but we can expect that they will differ substantially from what we and our forebears have taken for granted. Past and future provide one set of lenses; our expanding knowledge of human beings provides another."[16] It's this second lens, the expanding knowledge of human beings and their development, which we've focused on here.

A child's brain grows and strengthens as she experiences the world—as she plays, practises, reflects, enjoys the fullness of life, interacts with others, consolidates knowledge, and learns new things. When a child finds encouragement and guidance from those who care, from parents and others who are responsive to her, she's better able to cope with change and other eventualities.

We've discussed at length how parents can raise their children to become intelligent, creative, and capable adults—conscientious people with caring attitudes, positive mindsets, a desire to contribute to society, and the ability to make good decisions. And so, with that focus in mind, as informed by the work we've been doing with children, educators, and families for over three decades, what do we think parents should aspire to for their children? A feeling of well-being, and, ideally, happiness. Integrity. Character. Love. The recognition that change and challenge can be beneficial. The strength to welcome adversity, and to find resilience in the face of hardship. The ability to think, communicate, and act responsibly, creatively, thoughtfully, and wisely. A collaborative spirit. Inquiry. Self-confidence. Ample capacity for friendship, fun, and relaxation. And a lifelong commitment to happy productivity.

Our Final Secrets for Raising Happily Productive Kids

1. Reflective habits of mind—learning to process experiences carefully before reacting to them—contribute to a child's intelligence, creativity, and achievement.
2. Parents can foster their children's character and wisdom by valuing respect, honesty, kindness, integrity, responsibility, and patience, and by asking that these virtues be respected and modelled at school.
3. When children don't show advanced ability, it doesn't mean that parents haven't done a good job of supporting their abilities. People develop at different rates, and many successful adults were not academic stars in childhood.
4. Seven capacity-building essentials that we discuss in this book concern (i) paying attention to your child; (ii) nurturing his abilities, interests, and creativity; (iii) cultivating a growth mindset; (iv) finding an educational match for your child; (v) fostering his emotional and social intelligence; (vi) being collaborative; and (vii) recognizing what's central to your child's well-being.
5. Pay attention to challenge, change, and the power of experience—yours and your child's. Be aware. Be supportive. Be flexibly responsive. And above all, be there when it counts.

We opened chapter 1 with a quote from Stephen Hawking, who wrote, "Intelligence is the ability to adapt to change." We conclude now by coming back to that idea, thinking about its relevance for intelligence, achievement, and, ultimately, success in the fast-paced world of the twenty-first century. The best way to raise children is to live the promise of possibility—by seeing ourselves and our places within society as works in progress, by appreciating the myriad prospects that can result from change, by embracing opportunities to learn, and, perhaps most importantly, by teaching our children to do the same.

Endnotes

CHAPTER 1. STARTING WITH INTELLIGENCE

1   S. Hawking, *A Brief History of Time* (New York: Bantam Dell, 1988).

2   D. P. Keating, "Developmental Science and Giftedness: An Integrated Life Span Framework," in *The Development of Giftedness and Talent Across the Life Span*, eds. F. D. Horowitz, R. F. Subotnik, and D. J. Matthews (Washington, DC: American Psychological Association, 2009), 189–208 (hereafter cited in text as *DGT*).

3   U. Neisser et al., "Intelligence: Knowns and Unknowns," *American Psychologist 51*, no. 2 (1996): 77–101.

4   R. F. Subotnik, P. Olszewski-Kubilius, and K. D. Arnold, "Beyond Bloom: Revisiting Environmental Factors That Enhance or Impede Talent Development," in *Rethinking Gifted Education*, ed. H. Borland (New York: Teacher's College Press, 2003), 227–38.

5   N. Doidge, *The Brain That Changes Itself* (New York: Penguin, 2007); F. D. Horowitz, "A Developmental Understanding of Giftedness and Talent: Implications for Research, Policy, and Practice," in *DGT*, 3–20; D. P. Keating, ed., *Nature and Nurture in Early Child Development* (New York: Cambridge, 2011); R. E. Nisbett, *Intelligence and How To Get It: Why Schools and Cultures Count* (New York: Norton).

6   Intelligence test scores take age into account, and have an average score of 100 (50 percent of the same-age population falls above that score; 50 percent fall below). Anything above 120 (the top 10 percent of same-age people) is classified as "Superior," and above 132 (the top 2 percent) is "Very Superior."

7   The two most reputable tests are the current editions of the Wechsler and Stanford-Binet tests, both of which require a registered psychologist or specially

qualified psychometrist to administer them. These two tests are translated into many languages and are usually the only ones accepted by schools. Other tests vary enormously in their credibility, and, in general, the easier and quicker they are, the less reliable. We've not yet encountered an online intelligence test that has much validity or reliability.

8   Although IQ tests have historically been used to qualify children for some gifted programs, that practice is falling out of favour in most school jurisdictions, for all the reasons we discuss in this chapter, chapter 4, and elsewhere. For more on this topic, see D. J. Matthews and J. F. Foster, *Being Smart about Gifted Education* (Scottsdale, AZ: Great Potential Press, 2009).

9   Sometimes called "decontextualized tasks of abstract reasoning."

10 Based on statistical analyses, a child with an IQ of 140 ("Very Superior" range) on a test at age seven is likely to score 125 ("Superior" range) if she's tested ten years later, as a result of a statistical principle called "regression to the mean." For more on this topic, see the work of David Lohman. For example, D. F. Lohman and K. A. Korb, "Gifted Today But Not Tomorrow? Longitudinal Changes in Ability and Achievement During Elementary School," *Journal for the Education of the Gifted* 29 (2006): 451–84.

11 Best practice in intelligence testing prohibits taking the same test again before less than two years have passed. For research-based evidence and discussion about scoring variability across age, see A. W. Gottfried, A. E. Gottfried, and D. W. Guerin, "Issues in Early Prediction and Identification of Intellectual Giftedness," in *DGT*, 43–56.

12 Alfred Binet's original test has been revised many times since he began assessing children's learning problems in 1892; the Stanford-Binet Intelligence Scale is now in its fifth edition.

13 S. B. Kaufman, *Ungifted: Intelligence Redefined* (New York: Basic Books, 2013), 26–28.

14 S. Graham, "Giftedness in Adolescence: African American Gifted Youth and Their Challenges from a Motivational Perspective," in *DGT*, 43–56. Attempts to close the IQ scoring gaps have included modifying existing tests and designing new tests targeted to children growing up in rural and inner-city communities, and from Black and Hispanic backgrounds. See, for example, *DGT*.

15 H. Gardner, *Frames of Mind* (New York: Basic Books, 1983); H. Gardner, *The Unschooled Mind: How Children Think and How Schools Should Teach* (New York: Basic Books, 1991); H. Gardner, "A Multiplicity of Intelligences," *Scientific American* 9, no. 4 (1998): 18–23; H. Gardner, *Five Minds for the Future* (Cambridge, MA: Harvard Business School Press, 2007).

16 R. J. Sternberg, "Principles of Teaching for Successful Intelligence," *Educational Psychologist* 33, no. 2/3 (1998), 65–72; R. J. Sternberg, "Identifying and Developing Creative Giftedness," *Roeper Review* 23 (2000), 60–65; R. J. Sternberg, "Wisdom, Intelligence, Creativity, Synthesised: A Model of Giftedness,"

in *The Routledge International Companion to Gifted Education*, eds. T. Balchin, B. Hymer, and D. J. Matthews (Abingdon, UK: Routledge, 2009), 255–65.

17 W. Harris, "Can Music Make Your Kids Smarter?" *Music Education Online* http://www.childrensmusicworkshop.com/advocacy/canmusicmake.html. Donald Hodges is Covington Distinguished Professor of Music Education and director of the Music Research Institute at the University of North Carolina at Greensboro.

18 P. McKelvie and J. Low, "Listening to Mozart Does Not Improve Children's Spatial Ability: Final Curtains for the Mozart Effect," *British Journal of Developmental Psychology* 20 (2002): 241–58; K. M. Steele et al., "Prelude or Requiem for the 'Mozart Effect'?" *Nature 400*, no. 827 (1999): 6747; K. M. Steele, K. E. Bass, and M. D. Crook, "The Mystery of the Mozart Effect: Failure to Replicate," *Psychological Science 10*, no. 4 (1999): 366–9.

19 One study shows that nine- to eleven-year-old children who play musical instruments have significantly more grey matter volume in both the sensorimotor cortex—involved in planning and executing movement—and the occipital lobes—responsible for visual processing. E. Christensen, *The Neurosciences and Music: An Overview and Discussion* (2012). http://www.academia.edu/2407154/The_Neurosciences_and_Music_An_Overview_and_Discussion.

20 G. Schlaug et al., "Effects of Music Training on the Child's Brain and Cognitive Development," *Annals of the New York Academy of Science* 1060 (2005): 219–30.

21 G. M. Bidelman, J. T. Gandour, and A. Krishnan, "Musicians and Tone-Language Speakers Share Enhanced Brainstem Encoding but Not Perceptual Benefits for Musical Pitch," *Brain and Cognition* 77 (2011): 1–10.

22 S. Moreno et al., "Short-Term Music Training Enhances Verbal Intelligence and Executive Function," *Psychological Science* 11 (2011): 1425–33.

23 Ellen Bialystock, keynote address, Brainpower Initiative Conference, Toronto, May 2012.

24 Doidge, *The Brain That Changes Itself*, Keating, "Developmental Transitions in Giftedness and Talent," in *The Development of Giftedness and Talent Across the Life Span*, eds. F. D. Horowitz, R. F. Subotnik and D. J. Matthews (Washington, DC: American Psychological Association, 2009), 89–108; Nisbett, *Intelligence and How To Get It*.

25 *DGT*; Matthews and Foster, *Being Smart about Gifted Education*; R. F. Subotnik, P. Olszewski-Kubilius, and F. C. Worrell, "Rethinking Giftedness and Gifted Education: A Proposed Direction Forward Based on Psychological Science," *Psychological Science in the Public Interest* 12, no. 1 (2011): 3–54.

26 C. S. Dweck, *Mindset: The New Psychology of Success* (New York: Random House, 2006).

27 M. Gladwell, *Outliers: The Story of Success* (New York: Little, Brown, 2008).

CHAPTER 2: INTELLIGENCE AND CREATIVITY

1 For more information on mentorships—why they can be valuable learning experiences, how to structure them, and more—see Matthews and Foster, *Being Smart about Gifted Education,* 160–5.

2 Alexandre Da Silva Maia assisted in recounting aspects of this story. Alexandre was a preservice student at the University of Toronto who completed an internship with Joanne Foster in 2006.

3 D. H. Feldman, "Why Children Can't Be Creative," *Exceptionality Education Canada 1,* 1 (1991): 43–51.

4 M. Csikszentmihalyi, *Creativity: Flow and the Psychology of Discovery and Invention* (New York: Harper Perennial, 1996); J. Piirto, *Understanding Creativity* (Scottsdale, AZ: Great Potential Press, 2003).

5 E. P. Torrance, *Creativity in the Classroom: What Research Says to the Teacher* (Washington, DC: National Education Association, 1977).

6 D. N. Perkins, *The Mind's Best Work* (Cambridge, MA: Harvard University Press, 1981).

7 D. H. Feldman, M. Csikszentmihalyi, and H. Gardner, *Changing the World: A Framework for the Study of Creativity* (Westport, CT: Praeger, 1994).

8 Our approach to understanding creativity was inspired by Daniel Keating's 1980 article, "The Four Faces of Creativity" (D. Keating, "The Four Faces of Creativity," *Gifted Child Quarterly 24,* no. 2 [1980]: 56–61), in which he argues for content mastery, divergent thinking, critical thinking, and effective communication as essential components of creativity. We see giftedness and creativity as intertwined and interconnected, such that creativity is a potential outgrowth of all high-level ability, and high-level ability is an important foundation for creativity, something we discuss in more detail in *Being Smart about Gifted Education.*

9 See for example Howard Gardner's discussions of the lives of Freud, Einstein, Picasso, Stravinsky, T. S. Eliot, Martha Graham, and Gandhi, all of whose creativity rested on extraordinary mastery of their chosen domains: H. Gardner, *Creating Minds: An Anatomy of Creativity Seen through the Lives of Freud, Einstein, Picasso, Stravinsky, Eliot, Graham, and Gandhi* (New York: Basic Books, 1993).

10 Reprinted with permission from Judy Anne Breneman (http://usualdays.blogspot.ca/).

11 Another was that each persisted for years at a time, with very little hope of reward, foregoing normal lives and daily pleasures in pursuit of their creative goals.

12 Sternberg, "Identifying and Developing Creative Giftedness."

13 Ibid. In chapter 1, we introduce Sternberg's theory about intelligence including analytical, practical, and creative components. He's also known for his innovative approach to understanding creativity, which we discuss in this chapter.

14 Michele is Joanne Foster's daughter.

15 As it happened, Joanne's teacher gave her an A, so somehow or another, Joanne called that one right. It proved to be a good risk, but it was a risk.

16 Misha Abarbanel teaches at a Toronto high school where he's head of the English/Literacy department. He's past president of the Ontario Student Debating Union, and a recipient of both provincial and national awards for his outstanding contribution to debating. For more on his work, see http://www.educateforgood.com.

17 T. Balchin, "Recognising and Fostering Creative Production," in Balchin, Hymer, and Matthews, *The Routledge International Companion to Gifted Education*, 203–9; A. J. Cropley and K. K. Urban, "Programs and Strategies for Nurturing Creativity," in *International Handbook of Giftedness and Talent, 2nd edition*, eds. K. A. Heller et al. (Oxford, UK: Elsevier Science, 2000), 485–98; Csikszentmihalyi, *Creativity*; R. J. Sternberg, E. L. Grigorenko, and J. L. Singer, eds., *Creativity: From Potential to Realization* (Washington, DC: American Psychological Association, 2004); H. Wilson, "Challenge and Creativity: Making the Links," in Balchin, Hymer, and Matthews, *The Routledge International Companion to Gifted Education*, 235–42.

18 Csikszentmihalyi, *Creativity*.

19 M. Levine, *Teach Your Children Well: Parenting for Authentic Success* (New York: Harper, 2012), 65.

20 F. Dixon, "A Secondary Look: Chronically Curious and Driven to Discover," *Parenting for High Potential* (Winter 2012).

CHAPTER 3: THE CHANGING DEMANDS
OF PARENTING: DIAPERS TO DIPLOMAS

1 "Children Succeed with Character, Not Test Scores" (an interview with Paul Tough), NPR Staff, NPR, September 4, 2012, http://www.npr.org/2012/09/04/160258240/children-succeed-with-character-not-test-scores?utm_source=NPR&utm_medium=facebook&utm_campaign=20120904.

2 Subotnik, "Developmental Transitions in Giftedness and Talent."

3 J. Colombo et al., "High Cognitive Ability in Infancy and Early Childhood," in *DGT*, 23–42; A. W. Gottfried, A. E. Gottfried, and D. W. Guerin, "Issues in Early Prediction and Identification of Intellectual Giftedness."

4 "Five Simple Ways to Bond With Your Baby," Yummy Mummy Club, December 12, 2012, http://www.yummymummyclub.ca/family/babies/20131212/five-simple-ways-to-bond-with-your-baby.

5 Although Amy Chua's *Battle Hymn of the Tiger Mother* (New York: Penguin, 2011) has much that we agree with (the importance of discipline and skill acquisition, for example), we diverge strongly from its focus on obedience and top awards at the expense of play, autonomy, and imagination.

6   For a thoughtful, thorough, and well-written discussion of the basics of brain development, see C. A. Nelson III, "Neural Development and Lifelong Plasticity," in *Nature and Nurture in Early Child Development*, ed. D. P. Keating (Cambridge, UK: Cambridge University Press, 2011).

7   Keating, "Developmental Science and Giftedness."

8   J. Gilkerson and A. Richards, *Impact of Adult Talk, Conversational Turns, and TV During the Critical 0-4 Years of Child Development*, LENA Technical Talk, LTR-01-2, 2009, https://docs.google.com/viewer?url=http://www.lenababy.com/pdf/The_Power_of_Talk.pdf&pli=1.

9   S. Fraiberg, *The Magic Years: Understanding and Solving the Problems of Early Childhood* (New York: Charles Scribner's Sons, 1959.)

10 M. H. Immordino-Yang, J. A. Christodoulou, and V. Singh, "Rest Is Not Idleness: Implications of the Brain's Default Mode for Human Development and Education," *Perspectives on Psychological Science 7*, no. 4 (July 2012): 352–64; A. F. Lieberman, *The Emotional Life of the Toddler* (New York: The Free Press, 1993); C. A. Nelson, "Neural Plasticity and Human Development: The Role of Early Experience in Sculpting Memory Systems," *Developmental Science 3*, no. 2 (May 2000): 115–30.

11 S. Ashley and J. Pearson, "When More Equals Less: Overtraining Inhibits Perceptual Learning Owing to Lack of Wakeful Consolidation," *Proceedings of the Royal Society of Biological Sciences* (August 15, 2012): doi: 10.1098/rspb.2012.1423.

12 For more on the workings, and positive and negative consequences, of the Matthew Effect, see Keith Stanovich's *Progress in Understanding Reading: Scientific Foundations and New Frontiers* (New York: Guilford Press, 2000); M. Gladwell's *Outliers*; or S. B. Kaufman's *Ungifted*. The name of the "Matthew Effect" is taken from the Bible: "For to him who has shall be given and he shall have abundance; but from him who does not have, even that which he has shall be taken away." (Matthew 25:29)

13 Subotnik, "Developmental Transitions in Giftedness and Talent."

14 R. G. Barr, "Mother and Child: Preparing for a Life," in Keating, *Nature and Nurture in Early Child Development*.

15 E. Winner, *Gifted Children: Myths and Realities* (New York: Basic Books, 1996); E. Winner, "Toward Broadening Our Understanding of Giftedness: The Spatial Domain," in *DGT*, 59–74.

16 Robin is Dona Matthews's daughter.

17 The obsessive/harmonious passion distinction was made by Robert Vallerand and colleagues, and is discussed at some length by S. B. Kaufman in *Ungifted*.

18 Rena Subotnik and her colleagues have studied high-level talent development in music, science, technology, engineering, and math, and found this pattern of playful exploration leading to the hard work of engagement in talent development, and to a sense of playful mastery. See, for example, Subotnik, "Developmental Transitions in Giftedness and Talent."

19 For more information on the study, as well as the factors measured (for example, What is quality child care? What are family features?), go to http://www. nichd.nih.gov/news/resources/links/Pages/backgrounder051410.aspx.

20 Megan Gunnar has been studying stress in early childhood and its impact on brain and behavioural development for several decades now. See for example M. R. Gunnar et al., "The Rise in Cortisol in Family Day Care: Associations with Aspects of Care Quality, Child Behaviour, and Child Sex," *Child Development 81*, no. 3 (May-June 2010): 851–69.

21 Ibid.

22 When asked to explain possible reasons for the higher stress experienced by infants and toddlers in centre-based care, Gunnar suggests, "There is something about managing a complex peer setting for an extended time that triggers stress in young children." See http://www.cehd.umn.edu/research/highlights/Gunnar/.

23 *DGT*; M. Neihart, *Peak Performance for Smart Kids* (Waco, TX: Prufrock Press, 2008); P. Tough, *How Children Succeed: Grit, Curiosity, and the Hidden Power of Character* (Boston: Houghton Mifflin Harcourt, 2008).

24 Eric is Joanne Foster's son.

25 D. H. Pink, *Drive: The Surprising Truth about What Motivates Us* (Edinburgh: Canongate Books, 2010).

26 Keating, "Developmental Science and Giftedness."

27 Matching challenge to ability is important in all domains, but is particularly important in maths and sciences. If Roberto is going to have a chance to move his field forward in his twenties (the age at which most mathematical discoveries and advances are made), he needs to be mastering the relevant skills and content in his teen years. That means getting a solid foundation of knowledge in childhood.

28 For more about Amy Chua and her evolving position on parenting, see http:// amychua.com/.

29 This starts at a surprisingly young age. In fact, research shows that after a free-choice period, preschoolers are more likely to co-operate independently in cleaning up (see "Old-Fashioned Play Builds Serious Skills," Alix Spiegel, NPR, February 21, 2008, http://www.npr.org/templates/story/story. php?storyId=19212514).

30 J. L. Singer, "Delayed Gratification and Ego Development: Implications for Clinical and Experimental Research," *Journal of Consulting Psychology 19*, no. 4 (July 1955): 259–66. doi:10.1037/h0044541.

31 R. McMillan, S. B. Kaufman, and J. L. Singer, "Ode to Positive Constructive Daydreaming," *Frontiers in Psychology* (September 23, 2013). doi: 10.3389/fpsyg.2013.00626.

32 Companies like Google are recognizing that this principle also applies to adults, and allocating space and money to gyms, "chill-out rooms," and other

places where workers can ultimately become more productive by enjoying downtime for a while. See for example http://news.bbc.co.uk/2/hi/7290322. stm.

33 M. Price-Mitchell, "The Importance of Silence in a Noisy World," *Psychology Today*, December 8, 2013, http://www.psychologytoday.com/blog/the-moment-youth/201312/the-importance-silence-in-noisy-world.

34 E. Kolbert, "Spoiled Rotten: Why Do Kids Rule the Roost?" *The New Yorker*, July 2, 2012, http://www.newyorker.com/arts/critics/books/2012/07/02/120702crbo_books_kolbert?currentPage=all.

35 Kelly Bartlett, who writes a parenting blog (www.attachedfamily.com), has laid out a step-by-step plan for helping children become proficient around the house. See http://attachmentparenting.org/blog/2013/05/15/chores-without-threats-or-bribery/.

36 There's considerable evidence that raising adolescents is stressful. In fact, marital satisfaction in two-parent families is at its lowest during the teen years. See M. Cui and M. B. Donnellan, "Trajectories of Conflict Over Raising Adolescent Children and Marital Satisfaction," *Journal of Marriage and Family 71*, no. 3 (2009): 478–94.

37 R. F. Subotnik and L. Jarvin, "Beyond Expertise: Conceptions of Giftedness as Great Performance," in *Conceptions of Giftedness, 3rd Edition*, eds. R. J. Sternberg and J. E. Davidson (Cambridge, UK: Cambridge Press, 2005), 343–57; Subotnik, "Developmental Transitions in Giftedness and Talent."

38 D. J. Matthews, "Developmental Transitions in Giftedness and Talent: Childhood to Adolescence," in *DGT*, 89–108.

39 Keating, "Developmental Science and Giftedness."

40 Dona's story of her own experience.

41 M. Levine, *Teach Your Children Well*, 144.

42 Tough, *How Children Succeed*. "Grit" was originally used as a psychological construct by Angela Duckworth and colleagues. See A. L. Duckworth et al., "Grit: Perseverance and Passion for Long-Term Goals," *Personality and Individual Differences 92*, no. 6 (July 2007): 1087–101.

43 In fact, Juilliard has become very proactive and is now a leader in supporting the development of psychosocial skills such as those Tony would've needed in order to continue to develop his musical ability. Other institutions and programs are following suit.

44 Researchers studying the development of talent describe the "big-fish-small-pond effect" that can occur in settings where a child is easily the best in a given area of ability. This experience can lead to an inflated sense of ability that doesn't withstand the inevitable pressures that come with exposure to real competition, just as Tony experienced. See for example M. C. Makel, S-Y Lee, P. Olszewski-Kubilius, and M. Putalla, "Changing the Pond, Not the Fish: Following High-Ability Students Across Different Educational

Environments," *Journal of Educational Psychology, 104*(3), Aug 2012, 778-792.

45 Funding for the demo program that offers FACTOR awards is provided by Canada's Private Radio Broadcasters and the Department of Canadian Heritage's Canada Music Fund's New Musical Works Component. The awards are designed to encourage effort and talent. Michele won three of these awards while still in high school.

46 Michele is Joanne Foster's daughter.

47 M. Neihart, *Peak Performance for Smart Kids* (Waco, TX: Prufrock Press, 2008).

48 Erin is Dona Matthews's daughter.

49 https://college.harvard.edu/admissions/preparing-college/should-i-take-time.

50 S. Berger, How Can I Help My Gifted Child Plan for College? http://www.davidsongifted.org/db/Articles_id_10516.aspx

CHAPTER 4: A PARENTS' GUIDE TO TESTS AND ASSESSMENTS

1 Doidge, *The Brain That Changes Itself*; C. A. Nelson, "Neural Plasticity and Human Development"; C. A. Nelson, K. A. Thomas, and M. de Haan, *Neuroscience of Cognitive Development: The Role of Experience and the Developing Brain* (Hoboken, NJ: Wiley, 2006).

2 When children's abilities in different subject areas are highly variable—such as when they're extremely advanced in some areas, and considerably less advanced in others—it's sometimes referred to as asynchronous development, or developmental asynchrony.

3 Kaufman, *Ungifted.*

4 Keating, "Developmental Science and Giftedness."

5 Matthews and Foster, *Being Smart about Gifted Education*, 46.

6 C. A. Tomlinson et al., *The Parallel Curriculum in the Classroom: Book 2* (Thousand Oaks, CA: Corwin, 2006); C. A. Tomlinson and S. M. Reis, *Differentiation for Gifted and Talented Students* (Thousand Oaks, CA: Corwin Press, 2006); J. L. VanTassel-Baska and T. Stambaugh, *Comprehensive Curriculum for Gifted Learners, 3rd Edition* (Boston: Allyn & Bacon, 2006).

7 This book of IQ tests is sold alongside *Zombie Sudoku, Rock and Roll Jumble*, and *The Grid Reaper: Puzzles to Die For*. www.starstore.ca. Retrieved September 13, 2012.

8 B. Hymer, J. Whitehead, and M. Huxtable, *Gifts, Talents and Education: A Living Theory Approach* (Chichester, UK: Wiley-Blackwell, 2009), 17.

9 D. F. Lohman, "An Aptitude Perspective on Talent: Implications for Identification of Academically Gifted Minority Students," *Journal for the Education of the Gifted 28*, no. 3-4 (March 2005): 333–60. doi: 10.4219/jeg-2005-341.

10 Matthews and Foster, *Being Smart about Gifted Education*.

11 The goal of assessment is to acquire information that can inform programming initiatives, and so an intelligent assessment of giftedness aims to find students whose subject-area mastery so far exceeds grade-level programming that they're not learning much in the classroom unless appropriate adaptations are made. In *Being Smart about Gifted Education*, we briefly consider some of the recommended processes (for example, high-ceiling and above-level testing), and some that are more problematic, in relation to identifying children's heightened abilities.

12 Alexis is a teacher.

13 Graham, "Giftedness in Adolescence."

14 J. Ottmann and S. Mendaglio, "People's Conceptions of Giftedness" (presentation, National Association for Gifted Children, Indianapolis, IN, 2013).

15 For an article on this topic, see Dona Matthews, "Canadian Aboriginal Students: What They Can Teach Us All about Gifted Education," Dona Matthews (blog), November 6, 2013, http://donamatthews.wordpress.com/2013/11/06/canadian-aboriginal-students-what-they-can-teach-us-all-about-gifted-education/.

16 D. Y. Ford and J. L. Moore III, "Being Gifted and Adolescent: Issues and Needs of Students of Color," in *The Handbook of Secondary Gifted Education*, eds. F. A. Dixon and S. M. Moon (Waco, TX: Prufrock Press, 2006), 113–32; Graham, "Giftedness in Adolescence"; J. L. VanTassel-Baska, *Serving Gifted Learners Beyond the Traditional Classroom* (Waco, TX: Prufrock Press, 2007); B. Wallace and G. Eriksson, *Diversity in Gifted Education: International Perspectives on Global Issues* (London: Routledge, 2006); F. C. Worrell, "What Does Gifted Mean? Personal and Social Identity Perspectives on Giftedness in Adolescence," in *DGT*, 131–52.

17 J. H. Borland, "Gifted Education without Gifted Children: The Case for No Conception of Giftedness," in Sternberg and Davidson, *Conceptions of Giftedness*, 1–19; Hymer, Whitehead, and Huxtable, *Gifts, Talents and Education*; Matthews, Subotnik, and Horowitz, "A Developmental Perspective on Giftedness and Talent"; S. M. Reis, "Turning Points and Future Directions in Gifted Education and Talent Development," in Balchin, Hymer, and Matthews, *The Routledge International Companion to Gifted Education*, 317–24; Wallace and Eriksson, *Diversity in Gifted Education*; Worrell, "What Does Gifted Mean?"

18 Sandra Aamodt and Sam Wang, "Bright and early: Why opening schools for kids as young as six months makes economic sense," *New York Post*, October 7, 2012, http://www.nypost.com/p/news/opinion/opedcolumnists/bright_early_rHScLJoyQskl5yWCESwTdO.

19 J. L. VanTassel-Baska, "Using Performance-Based Assessment to Document Authentic Learning," in *Alternative Assessments with Gifted and Talented Students*, ed. J. L. VanTassel-Baska (Waco, TX: Prufrock Press, 2008), 285–308.

20 A. Robinson, B. M. Shore, and D. L. Enersen, *Best Practices in Gifted Educa-*

tion: An Evidence-Based Guide (Waco, TX: Prufrock Press, 2007).

21 We discuss this topic in depth in *Being Smart about Gifted Education*.

22 Lead quote (no author, no title), *The Robesonian* (Lumberton, NC: August 9, 2005), 10.

23 Matthews and Foster, *Being Smart about Gifted Education*.

24 We define giftedness as follows: "Giftedness is exceptionally advanced subject-specific ability at a particular point in time, and in a particular context, such that an individual's educational needs cannot be well met without making significant adaptations to the curriculum, or providing other learning opportunities." (Matthews and Foster, *Being Smart about Gifted Education*)

25 Gerry Ugalde is a teacher and trainer. She focuses on health and wellness, nutrition, and athletic performance.

26 S. B. Kaufman, "The Pesky Persistence of Labels," *Psychology Today*, October 13, 2012, http://www.psychologytoday.com/blog/beautiful-minds/201210/the-pesky-persistence-labels. For a deeper understanding of the danger and potential damage of labelling, see S. B. Kaufman's *Ungifted*, in which he discusses his personal experience as a child labelled learning disabled and originally slotted for a substandard education.

26 Personal communication between Nancy Steinhauer and Dona Matthews.

CHAPTER 5: EDUCATION: PARENTS' ROLES AT SCHOOL

1 Robinson, Shore, and Enersen, *Best Practices in Gifted Education*, 251.

2 Mrs. Obama's talk took place on April 2, 2009. Subsequent to this talk we wrote an open letter to Mrs. Obama about many of these topics, a letter which was published in *Education News* on April 6, 2009 (http://ednews.org/articles/36205/1/Open-Letter-to-Michelle-Obama/Page1.html) and reprinted in the summer 2009 issue of *Roeper Review*. It was also posted to listservs throughout North America and the United Kingdom.

3 The Elizabeth Garrett Anderson School has been designated a leading-edge school, funded by a government initiative in the United Kingdom that recognizes schools' achievements in supporting students' learning, allowing them to work collaboratively with other schools to support optimal learning outcomes in all students.

4 D. J. Matthews and J. F. Foster, "Creating a Culture Where It's Cool to Be Smart," Frontispiece, *Gifted Education International* 25 (2009).

5 Haim Ginott was a school teacher, child psychologist, and psychotherapist.

6 In many schools, teachers are required to follow a "two years behind" policy, whereby a student has to be two years behind what's expected for his age before teachers can initiate formal testing procedures. In some jurisdictions, however, parents' expressed concerns can open the door for proactive educational address.

7 As initially told to Maria Fara-On and recounted here. Maria was a preservice student at the University of Toronto who completed an internship with Joanne Foster in 2006.

8 R. Weinfeld and M. Davis, *Special Needs Advocacy Resource Book* (Waco, TX: Prufrock Press, 2009).

9 For more information about the National Association for Gifted Children, see http://www.nagc.org/. For links to other organizations, visit the Resources page at http://www.raisingsmarterkids.net.

10 For more information about Luc Kump's parent advocacy group in Belgium, visit http://www.eduratio.be/.

11 For more on this topic, see K. Nilles, "Parents Need Support, Too," *Parenting for High Potential 3*, no. 4 (2014), 8–11; N. A. Cohen "The Importance of Teaching Children Self-Advocacy," *Parenting for High Potential 3*, no. 4 (2014), 12–14.

CHAPTER 6: EDUCATION: TEACHERS'
ROLES, RESPONSIBILITIES, AND REQUIREMENTS

1 C. A. Tomlinson, "Grading and Differentiation: Paradox or Good Practice?" *Theory into Practice 44*, no. 3 (2005): 269.

2 Julie is a parent who attended a workshop with us.

3 E. Fromm, *To Have or To Be* (London: Bloomsbury, 1976).

4 J. A. Plucker and C. M. Callahan, eds., *Critical Issues and Practices in Gifted Education* (Waco, TX: Prufrock Press, 2008); Robinson, Shore, and Enersen, *Best Practices in Gifted Education*.

5 Thomas Friedman, "Can't we do better?" *New York Times*, December 8, 2013.

6 Susan Miller was a teacher-candidate when she took Joanne's gifted education class a few years ago. She is now a caring and conscientious teacher who works hard both independently and collaboratively to continue to learn all she can about gifted-level development.

7 C. A. Tomlinson, "Differentiated Instruction," in Plucker and Callahan, *Critical Issues and Practices in Gifted Education*.

8 L. Kanevsky, "Deferential Differentiation: What Types of Differentiation Do Students Want?" *Gifted Child Quarterly 55*, no. 4 (2011): 279–99.

9 P. A. Dettmer, M. S. Landrum, and T. N. Miller, "Professional Development for the Education of Secondary Gifted Students," in Dixon and Moon, *The Handbook of Secondary Gifted Education*, 611–48; J. Geake, "Neural Interconnectivity and Intellectual Creativity: Giftedness, Savants, and Learning Styles," in Balchin, Hymer, and Matthews, *The Routledge International Companion to Gifted Education*, 10–17; Robinson, Shore, and Enersen, *Best Practices in Gifted Education*; Tomlinson, "Differentiated Instruction."

10 Visit our web site at www.beyondintelligence.net for more information about

planning, as well as additional details about assessment, activities, and learning environments.

11 Karen Rogers, an expert in gifted education who wrote *Re-forming Gifted Education: How Parents and Teachers Can Match the Program to the Child* (Scottsdale, AZ: Great Potential Press, 2002), provided these points at an Association for Bright Children parents' group presentation, May 2007, Toronto.

12 For example, C. A. Tomlinson's parallel curriculum model and J. VanTassel-Baska's integrated curriculum model.

13 B. S. Bloom, *Taxonomy of Educational Objectives, Handbook I: The Cognitive Domain* (New York: David McKay, 1956). Bloom's work focused on educational objectives in the cognitive domain. Since then, others (e.g., Anderson et al., 2001) have supplemented the original taxonomy with objectives in the emotional and kinesthetic domains: L. Anderson et al., *A Taxonomy for Learning, Teaching, and Assessing: A Revision of Bloom's Taxonomy of Educational Objectives* (New York: Longman, 2001).

14 Additional information about Bloom's Taxonomy can be found in resource material accessible at www.beyondintelligence.net.

15 H. Gardner, *Frames of Mind*; H. Gardner, "A Multiplicity of Intelligences."

16 R. J. Sternberg, *Beyond IQ: A Triarchic Theory of Human Intelligence* (New York: Cambridge University Press, 1985); R. J. Sternberg, *Successful Intelligence* (New York: Plume, 1997).

17 J. S. Renzulli and S. M. Reis, *The Schoolwide Enrichment Model: A Comprehensive Plan for Educational Excellence* (Mansfield Center, CT: Creative Learning Press, 1985); J. S. Renzulli and S. M. Reis, *Enriching Curriculum for All Students, 2nd Edition* (Thousand Oaks, CA: Corwin Press, 2008).

18 Matthews and Foster, *Being Smart about Gifted Education*, 115.

19 "Educators strengthen children's learning spirit when they are proactive, motivating, supportive, nurturing, well-informed, and attentive to diversity in all its forms." From Matthews and Foster, *Being Smart about Gifted Education*, 116.

20 Professional development workshops listings can be found in educational journals. There are many of these published, and one example is *Teaching for High Potential*, available online at http://www.nagc.org/php.aspx. Other education-based sites have links to journals as well.

21 Collette is a frustrated first-year teacher we spoke with who is nevertheless making an effort to provide advanced-level curriculum to students whose learning profiles indicate a need for such programming.

22 Both Michelle Obama and President Obama have said that it is "cool to be smart," she in an address to the Elizabeth Garrett Anderson School for girls in London, England, on April 2, 2009, and he in St. Louis, Missouri, on April 29, 2009, at the one-hundredth-day mark of his presidency. We heartily

concur, as this kind of attitude is an important component of raising smarter kids across countries, cultures, and languages. Our commentary on Michele Obama's address has been published elsewhere. Foster and Matthews, "Open letter to Michelle Obama."

CHAPTER 7: DECISION-MAKING ABOUT SCHOOLING

1 M. J. Dufur, T. L. Parcel, and K. P. Troutman, "Does Capital at Home Matter More than Capital at School? Social Capital Effects on Academic Achievement," *Research in Social Stratification and Mobility* 31 (March 2013); 1–21. doi:10.1016/j.rssm.2012.08.002.

2 M. Gladwell, *Blink: The Power of Thinking Without Thinking* (New York: Little Brown, 2006).

3 A. Ripley, *The Smartest Kids in the World and How They Got That Way* (New York: Simon & Schuster, 2013), 215.

4 M. Gentry, "No Child Left Behind: Neglecting Excellence," *Roeper Review 29*, no. 1 (2005): 25.

5 M. G. Fullan, *The New Meaning of Educational Change, 3rd Edition* (New York: Teachers College Press, 2001); *DGT*; Nisbett, *Intelligence and How to Get It*; Robinson, Shore, and Enersen, *Best Practices in Gifted Education*; Rogers, *Re-forming Gifted Education*.

6 The factors aren't listed by priority; that varies, depending on what matters most to a particular family in a particular situation.

7 Robin and Erin are Dona Matthews's daughters.

8 In *Being Smart about Gifted Education* (2009), we tell the story of Thomas and his parents' dilemmas about elementary school choice. In the end, Thomas went to his neighbourhood school, where the principal worked with the teachers to make sure Thomas's learning needs were well met and he was provided with the right mix of autonomy and challenge. When it came time to choose a high school, Thomas's parents did the initial spadework, and then allowed Thomas to make an informed choice. Thomas selected one because of the course options it provided, and the opportunities to get to know people from a wide range of backgrounds. He's just completed his final year at this school, and although there were some ups and downs, overall it was a great success. The decision-making process, however, took a lot of time and effort.

9 For a more detailed discussion of these schooling options, see *Being Smart about Gifted Education* (2009).

10 We discuss in more detail elsewhere the advantages of public schools: "While competitive independent schools can work very well for bright highly-motivated children, such schools often have a one-size-fits-all approach to learning that fails to address exceptional advancement, particularly when advancement is combined with individualistic or idiosyncratic temperament or personality characteristics. For one example, most private schools

do not address systematically or well the learning needs of the student who is extremely gifted mathematically. Our clinical experience suggests that the more highly gifted the child, and/or the more domain-specific the giftedness, the less likely it is that a private school will be able to provide a good educational fit. Publicly funded schools are legislatively mandated to accommodate many different kinds of learners, and are therefore often more ready, willing, and able to address diversity in students' learning ability"; from D. J. Matthews and J. Kitchen, "Allowing Idiosyncratic Learners to Thrive: Policy Implications of a Study of School-within-a-School Gifted Programs," *Journal of School Choice 1*, no. 4 (2007): 27–53, p. 30. Also see J. Andrews and J. Lupart, *The Inclusive Classroom: Educating Exceptional Children, 2nd edition* (Toronto: Nelson, 2000): S. E. Eckes and J. A. Plucker, "Charter Schools and Gifted Education: Legal Obligations," *Journal of Law and Education 34*, no. 3 (2005): 421–36; Matthews and Foster, *Being Smart about Gifted Education.*

11 See also Matthews and Foster, *Being Smart about Gifted Education*, 152-3.

12 For information about the effectiveness of various approaches to gifted programs, see Robinson, Shore, and Enersen, *Best Practices in Gifted Education*; Plucker and Callahan, *Critical Issues and Practices in Gifted Education.*

13 Matthews and Foster, *Being Smart about Gifted Education.*

14 S. Assouline, N. Colangelo, and A. Lupkowski-Shoplik, *Iowa Acceleration Scale Manual, 3rd Edition* (Scottsdale, AZ: Great Potential Press, 2009); N. Colangelo, S. Assouline, and M. U. M. Gross, *A Nation Deceived: How Schools Hold Back America's Brightest Students* (Iowa City, IO: The Connie Belin & Jacqueline N. Blank International Center for Gifted Education and Talent Development, 2004).

15 J. VanTassel-Baska, "Theory and Research on Curriculum Development for the Gifted," in K. A. Heller et al., *International Handbook of Giftedness and Talent*, 345–66.

16 L. Rivero, *The Homeschooling Option: How to Decide When It's Right for Your Family* (New York: Palgrave Macmillan, 2007).

17 *Parenting for High Potential 2*, 8 (2013), has a homeschooling focus. This journal can be found under publications at http://www.nagc.org.

18 C. M. Callahan and T. R. Moon, "Sorting the Wheat from the Chaff: What Makes for Good Evidence of Effectiveness in the Literature in Gifted Education?" *Gifted Child Quarterly 51*, no. 4 (2007): 305–19.

19 A. C. Doyle, *The Sign of Four* (London: Spencer-Blackett, 1890).

20 J. F. Foster, "Extracurricular Activities," *Encyclopedia of Giftedness, Creativity, and Talent, Volume 1*, ed. B. A. Kerr (Thousand Oaks, CA: Sage, 2009), 343–5.

21 Kate Allen, "Lego Man in space," *Toronto Star*, January 25, 2012, http://www.therecord.com/news/canada/article/660528--toronto-teens-send-lego-man-into-space. Follow-up: http://www.thestar.com/news/gta/article/1122175--lego-man-creates-a-stir-in-public.

22 Information about mentoring can be found on the Davidson Institute web site, at http://davidsongifted.org. Some organizations that match mentors with mentees are Dreamcatcher (http://www.dreamcatcheryukon.ca), the National Mentoring Partnership, iMentor, the Mentoring Group, the International Telementor Program, and UConn Mentor Connection. See also J. Reilly, *Mentorship: The Essential Guide for Schools and Business* (Scottsdale, AZ: Great Potential Press, 1992).

23 As initially told to Alexandre Da Silva Maia and recounted here. Alexandre was a preservice student at the University of Toronto who completed an internship with Joanne Foster in 2006.

24 As initially told to Maria Fara-On and recounted here. Maria was a preservice student at the University of Toronto who completed an internship with Joanne Foster in 2006.

25 R. Frost, "The Secret Sits," *Poetry Magazine*, April, 1936.

26 The principal rarely has full autonomy, however, and is more or less constrained by the board, superintendents, district supervisors, and other administrators within the system.

CHAPTER 8: POSSIBLE COMPLICATIONS

1 Renata is a parent we have done some work with.

2 Paul Broca was a surgeon and anthropologist, best known for his pioneering studies on the brain.

3 Karla was a teacher candidate at the Ontario Institute for Studies in Education of the University of Toronto when she stated this.

4 B. A. Kerr and M. F. Nicpon, "Gender and Giftedness," in *Handbook of Gifted Education*, eds. N. Colangelo and G. A. Davis (Boston: Allyn & Bacon, 2003), 493–505; Reis, "Gender, Adolescence, and Giftedness," 87–112.

5 Tough, *How Children Succeed.*

6 Goleman, *Emotional Intelligence.*

7 Stuart Shanker is a Distinguished Research Professor of psychology and philosophy at York University. For an interview with Michael Enright, see http://www.youtube.com/watch?v=wJRtbcChyoY. For an article on Dr. Shanker's approach to teaching self-regulation, see http://www.cea-ace.ca/education-canada/article/self-regulation-calm-alert-and-learning.

8 C. Folsom, *Teaching for Intellectual and Emotional Learning (TIEL)* (Lanham, MD: Rowman & Littlefield, 2008).

9 Based on the work of Lev Vygotsky, which emphasizes engagement in authentic learning, and a balance between challenge and support, the Tools of the Mind curriculum was developed by Elena Bodrova and Deborah Leong. S. B. Kaufman discusses it in some detail in *Ungifted* (2013), as does Paul Tough in *How Children Succeed* (2012). For more on this approach, see http://www.toolsofthemind.org/.

10 S. B. Kaufman discusses the research on Montessori approaches in *Ungifted* (2013).

11 D. B. Peters, *Make Your Worrier a Warrior: A Guide to Conquering Your Child's Fears* (Tucson, AZ: Great Potential Press, 2013).

12 S. C. Radcliffe, *The Fear Fix: Solutions for Every Child's Moments of Worry, Panic and Fear* (New York: HarperCollins, 2013).

13 These strategies were published originally in our blog: http://beyondintelligenceblog.wordpress.com/2013/09/01/reassurance-coping-skills-action-and-resilience-handling-tragedy-with-kids/.

14 Querobin (Qb) Mascarenhas, now a science teacher and an athletic coach, was switching careers from engineering to teaching in 2008, and spoke about the connections.

15 Although some people think perfectionism is more prevalent among gifted learners, that belief isn't borne out in the research. J. F. Foster, "Procrastination and Perfectionism: Connections, Understandings, and Control," *Gifted Education International 23*, no. 3 (2007): 132–40; S. Mendaglio, "Should Perfectionism Be a Characteristic of Giftedness?" *Gifted Education International 23*, no. 3 (2007), 229–30; J. Stober and J. Joormann, "Worry, Procrastination, and Perfectionism: Differentiating Amount of Worry, Pathological Worry, Anxiety, and Depression," *Cognitive Therapy and Research 25*, no. 1 (February 2001): 49–60.

16 Attributed to Martha Graham.

17 For more on this, see http://amychua.com/.

18 Foster, "Procrastination and Perfectionism."

19 For more on why children procrastinate, and what parents can do to help them overcome avoidance behaviour, see J. Foster, *Not Now, Maybe Later: Helping Children Overcome Procrastination* (Tucson, AZ: Great Potential Press, forthcoming).

20 S. Aamodt and S. Wang, *Welcome to Your Child's Brain: How the Mind Grows from Conception to College* (London: Bloomsbury, 2012).

21 S. Harter, *The Construction of the Self: A Developmental Perspective* (New York: The Guilford Press, 1999); C. S. Dweck, *Self-Theories: Their Role in Motivation, Personality, and Development* (Philadelphia, PA: Psychology Press, 1999); C. S. Dweck, *Mindset: The New Psychology of Success* (New York: Random House, 2006).

22 As recounted by Alexandre Da Silva Maia, who interned with Joanne Foster in 2006, with information provided by Luis, who is now an experienced and confident teacher.

CHAPTER 9: THE SOCIAL CONTEXT: FRIENDS AND OTHERS

1 M. Thompson and C. O'Neill-Grace, *Best Friends, Worst Enemies: Understanding the Social Lives of Children* (New York: Random House, 2001), 66.

2   Graham, "Giftedness in Adolescence"; Keating, "Developmental Science and Giftedness"; D. P. Keating and C. Hertzman, eds., *Developmental Health and the Wealth of Nations: Social, Biological, and Educational Dynamics* (New York: Guilford Press, 1999); J. L. VanTassel-Baska, T. L. Cross, and F. R. Olenchak, *Social-Emotional Curriculum with Gifted and Talented Students* (Waco, TX: Prufrock Press, 2009).

3   B. M. Shore, C. L. Walker, and P. D. T. Gyles, "The Gifted Friends Wish List: Qualities Highly Able Teens and Young Adults Value in Their Friends" (paper, National Association for Gifted Children, Denver, CO, November 2012).

4   Parents may also be interested in learning about Peacebuilders, which offers professional development and curricular strategies designed to promote cooperative, safe, and productive environments for children and teenagers. For information, visit www.peacebuilders.com.

5   Kids Now is an organization that provides extracurricular programs for students. With mentorships focusing on bullying prevention, leadership, confidence, and more, a range of skill-building opportunities are offered to grades seven and eight students in over two hundred schools in Canada. For more information, visit www.kidsnowcanada.org.

6   Eileen Kennedy Moore is the author of *The Unwritten Rules of Friendship* (2003), and writes a blog on children's friendships: http://www.psychology-today.com/blog/growing-friendships/201209/how-children-make-friends-part-1.

7   W. Craig, T. Vaillancourt, and D. Pepler, "Bullying: Why don't we intervene?" *The Globe and Mail* commentary, May 7, 2010. http://www.theglobeandmail.com/commentary/bullying---why-dont-we-intervene/article4317968/.

8   Parents can consult the literature (Barbara Coloroso's books are excellent), and check kids' help lines and other sites that address bullying, cyberbullying, and victimhood, for more.

9   These steps also contribute to mindfulness, which we discuss in chapter 10.

10 The Friends of Simon Wiesenthal Center for Holocaust Studies (in Toronto) and the Center for Tolerance (in New York City) provide excellent resource materials and informative learning sessions for educators and student groups.

11 Seth Rudetsky, Sirius XM Radio, September 19, 2012.

12 Information can be found at Cyberbullying Research Center: www.cyberbullying.us/resources.php.

13 On October 22, 2012, Jesse Hirsh did an article on cyberbullying, on Metro Morning, CBC Radio, Toronto, where he described cyberbullyies as a "Virtual Lynch Mob." http://www.cbc.ca/player/News/Canada/Toronto/Audio/ID/2295001529/?page=7&sort=MostPopular.

14 Craig, Vaillancourt, and Pepler, "Bullying: Why Don't We Intervene?"

15 The Friends of Simon Wiesenthal Center for Holocaust Studies (in Toronto) offers resource material and educational programs on tolerance and conflict resolution. See www.friendsofsimonwiesenthalcenter.com.

16 Chris Colfer is an Emmy Award–winning actor on the television show *Glee*.

17 The issue of legislation is carefully considered in a *CBC News* story, "Can Cyberbullying Laws Really Work?" (Janet Davison, August 13, 2013). Nova Scotia passed a law in August 2013, in the wake of the tragic death of seventeen-year-old Rehtaeh Parsons, who committed suicide as a result of cyberbullying that she could no longer endure. The legislation, which serves as a starting point to combat cyberbullying and as a template for other provinces to consider, is designed to protect future victims and hold perpetrators (and sometimes their parents) responsible for "insidious online behaviour." Media outlets across Canada and beyond have weighed in on this law, and on what else can be done to help put an end to cyberbullying. Readers can find out more by searching "cyberbullying legislation" or by going to http://www.cbc.ca/news/canada/story/2013/08/09/f-cyberbullying-legislation-rehtaeh-parsons.html.

18 Recommendations for a national anti-bullying strategy were made by Debra Pepler, scientific co-director of the Promoting Relationships and Eliminating Violence Network at York University, and a founding member of the Canadian Initiative for the Prevention of Bullying. The need to reinvent the PTA as a twenty-four-hour-a-day online resource for kids in trouble is a strategy we first heard about from Jesse Hirsh, CBC Radio media commentator. http://www.cbc.ca/player/News/Canada/Toronto/Audio/ID/2295001529/?page=7 &sort=MostPopular.

19 Annie Murphy Paul, quoting Joshua Aronson, in "It's Not Me, It's You," *New York Times*, October 6, 2012.

20 Hymer, Whitehead, and Huxtable, *Gifts, Talents and Education*, 18.

21 R. D. Putnam, *Making Democracy Work: Civic Traditions in Modern Italy* (Princeton, NJ: Princeton University Press, 1993).

22 Keating, "Developmental Science and Giftedness"; Matthews, "Developmental Transitions in Giftedness and Talent: Childhood to Adolescence."

23 Joseph Renzulli and colleagues run the Neag Center for Gifted Education and Talent Development at the University of Connecticut. They have a long history of innovation and research on creativity, mentoring, giftedness, and talent development. For more information, see http://www.gifted.uconn.edu/.

24 NBC Sports Group, Sochi Winter Games coverage, February 23, 2014: http://nbcsportsgrouppressbox.com/2014/02/23/2014-sochi-winter-games-feb-23-nbc-daytime-highlights/.

25 You may recall the story of Tony, the talented young trumpet player who was on the fast track to success until he went to Juilliard and encountered other trumpet players with expertise he had not yet developed. In chapter 8, we

discuss how to foster psychosocial strengths in order to prevent problems like those Tony experienced, and we discuss more explicitly how to help children build self-confidence.

26 Subotnik and Jarvin, "Beyond Expertise"; *DGT*.

27 When we advocate that young people learn how to "play the game," we aren't suggesting they subdue their individuality in the service of conformity. Quite the reverse, because it's one's individuality that sets one apart and gives one something special to contribute. However, smart people who don't learn how to get along in their field are soon excluded from it, which means they can lose their chance at success, or at the very least take longer to get there. The research on talent development shows that there are big consequences for those who don't know how to negotiate the social landscape, or choose not to.

28 Journalist and author of books on sisters.

29 Joyce Maynard is a novelist and columnist who often writes about family and parenting issues. This is a frequently cited quote that can be found on Joyce Maynard's *Goodreads* profile: https://www.goodreads.com/author/show/71438.Joyce_Maynard.

CHAPTER 10

1 J. Higley, "Nearly 25 Years of Fathering—and All I've Got Are These Lousy Tips," Huffington Post (HuffPost Parenting), December 3, 2013, http://www.huffingtonpost.com/jim-higley/nearly-25-years-of-fathering-and-all-ive-got-are-these-3-lousy-tips_b_4369677.html?utm_hp_ref=parents&ir=Parents.

2 R. Sternberg, "Developing Your Child's Successful Intelligence," in *Parenting Gifted Children,* eds. J. L. Jolly, D. J. Treffinger, T. F. Inman, and J. F. Smutny (Waco, TX: Prufrock Press, 2011), 15.

3 We describe some of the techniques for creating a gap between an event and a response when we address bullying in chapter 9. Mindfulness can be an effective tool for helping bullies and their victims break the bully-victim loop.

4 For more information about this organization and its worldwide events, visit www.weday.com.

5 R. Sternberg, L. Jarvin, and E. Grigorenko, *Explorations in Giftedness* (New York: Cambridge University Press, 2011).

6 Levine, *Teach Your Children Well.*

7 A. Nair, "Seven Stops to Being Less Hard on Our Kids," Yummy Mummy Club, December 12, 2013, http://www.yummymummyclub.ca/blogs/andrea-nair-button-pushing/20131212/steps-to-being-less-harsh-on-our-kids.

8 "Parenting and Multi-Tasking in the Digital Age," Psyche's Circuitry (blog), March 28, 2013, http://psychescircuitry.wordpress.com/2012/03/28/parenting-and-multi-tasking-in-the-digital-age/.

9 Ibid.

10 C. Steiner-Adair with T. H. Barker, *The Big Disconnect: Protecting Childhood and Family Relationships in the Digital Age* (New York: HarperCollins, 2013), 10.

11 Ibid.

12 D. K. Simonton, *Greatness: Who Makes History and Why* (New York: Guilford Press, 1994); *DGT*.

13 Extracted from a copy of a report card from St. George's School, Ascot, dated 1884, which Joanne received from a colleague who teaches at the University of Toronto. The information from Winston Churchill's report card is duplicated online at http://www.dailymail.co.uk/news/article- 507221/churchill. Accessed September 21, 2013. Taken from C. Hurley, ed., *Could Do Better: School Reports of the Great and the Good* (New York: Simon and Schuster, 2003).

14 From http://www.forbes.com/sites/davidewalt/2012/11/05/gurdon-makes-the-grade/ Accessed February 25, 2014.

15 Hillary Clinton wrote a wonderful book on child development, pulling together current research in a number of fields, emphasizing the importance of communities in children's optimal development: H. R. Clinton, *It Takes a Village and Other Lessons Children Teach Us* (New York: Simon and Schuster, 1996).

16 H. Gardner, *The Disciplined Mind: Beyond Facts and Standardized Tests, the K–12 Education That Every Child Deserves* (New York: Penguin Books, 2000).

Index

A

Aamodt, Sandra, 96, 265n20
Abarbanel, Misha, 43
abstract reasoning, 9, 16, 250n9
academic achievement
  factors, 108, 127
  labelling, 98–104
  mindset, 20, 24
  profiles of intelligence, 13, 16, 87
  tests and assessments, 15, 16, 89,
    91–97, 141
acceleration, 75, 102, 162, 166
acceptance, 179, 207, 226
accommodation
  friendships, 215
  labelling, 101
  schools, 118, 148, 173
administrative support
  teachers, 131–32, 134, 136, 139,
    148–49, 150, 152
adolescence
  decision-making, 78–80
  early adolescence, 72–76
  education, 79–80
  gap year, 81–82, 86
  goal-setting, 78–79
  guidance counsellors, 75, 80, 136,
    223

  identity, 73, 79
  late adolescence, 80–85
  psychosocial skills, 73, 223
  relationship-building skills, 73, 83,
    188, 222, 225
  resilience, 85
adulthood See early adulthood
advanced intellectual ability See
  giftedness
advanced learning See gifted education
advanced placement (AP) courses,
  74–75, 90, 163, 180, 183
adversity See under coping skills
advocacy, 122–28. See also parenting
  strategies
aggression, 63, 216, 230
Aikido lessons, 206
Alcott, Louisa May, 205
Allen, Kate, 263n21
alternative schools, 163
Alvarez, Luis, 224
ambiguity tolerance, 42–43
American Psychological Association
  (APA)
  task force on intelligence, 7–9, 14, 24
analytical intelligence, 9, 16, 17, 143
Anderson, L., 261n13
Andrews, J., 262n10

anger, 185, 193, 202
apprenticeships, 81, 86
Aristotle, 65
Arnold, Karen D., 249n4
Aronson, Joshua, 267n19
arrogance, 103
art and creativity, 36
Ashley, S., 254n11
assessments. *See also* tests
  approaches, 94–96, 105–6, 131,
    140–41, 151
  boredom, 190–93
  concerns, 91–93
  definition, 88
  educational practices, 96–97, 104,
    259n6
  giftedness, 89–91, 96–100, 258n11
  information sources, 89–90, 94
  intelligence continuum, 12–13,
    90–91
  principles, 88–91
  race and social class disparities, 12,
    91, 95–97
Association for Bright Children
  (ABC), 123
Assouline, S., 263n14
athletics *See* sports
attention-deficit/hyperactivity disorder
  (ADHD)
  labelling, 101
autonomy. *See also* decision-making;
  independence
  adolescence, 78–80
  childhood, 67
  early adulthood, 83–85
  parenting strategies, 120

B
babies *See* early years
balance
  between ability level and degree of
    challenge, 45
  priorities, 68, 109
  between work and play, 56–57,
    67–69

Balchin, T., 250n16, 253n17, 258n17,
  260n9
Barker, T. H., 269n10, 269n11
Barr, R.G., 254n14
Bartlett, Kelly, 256n35
Bass, K.E., 251n18
Beales, Bernie, 287
behaviour problems
  aggression, 63, 216, 230
  anger, 185, 193, 202
  being different, 178–80, 230
  boredom, 190–93
  bullying, 216–22
  coping mechanisms, 181–84
  emotional intelligence, 180–84
  fear of failure, 193–97
  fear of success, 195–97
  inferences and assumptions,
    176–77
  laziness, 200–202
  perfectionism, 197–200, 265n15
  procrastination, 202–4
  resilience and coping skills,
    184–90, 265n13
  self-confidence, 204–7, 267n25
  self-esteem, 178–80
  social and emotional well-being,
    175–208
  worry, 102, 185–87
Berger, S., 257n50
Bergman, Ingmar, 15, 16
Bialystock, Ellen, 251n23
Bidelman, G. M., 251n21
Binet, Alfred, 11–12, 250n12
Bloom's Taxonomy, 142–43, 261n13,
  261n14
bodily-kinesthetic intelligence, 14
Bodrova, Elena, 264n9
boredom, 69–70, 117, 190–93
Borland, J. H., 258n17
brain development
  assessment, 88–89
  childhood, 65–66
  disparities in early years, 96
  early adolescence, 73–74

intelligence, 19
music education, 17–18
neuroscience, 12, 17–19, 53–55, 89
brain-building, 53–55
Branson, Richard, 12, 81
Breneman, Judy Anne, 31
Broca, Paul, 177, 264n2
Buck, Pearl S., 34
bullying. *See also* cyberbullying
   behaviour problems, 216–22,
     268n3
   rejection, 213, 216

C
Callahan, C. M., 260n4, 260n7,
   263n12, 263n18
Calm, Alert, and Ready for Learning,
   181–83
capacity-building essentials, 129–31,
   150, 152, 247
career decision-making, 2, 78–79,
   80–82, 86
Center for Tolerance, 266n10
character, 233–36, 246–47
charter schools, 161
checklists
   advocacy strategies for parents,
     125–26
   brain-building experiences, 55–56
   child's educational experience, 120
   classroom strategies to reduce
     bullying, 221–22
   drawbacks of the gifted label,
     102–4
   elements of a good school, 156
   five questions to ask when kids have
     problems, 177–78
   four practices parents can teach
     kids to prevent bullying, 217–18
   good assessment practices, 140–41
   options to challenge learners, 142
   problem-based learning, 145
   professional development options
     for teachers, 132–33
   resilience and coping skills: helping

kids deal with challenges,
   187–90
   successful learning environments,
   148–49
   what do teachers need for
     intelligence-building?, 134
child-care study, 62–64
childhood. *See also* early years
   brain development, 65–66
   decision making, 67
   developmental stage, 64–72
   parenting strategies, 85–86
   racial disparities, 96
   work habits, 85
chores, 71–72
Christensen, E., 251n19
Christodoulou, J.A., 254n10
Chua, Amy, 69, 200, 253n5
Churchill, Winston, 13, 87, 238,
   269n13
clearly defined goals, 44–45
Clinton, Hillary Rodham, 269n15
Cohen, N. A., 260n11
Colangelo, N., 263n14, 264n4
Colfer, Chris, 221
college, 80–84, 163
Colombo, J., 253n3
Coloroso, Barbara, 266n8
comfort zone, 24, 77, 194, 225
common sense *See* practical
   intelligence
community-based learning, 171–72,
   235, 244
competition, 43, 67–68, 77, 83, 172,
   198, 229
computers
   cyberbullying, 219–22
   learning opportunities, 133, 169,
     238
confidence *See* self-confidence
conflict resolution, 181, 206, 214, 220
Cooke, Alistair, 46
coping skills. *See also* emotional well-
   being; social well-being
   adversity, 184–90, 246

early adulthood, 82 – 84
mechanisms, 181 – 84
perfectionism, 199 – 200
procrastination, 204
self-confidence, 207
setbacks, 76 – 78
Craig, W., 266n7, 266n14
creative ideas, 32 – 49
creative intelligence, 15, 16
creative or experiential intelligence
   triarchic intelligences approach,
   144
creative productivity, 33, 224
creative writing, 15, 39 – 41, 118, 122,
   169 – 70, 172, 189, 205
creativity
   analyzing ideas, 36 – 37
   belief in self, 41 – 42
   challenges, 38 – 41, 45
   communication, 34 – 35
   critical thinking, 33 – 34
   curiosity, 45 – 46
   divergent thinking, 32 – 33
   domain-specific knowledge, 30 – 31
   enjoyment, 43 – 44
   flow, 44 – 45
   intelligence, 27 – 28, 48 – 49
   obstacles, 38 – 39
   parental modeling, 241
   problem-solving, 36
   productive balance, 34 – 35
   rejection, 39 – 41
   risk-taking, 39 – 40
   selling ideas, 37 – 38
   teachers, 131
   tests and assessments, 94 – 95
   thinking habits, 35 – 44
   tolerating ambiguity, 42 – 43
   understanding, 29 – 35, 252n8
   video game design, 27 – 30, 34, 37,
   44 – 45
critical thinking, 11, 33 – 37, 252n8
Crook, M.D., 251n18
Cropley, A. J., 253n17
Crosby, Sidney, 224

Cross, T. L., 266n2
Csikszentmihalyi, Mihaly, 44, 252n4,
   252n7, 253n17
Cui, M., 256n36
Curie, Marie, 194, 240
curiosity, 7, 45 – 46, 49, 69, 71, 240
curriculum. *See also* learning match
   differentiation, 137 – 39, 142 – 48
   modification, 109 – 11, 119, 131,
   159, 183 – 84
   Tools of the Mind, 184
cyberbullying. *See also* bullying
   definition, 219
   law enforcement and legislation,
   221, 267n17
   parenting strategies, 220 – 22
   parents' questions, 218 – 21

D
Da Silva Maia, Alexandre, 252n2,
   264n23, 265n22
da Vinci, Leonardo, 224
Dali, Salvador, 198, 203
Darwin, Charles, 98 – 99, 245
Davidson, J. E., 256n37, 258n17
Davis, G. A., 264n4
Davis, M, 260n8
Davis, Miles, 76
daycare, 62 – 64
daydreaming, 69 – 71
de Haan, M., 257n1
decision-making
   adolescence, 78 – 80
   childhood, 67
   early adulthood, 80 – 85, 86
   school choice, 153 – 60, 172 – 74
Dennis, Tracy, 236 – 37, 287
depression, 193, 202
Dettmer, P. A., 260n9
developmental asynchrony, 257n2
developmental stages
   childhood, 64 – 72
   early adolescence to mid-
      adolescence, 72 – 80
   early years, 53 – 64

late-adolescence to early adulthood, 80 – 85
Dewey, John, 107
Dibb, Jo, 108
differentiation
  individual curriculum, 137 – 39, 142 – 48
  parenting strategies, 228 – 29
discovery, 11, 46, 69
disengagement from school, 90, 101
Disraeli, Benjamin, 165
divergent thinking and creativity, 32 – 33, 151, 252n8
diversity, 151, 152, 157, 214, 230
Dixon, F., 253n20, 258n16, 260n9
Doidge, Norman, 249n5, 251n24, 257n1
domain-specific knowledge and reasoning, 30 – 31, 104
Donnellan, M.B., 256n36
Doyle, Sir Arthur Conan, 167
drama activities, 56, 118, 144, 162, 169 – 70
dual track programs, 162
Duckworth, Angela, 256n42
Dufur, M. J., 262n1
Dweck, Carol, 19 – 21, 78, 101, 166, 265n21

E
early adolescence. *See also* adolescence
  adolescence, 72 – 76
  behaviour problems, 178 – 80
  brain development, 73 – 74
  developmental stage, 72 – 80
  failure, 75 – 78
  stress, 72 – 78, 256n36
  transitions, 74 – 75, 86, 179
early adulthood
  autonomy, 83 – 85
  education, 80 – 85, 86
  encouragement by parents, 82 – 84
  entitlement, 71
  mentorship, 82
  psychosocial skills, 73, 225

transitions, 83 – 84, 86
early childhood education, 62 – 64, 96
early years
  affection and play, 85, 255n29
  child-care, 62 – 64
  developmental stage, 53 – 64
  racial disparities, 96
Eckes, S. E., 262n10
Edison, Thomas, 53, 134
education. *See also* learning; schools
  adolescence, 79 – 80
  early adulthood, 80 – 85
  parental role, 107 – 8, 127 – 28
  special education, 123, 140, 149, 150 – 51, 161
  teachers, 109 – 19
  university, 80 – 85
educational measurement *See* assessments; tests
Einstein, Alfred, 13, 26, 29, 33, 38, 87, 99, 120 – 21, 237, 252n9
electronic devices, 66, 69, 234
Eliot, T.S., 33, 252n9
Elizabeth Garrett Anderson School (EGAS), 107 – 8, 259n3, 261n22
emotional intelligence
  behaviour problems, 6, 101, 178 – 80, 190 – 207
  concerns, 70, 79, 175 – 80
  definition, 14
  development, 63, 70, 75, 96, 130 – 31, 178 – 80
  parenting strategies, 53, 58, 181 – 84, 207 – 8, 241 – 42
  resilience and coping skills, 180 – 89
emotional well-being *See* emotional intelligence
encouragement by parents, 108, 119, 127, 245 – 47
Enersen, D. L., 258n20, 259n1, 260n4, 260n9, 262n5, 263n12
engagement
  development, 19, 58, 64
  disengagement from school, 90, 101
  flow and creativity, 44

in learning, 61 – 62, 116, 127, 133,
    264n9
playful exploration, 52, 61 – 62, 225,
    254n18
in school, 90, 153, 167
enjoyment of creativity, 43 – 44
enrichment, 70, 97, 121 – 22, 146. *See
    also* gifted education
enthusiasm
    lack of, 104, 197
    for learning, 111, 121 – 22
envy, 103, 216, 220, 230
Eriksson, G., 258n16, 258n17
evaluation *See* assessments; tests
existential intelligence, 14
expectations, 98, 102, 151, 159, 196,
    198 – 99
experiential intelligence, 144
extracurricular activities
    community-based learning
        experiences, 167 – 72, 244
    leadership development, 170 – 71
    mentorships, 169, 266n5
    value of, 28 – 29

F
failure. *See also* setbacks
    attitude to, 181
    early adolescence, 75 – 78
    fear of, 193 – 95
families
    grandparents, 186, 227
    sibling relationships and learning
        social skills, 226 – 30
family social capital
    factors in academic achievement,
        153 – 55
Fara-On, Maria, 260n7, 264n24
fears, 185 – 87, 193 – 97
feedback, 22, 45, 47
Feldman, D. H., 7, 252n3
finances
    considerations, 1, 66 – 67, 114, 174,
        242
    pressures, 121 – 22, 128, 228

Fishel, Elizabeth, 227
Fitzgerald, F. Scott, 42
Fitzsimmons, William, 82
fixed mindset, 19 – 24, 110, 239. *See
    also* growth mindset
flow
    balance between ability level and
        degree of challenge, 45
    clearly defined goals, 44 – 45
    creativity, 44 – 45
    feedback, 45
Folsom, C., 264n8
Forbes, Malcolm S., 119
Ford, D. Y., 258n16
Foster, Joanne, 87 – 88, 91, 250n8,
    251n25, 252n1, 252n2, 257n10,
    259n4, 259n21, 259n23, 259n24,
    260n7, 261n18, 261n19, 261n22,
    262n8, 262n9, 262n10, 263n10,
    263n11, 263n13, 263n20, 264n23,
    264n24, 265n15, 265n18, 265n19,
    265n22, 267n25
Fraiberg, Selma, 55
Franklin, Benjamin, 31
Free the Children, 235
Freud, Sigmund, 33, 40, 252n9
Friedman, Thomas, 133
Friends of Simon Wiesenthal Center
    for Holocaust Studies, 266n10,
    267n15
friendship-building
    accommodation, 215
    importance, 210 – 12
    misconceptions, 215
    parenting strategies, 212 – 15,
        230 – 31
    social acceptance, 207
    social intelligence, 206, 209 – 31,
        247
    social networks, 210 – 11
Fromm, Erich, 131
Frost, Robert, 172
frustration, 113 – 14, 192 – 93
Fullan, M. G., 262n5
Fuller, Buckminster, 51

fun *See* engagement

G

Galileo, 38 – 39
Gandhi, Mahatma, 33, 252n9
Gandour, J. T., 251n21
gap year, 81 – 82, 86
Gardner, Howard, 13 – 16, 33 – 34,
    165 – 66, 246, 252n7, 252n9, 261n15
Gates, Bill, 81
Geake, J., 260n9
Gentry, Marcia, 156
gifted education
    elitism, 102 – 3
    school criteria, 148 – 51, 162
giftedness
    advanced intellectual ability,
        98 – 100
    assessment measures, 10, 89 – 97,
        105, 141, 173, 224, 250n8
    definition, 259n24
    development, 31, 58 – 59
    envy, 103, 216, 220, 230
    expectations, 98, 102, 151, 159, 196,
        198 – 99
    higher-order thinking skills, 143,
        145
    labelling, 98 – 104, 230
    models, 99
    multipotentiality, 82
    self-doubt, 102, 103
Gilkerson, J., 254n8
Ginott, Haim, 110
Gladwell, Malcolm, 23, 154, 254n12
global awareness, 235
goal-setting, 78 – 79
Goleman, Daniel, 181
Gottfried, A.E., 250n11, 253n3
Gottfried, A.W., 250n11, 253n3
Graham, Martha, 33, 252n9, 265n16
Graham, S., 250n14, 258n13, 258n16,
    266n2
Gretzky, Wayne, 98 – 99
Grigorenko, E. L., 253n17, 268n5
Grisham, John, 37

grit, 75 – 76, 256n42
Gross, M. U. M., 263n14
growth mindset, 19 – 24, 241. *See also*
    fixed mindset
Guerin, D.W., 250n11, 253n3
guidance counsellors, 75, 80, 136, 223
Gunnar, Megan, 62 – 63
Gurdon, John, 238 – 39
Gurley Brown, Helen, 15, 16
Gyles, P. D. T., 266n3

H

Habitat for Humanity, 244
habits
    creative thinking, 35 – 44
    work habits, 85, 199, 201
habits of mind, 28, 64 – 66, 247
happy productivity, 240, 247 – 48
hard work, 22 – 23, 26, 53, 61, 64, 99,
    108, 127, 202
Harris, W., 251n17
Harter, S., 265n21
Hawking, Stephen, 5, 9, 15, 247 – 48
healthy life balance, 56 – 57, 67 – 69
Heller, K. A., 253n17, 263n15
Hemingway, Ernest, 37
Hertzman, C., 266n2
high-ability learners *See* giftedness
high-level development, 19, 59, 64, 89,
    91, 108, 124, 139, 142, 146, 166, 178,
    252n8, 254n18. *See also* giftedness
Higley, Jim, 234
Hillary, Edmund, 225
Hirsh, Jesse, 266n13
Hodges, Donald, 17
Holmes, Sherlock, 143, 167
homeschooling, 164
homework, 113, 142, 159, 176, 177,
    191, 200, 203
Horowitz, Frances Degen, 9, 249n2,
    251n24, 258n17
Hurley, C., 269n13
Huxtable, Marie, 223, 257n8, 258n17
Hymer, Barry, 223, 250n16, 253n17,
    257n8, 258n17, 260n9, 287

I

ideas *See* creative ideas
identity
    adolescence, 73, 79
    being different, 178 – 80
    imagination, 26, 32 – 33, 46
Immordino-Yang, M.H., 254n10
independence. *See also* autonomy
    challenges, 52, 73
    chores, 71 – 72
independent schools, 161
individuality and learning
    differentiation, 118 – 19, 137 – 39,
        142 – 48
    parenting strategies, 227 – 29, 231,
        243 – 45, 268n27
infancy *See* early years
inferences and assumptions
    behaviour problems, 176 – 77
intellectually advanced. *See also*
    giftedness
    abilities, 13, 19 – 20, 64, 73, 98 – 100,
        242
    challenges, 90, 92 – 94, 157 – 59,
        167 – 69, 208, 216
    peers, 179 – 80, 207, 211 – 12
intelligence. *See also* brain
    development
    analytical intelligence, 15, 16
    definitions, 7, 24 – 25
    existential intelligence, 14
    experiential intelligence, 144
    language study, 18 – 19, 25, 122, 154
    misconceptions, 5 – 6
    multiple intelligences (MI)
        approach, 14, 143, 165 – 66
    praise for, 21 – 22, 26, 183
    as a process, 9
    profiles of, 13 – 15, 16
    spatial reasoning, 8, 14, 17, 110
    task force, 7 – 9, 14, 24
    triarchic intelligences approach, 143
intelligence continuum, 12 – 13, 90 – 91
intelligence quotient (IQ). *See also* tests
    limitations of test, 11 – 13, 250n8,

250n11, 250n14
    misconceptions, 6 – 8
    scores, 8, 9 – 12, 25, 88, 89, 91, 93,
        98, 249n6, 250n10
    types of tests, 8, 92 – 93, 249n7,
        250n12
intelligence-building
    child-care, 62 – 64
    imagination, 26, 32 – 33, 46
    learning opportunities, 121 – 22,
        237 – 38
    parenting strategies, 25 – 26,
        237 – 48
    problem-based learning, 144 – 46
    social context, 222 – 24
    taking responsibility, 116 – 17, 190
    work vs play, 22 – 23, 52 – 53
International Baccalaureate (IB), 163
interpersonal (social) intelligence, 14
intrapersonal (emotional) intelligence,
    14

J

Jarvin, L., 256n37, 268n5, 268n26
Jobs, Steve, 81
Joormann, J., 265n15
Juilliard, 76, 83, 256n43

K

Kanevsky, Lannie, 137
Kaufman, Scott Barry, 12, 70, 101,
    254n12, 254n17, 257n3, 259n26,
    264n9, 265n10
Keating, Daniel, 30, 249n2, 249n5,
    251n24, 252n8, 254n6, 254n7,
    254n14, 255n26, 256n39, 257n4,
    266n2, 267n22
keep growing in creativity, 40 – 41
Keller, Helen, 210
Kennedy-Moore, Eileen, 266n6
Kerr, B. A., 263n20, 264n4
Kielburger, Craig, 235
Kielburger, Marc, 235
King, Martin Luther, Jr., 234 – 35
Kitchen, J., 262n10

knowledge. *See also* intelligence
  domain-specific knowledge, 30 – 31
  as double-edged sword, 38
Kolbert, E., 256n34
Korb, K. A., 250n10
Krishnan, A., 251n21
Kump, Luc, 260n10
Kwan, Sylvia, 287

L
labelling
  accommodation, 101
  attention-deficit/hyperactivity
    disorder (ADHD), 101
  giftedness, 92, 98 – 104
  learning disabilities, 101
Landrum, M. S., 260n9
language immersion and dual track
    programs, 162, 174
language learning
  intelligence, 14, 18 – 19, 25, 122, 154
  motivation at early age, 60 – 61
  reading, 64 – 65
late adolescence *See under* adolescence
laziness
  behaviour problems, 200 – 202
  fear of success, 197
leadership development
  extracurricular activities, 170 – 71
learning
  activities, 141 – 48
  comfort zone, 24, 77, 194, 225
  disabilities labelling, 101
  ownership of, 67, 69, 117
  passion for learning, 60 – 61
  praise, 21 – 24
  time management, 84, 125, 176 – 77,
    192, 200, 203 – 4
learning environment. *See also* schools
  accommodating students, 118 – 19,
    147 – 48, 173
  capacity-building essentials,
    129 – 31, 150, 152, 247
  decision-making, 153 – 74
  diversity, 151, 157, 214, 230

extracurricular activities, 167 – 72
  intelligence-building, 222 – 24,
    237 – 39, 241 – 42
  leadership development, 170 – 71
  mentorships, 169
  Renaissance, 224
  teachers, 148 – 51
learning gap
  racial disparities, 95 – 97
learning match, 68, 255n27
learning styles, 67
Lee, S-Y, 256n44
Leong, Deborah, 264n9
Levine, Madeline, 46, 75, 236
Lieberman, A.F., 254n10
Lincoln, Abraham, 123
linguistic intelligence, 14
logical-mathematical intelligence, 14
Lohman, David, 250n10, 257n9
Lombardi, Vince, 198
Low, J., 251n18
Lupart, J., 262n10
Lupkowski-Shoplik, A., 263n14

M
Machiavelli, Niccolo, 224
magnet schools and programs, 162 – 63
Makel, M. C., 256n44
Manet, Eduoard, 36
Mascarenhas, Querobin (Qb), 265n14
Masci, Kelly, 59
mastery model of giftedness, 9, 99,
    252n8
mathematics, 57, 67, 68, 89, 90, 96,
    103, 142, 143, 162
"Matthew Effect, The," 58
Matthews, Dona, 87, 91, 227, 249n2,
    250n8, 250n16, 251n24, 251n25,
    252n1, 253n17, 256n38, 256n40,
    257n10, 258n15, 258n17, 259n4,
    259n21, 259n23, 259n24, 259n26,
    260n9, 261n18, 261n19, 261n22,
    262n8, 262n9, 262n10, 263n11,
    263n13, 267n22
Matthews, Robin, 254n16

May, Rollo, 33
Maynard, Joyce, 229
McArthur, David, 22 – 23
McKelvie, P., 251n18
McMillan, Rebecca, 70
Mendaglio, S., 258n14, 265n15
mentorships, 82, 169, 252n1, 264n22
Michelangelo, 30, 224
mid adolescence *See* adolescence
Miller, Susan, 136 – 37, 260n6
Miller, T. N., 260n9
mindfulness and parenting strategies,
    233 – 37, 266n9, 268n3
mindsets, 19 – 24, 110, 166, 239, 241
misconceptions
    friendship-building, 215
    intelligence, 5 – 8
    self-confidence, 204 – 5
modelling. *See also* parenting strategies
    creativity, 241
    friendship-building, 214 – 15
    mindfulness, 233 – 37
    resilience and coping skills,
        187 – 90, 195, 199
    social skills, 225 – 26, 242 – 43
money
    financial considerations, 1, 66 – 67,
        114, 174, 242
    financial pressures, 121 – 22, 128, 228
Montessori schools
    school choices, 163 – 64
    self-regulation skills, 184
Moon, S. M., 258n16, 260n9, 263n18
Moore III, J. L., 258n16
Moreno, S., 251n22
motivation to learn, 21, 57 – 60, 66
Mozart, Wolfgang Amadeus, 43
"Mozart Effect," The, 17
multiple intelligences (MI) approach,
    14, 143, 165 – 66
multipotentiality, 82
multi-sensory stimulation, 53, 56, 63
multi-tasking by parents, 236 – 37
music education
    brain development, 17 – 18, 251n19

motivation, 59
parenting strategies, 66 – 67
setbacks, 76 – 78
musical intelligence, 14, 17 – 18
mystery model of giftedness, 99

N
Naimji, Senka, 32 – 33
Nair, Andrea, 53, 236
National Association for Gifted
    Children (NAGC), 123
National Institute for Child Health and
    Human Development (NICHD),
    62 – 63
naturalistic intelligence, 14
Navratilova, Martina, 104
Neag Center for Gifted Education and
    Talent Development, 267n23
Neihart, Maureen, 78, 255n23
Neisser, Ulric, 249n3
Nelson, C.A., 254n6, 254n10, 257n1
neuroscience *See under* brain
    development
Nicpon, M. F., 264n4
Nietzsche, Friedrich, 115
Nilles, K., 260n11
Nin, Anais, 209
Nisbett, Richard E., 249n5, 251n24,
    262n5

O
Obama, Barack, 24, 261n22
Obama, Michelle, 108, 259n2, 261n22
obstacles to creativity, 38 – 39
Olenchuk, F. R., 266n2
Olszewski-Kubilius, Paula, 249n4,
    251n25, 256n44
O'Neill-Grace, C., 265n1
online learning, 138, 169
Orwell, George, 37
Ottman, J., 258n14
outcomes
    achievement, 116, 146, 151, 184
    educational, 107, 116, 127, 155, 242
    mindsets, 19

P
Parcel, T. L., 262n1
parenting strategies
    advocacy role at school, 107–8,
        120–28
    childhood development, 85–86
    collaboration with teachers,
        110–19, 129–30
    conflict resolution, 181, 206, 214,
        220
    cyberbullying, 220–22
    differentiation skills between
        children, 228–29
    emotional intelligence, 207–8, 242
    intelligence-building, 1–3, 25–26,
        238–48
    laziness, 202
    mindfulness, 233–37
    multi-tasking, 236–37
    nurturing creativity, 48–49, 241
    nurturing friendship-building,
        212–15, 230–31
    nurturing productive children,
        247–48, 266n4
    perfectionism, 199–200
    procrastination, 204
    reflectivity, 233–37
    resilience and coping skills,
        187–90, 195, 199, 265n13
    self-confidence, 207
    sense of humour, 200, 236
    setbacks, 6, 207, 241, 246
    sibling relationships, 226–30
    social skills, 225–26, 242–43,
        268n27
Parker, Dorothy, 69
Parsons, Rahteah, 267n17
passion for learning, 60–61
Pasteur, Louis, 153
Pauling, Linus, 32
Pearce, Joseph Chilton, 53, 61
Pearson, J., 254n11
peers. *See also* friendship-building
    group, 75, 90, 96, 99, 102, 175, 230
    intellectual, 179–80, 207, 211–12

mediation, 214, 221
pressure, 72, 81, 84, 102–3,
    178–80, 210, 212
Pepler, Debra, 266n7, 266n14, 267n18
perfectionism
    behaviour problems, 197–200,
        265n15
    parenting strategies, 199–200
Perkins, D. N., 252n6
perseverance
    creativity, 43–44
    habits of mind, 28
    self-confidence, 240
    tests and assessments, 94
Peters, D. B., 265n11
physical exercise *See* sports
Picasso, Pablo, 13, 29, 33, 40, 87, 252n9
Piirto, J., 252n4
Pink, D.H., 255n25
play vs work, 52–53, 56–62, 69–72
playful exploration, 52, 61–62, 85, 225
playtime, unstructured, 56–63, 69–71,
    85, 253n5, 255n32
Plucker, J. A., 260n4, 260n7, 262n10,
    263n12
Porath, Marion, 287
positive attitudes, 181, 187, 195, 207,
    215, 217, 246
practical intelligence, 15, 16, 144
praise
    being intelligent, 21–22, 26, 183
    problems with, 20–22, 26, 184, 205
    self-confidence, 5, 205
Prather, Hugh, 198
Price-Mitchell, Marilyn, 70–71
private schools, 161
problem-based learning, 70–71,
    144–46, 178, 180, 207
problems *See* behaviour problems
problem-solving
    creativity, 36
    procrastination, 202–4
productivity
    creative productivity, 33, 224
    happy productivity, 240, 247–48

professional development for teachers, 131–33
Program for International Student Assessment (PISA), 133
psychosocial skills, 73, 225
public schools, 161
Putalla, M., 256n44
Putnam, Robert, 224
Pythagoras, 160

Q
quizzes
are you raising your child to thrive?, 240–43
do you foster your child's emotional intelligence?, 182–83
does this school support children's optimal development?, 156–57
intelligence misconceptions, 5–6
parental support at home and school, 126–27
parenting for creativity, 47–48
your child's school, 150–51

R
race and social class disparities
learning gap, 95–97
tests and assessments, 12, 91, 95–97
Radcliffe, Sarah Chana, 186
rage to master, 60–61
reassurance, 188–89
reflectivity, 233–37, 247
Reilly, J., 264n22
Reis, S. M., 257n6, 258n17, 261n17, 264n4
rejection
bullying, 213, 216
creativity, 39–41
fear of failure, 193
gifted label, 98–104, 230
relationship-building skills. *See also* friendship-building
adolescence, 73, 83, 188, 222, 225
Renaissance and learning environment, 224

Renzulli, Joseph, 224, 261n17
resilience and coping skills
adolescence, 73–74, 85
behaviour problems, 184–90
parenting strategies, 190
setbacks, 77
Richards, A., 254n8
Ripley, Amanda, 155
risk-taking and creativity, 39–40
Rivero, L., 263n16
Robinson, A., 258n20, 259n1, 260n4, 260n9, 262n5, 263n12
Rogers, Karen, 261n11
Roosevelt, Eleanor, 46
Roosevelt, Franklin D., 185
Rowling, J.K., 37
Rudetsky, Seth, 266n11
Russell, Bertrand, 109

S
Schlaug, G., 251n20
Schleicher, Andreas, 133
school choices
acceleration, 162
advanced placement, 163
alternative, 163
charter, 161
decision-making, 153–58, 160–64, 172–74, 262n6, 262n8, 262n9
evidence of quality, 164–67
gifted education, 162
homeschooling, 164, 263n17
independent, 161, 262n10
International Baccalaureate (IB), 163
language immersion and dual track, 162
magnet schools and programs, 162–63
Montessori, 163–64
private, 161, 262n10
public, 161, 262n10
specialty subject focus, 162
school culture, 131, 148–51, 153–55, 174
schools. *See also* education; learning environment

accommodating needs, 118, 148, 173
flexibility, 150–51
individual choice, 158–60
quality, 155–58
special education, 123, 140, 149, 150–51, 161
teachers, 148–51
second language learning *See* language learning
secrets
child development and parenting strategies, 85–86
decision-making about schooling, 173–74
emotional intelligence: addressing possible complications, 207–8
intelligence and creativity, 48–49
parents' roles at school, 127–28
raising happily productive kids, 247–48
social context, 230–31
starting with intelligence, 25–26
teachers' roles, responsibilities, and requirements, 152
tests and assessments, 105–6
self-acceptance, 179, 226
self-awareness, 70, 182, 185, 233
self-confidence
behaviour problems, 204–8
misconceptions, 204–5
praise, 5, 205
strategies, 41, 71, 90, 102, 207, 225–26, 240–41, 267n25
self-critical, 20
self-discipline, 116, 127, 201, 202
self-discovery, 24, 70
self-doubt, 102, 103
self-esteem, 178–80
self-regulation skills, 180–84, 242
self-sabotage, 197
selling ideas and creativity, 37–38
sensitivity, 14, 73, 185, 187, 189
setbacks
early adulthood, 225

emotional intelligence, 180
fear of failure, 194–95
growth mindset, 24
management of, 76–77, 256n44
modelling, 199
parenting strategies, 6, 207, 241, 246
Shanker, Stuart, 181–83, 264n7
Shaw, George Bernard, 190
Shockley, William, 224
Shore, B. M., 258n20, 259n1, 260n4, 260n9, 262n5, 263n12, 266n3
sibling relationships
families, 226–30
rivalry, 228–29
Silicon Valley, 224
Simonton, D. K., 269n12
Singer, Jerome, 69–70, 253n17
Singh, V., 254n10
"SMART" goal-setting, 78
social class disparities on tests and assessments, 95–96
social context and learning environment, 222–24, 241–42
social intelligence
empathy, 14, 233
friendships, 206, 209–31, 247
parenting strategies, 242
social media, 218
social networks, 210–11
social skills
self-acceptance, 226
siblings, 226–30
training, 213–14, 225–26, 231, 242–43
social well-being
behaviour problems, 175–208
socio-economic status, 12, 91, 95–96, 210
socio-economic status, 12, 91, 95–96, 210
Socrates, 27
spatial reasoning, 8, 14, 17, 110
specialty subject focus schools, 162
spontaneity, 32–33, 151
sports, 56, 60, 161, 171, 206, 229

Stambaugh, T., 257n6
standardized tests *See* intelligence
    quotient (IQ)
Stanovich, Keith, 254n12
Steele, K.M., 251n18
Steiner-Adair, Catherine, 237
Steinhauer, Nancy, 103, 287
Sternberg, Robert, 15 – 17, 35 – 36, 234,
    253n17, 258n17, 261n16, 268n5
Stober, J., 265n15
Stockett, Kathryn, 37
strategies *See* parenting strategies
Stravinsky, Igor, 33, 38, 252n9
stress in early adolescence, 72 – 78
student teachers *See* teacher training
Subotnik, Rena, 52, 249n2, 249n4,
    251n24, 251n25, 254n13, 254n18,
    256n37, 258n17, 268n26, 287
Suzuki, David, 235

T
task force on intelligence, 7 – 9, 14, 24
teacher training, 132, 134 – 36, 138 – 39
teachers
    administrative support, 131 – 32,
        134, 136, 139, 148 – 49, 150, 152,
        264n26
    attention to the individual student,
        130 – 31, 136 – 37
    autonomy, 133, 163
    classroom strategies, 130 – 32,
        134 – 48, 260n10
    collaboration with parents, 109 – 19,
        129 – 30, 242
    creativity, 131
    curriculum and assessment, 139 – 41
    experienced teachers, 136 – 37
    learning environment, 148 – 51
    professional development, 131 – 33,
        261n20
    respect for diversity, 151, 152, 157,
        230, 261n19
    responsibilities, 129 – 52
    student teacher observations,
        134 – 36

Teaching for Intellectual and
    Emotional Learning (TIEL), 183
technology
    cyberbullying, 219 – 22
    electronic devices, 66, 69, 234
    learning opportunities, 133, 169,
        238
    multi-tasking, 236 – 37
    online learning, 138, 169
    social media, 69, 218, 234
    television, 56, 117, 182
    video game design, 27 – 30, 34, 37,
        44 – 45
teenagers *See* adolescence
television, 56, 117, 182
Terman, Lewis, 224
tests. *See also* assessments; intelligence
    quotient (IQ)
    creativity, 94 – 95
    definition, 88
    educational measurement, 14,
        91 – 97
    goals, 105 – 6
    intelligence continuum, 12 – 13,
        90 – 91
    limitations, 7 – 8, 88 – 89
    principles, 88 – 91
    race and social class disparities, 12,
        91, 95 – 97
    score reliability, 7 – 9, 11, 25, 88 – 89, 91
    types, 92 – 93
thinking habits and creativity, 35 – 44
Thomas, K. A., 257n1
Thompson, M., 265n1
"Tiger Mother," 53, 69, 200
time management, 84, 125, 176 – 77,
    192, 200, 203 – 4
toddlers *See* early years
tolerate ambiguity, 42 – 43
Tomlinson, Carol Ann, 129, 257n6,
    260n7, 260n9, 261n12
Tools of the Mind, 184
Torrance, E.P., 252n5
Tough, Paul, 52, 255n23, 256n42,
    264n5, 264n9

transitions
  early adolescence, 74–75, 86, 179
  early adulthood, 83–84, 86
triarchic intelligences approach
  analytical intelligence, 143
  creative intelligence, 144
  intelligence-building, 143–44
  practical intelligence, 144
Troutman, K. P., 262n1
Tzu, Lao, 233

U
Ugalde, Gerry, 259n25
university, 80–85
unstructured play, 56–63, 69–71, 85,
  253n5, 255n32
Urban, K.K., 253n17

V
Vaillancourt, T., 266n7, 266n14
Vallerand, Robert, 254n17
Van Gogh, Vincent, 205
VanTassel-Baska, J. L., 257n6, 258n16,
  258n19, 261n12, 263n15, 266n2
video game design and creativity,
  27–30, 34, 37, 44–45
Vygotsky, Lev, 264n9

W
Walker, C. L., 266n3
Wallace, B., 258n16, 258n17
Wang, Sam, 96, 265n20
Weinfeld, R., 260n8
Whitehead, Jack, 223, 257n8, 258n17
Wilson, H., 253n17
Winberg, Judy, 287
Winfrey, Oprah, 144
Winner, Ellen, 60
wisdom, 226, 235–36
work habits
  chores, 71–72
  hard work, 22, 26, 53, 61, 64, 99,
    108, 127, 202
work vs play, 52–53, 56–62, 69–72

World Wildlife Education Fund, 171
Worrell, F.C., 251n25, 258n16, 258n17
worry, 102, 185–87
Wright, Frank Lloyd, 158
writing, 15, 39–41, 118, 122, 169–70,
  172, 189, 205

Y
Yummy Mummy Club, 253n4, 268n7

Acknowledgements

We are grateful to so many people for their help in bringing *Beyond Intelligence* to these pages.

Beverley Slopen, our literary agent, has also become our good friend. She believed in *Beyond Intelligence* from the moment we brought the idea to her. She encouraged us to write in a non-academic style—something we found more difficult than we would've thought possible—and shepherded the book through countless drafts with patience, affection, and good humour.

Bernie Beales, Tracy Dennis, Barry Hymer, Sylvia Kwan, Marion Porath, Nancy Steinhauer, Rena Subotnik, and Judy Winberg are colleagues and friends who reviewed *Beyond Intelligence* as we were writing it. Their questions, comments, and suggestions helped us shape the book to reflect the most relevant current research findings.

Mona Diamond, Chloe Dirksen, Meredith Englander, Daphne Fenwick, Michelle Grinstein, Carole Matthews, Toby Molouba, Christie Nash, Michelle Osry, Shelley Peterson, Katie Waks, and Mark Wallace read preliminary chapters of the manuscript, and provided valuable feedback that contributed in innumerable ways to the book's final format and content. Their ideas kept us focused on how parents can benefit from the research and make practical use of the information we convey.

Jane Bertrand, Diana Brecher, and Felice Kaufmann were wise and thoughtful sounding boards throughout the process, and helped ensure we stayed on track and up to date.

Robin Spano, Keith Whybrow, Erin Kawalecki, James Kawalecki, Alex Gross, and Ashley Gross were generous in their suggestions for getting *Beyond Intelligence* ready for publication. From thinking about the book's format and content, through to the creation of a web site, generating ideas for a title, and ensuring the book reaches as wide an audience as possible, they've been insightful in their responses to our requests for help.

Eric and Cheryl Foster and Michele and Aaron Harlang offered opinions from their unique perspectives, and were always encouraging of our efforts as the book unfolded.

Sarah MacLachlan, Janice Zawerbny, Linda Pruessen, Laura Repas, Janie Yoon, Meredith Dees, and everyone else at House of Anansi Press have been enthusiastic in their support, and generous with their expertise. They've made the process of moving from manuscript to finished book a pleasure.

To all the parents, children, educators, teacher candidates, professionals, and others with whom we consulted and whose "stories" we tell, thank you for letting us share bits and pieces of your experience.

And finally, we want to thank Stephen Gross and Garry Foster for their unwavering belief in our work. They've been a strong and steady presence for each of us, providing the loving foundation that enabled us to bring this book to fruition.

About the Authors

Dona Matthews has worked with children, families, teachers, and schools since 1990. She has a Master of Education and a Ph.D. from the University of Toronto, where she taught courses in child and adolescent development, educational psychology, special education, and gifted education for twenty years, and was executive director of the Millennium Dialogue on Early Child Development. She has also taught at the University of British Columbia, Ryerson University, and Brock University. From 2003–2007 she was associate professor at Hunter College, City University of New York, where she was the founding director of the Center for Gifted Studies and Education. Dr. Matthews has presented extensively in Canada, the United States, and the United Kingdom, and has published dozens of articles and book chapters on various aspects of child and adolescent development and education. Her previous books include *The Development of Giftedness and Talent Across the Life Span* and *The Routledge International Companion to Gifted Education*. She now lives in Toronto, where she contributes to *Creativity Post* and *Parents Space*, writes a blog, and consults to families and schools on ways to support children's optimal development.

Joanne Foster has a Master of Education from the University of Toronto in special education and adaptive instruction, and a

Doctorate of Education from the University of Toronto in human development and applied psychology. She has worked in the capacity of teacher, gifted education specialist, enrichment program coordinator, and educational consultant, and for over thirty years has been active in promoting the best possible learning opportunities for children and adolescents. She conducts teacher-training workshops, gives presentations to teachers and parents in local, national, and international forums, works with policy makers, and serves on several committees concerning children's education and development. She teaches educational psychology courses at the Ontario Institute for Studies in Education of the University of Toronto where she also provides leadership in the areas of giftedness and programming for high-level development by advising and networking with faculty, partnership schools, and parent organizations. Dr. Foster writes a series of articles for the journal *Parenting for High Potential,* and her writing has been featured in many other peer-reviewed and popular publications. She's also the author of *Not Now, Maybe Later: Helping Children Overcome Procrastination.*

Dona Matthews and Joanne Foster have worked together for almost twenty years, and have collaborated on several projects. Drs. Matthews and Foster are co-authors of the award-winning *Being Smart About Gifted Education* (2nd edition), as well as many articles in professional and parenting publications. Recognized experts in education and child development, the authors are also dedicated parents who continue to participate actively in advocacy initiatives. They've done joint presentations at conferences and other venues across North America. For more on their work, and to see their blogs and material related to various topics covered in *Beyond Intelligence: Secrets for Raising Happily Productive Kids,* go to www.beyondintelligence.net.